The Weekly Curriculum

Dedication

To all those early childhood educators who led the way, to those who follow, and to the children whose lives we touch: may your lives be full of the joy of learning.

Acknowledgment

To Don, whose patience and support contributed to the joy of writing this book.

The Weekly Curriculum

52 Complete

Preschool

Themes

Barbara Backer

Illustrations by Joan Waites

gryphon house
Beltsville, MD

Published by Gryphon House, Inc.
10726 Tucker Street, Beltsville, MD 20705-0207
301.595.9500; 301.595.0051 (fax); 800.638.0928

Visit us on the web at www.gryphonhouse.com

Illustrated by Joan Waites

Library of Congress Cataloging-in-Publication Data

Backer, Barbara.
  The weekly curriculum : 52 complete preschool themes
/ Barbara Backer ; illustrations, Joan Waites.
     p. cm.
Includes index.
  ISBN-13: 978-0-87659-282-3
  ISBN-10: 0-87659-282-5
  1. Education, Preschool--Curricula. 2. Education, Preschool--Activity programs. 3. Curriculum planning. I. Title.
  LB1140.4.B317 2003
  372.19--dc21   2002155533

Bulk purchase
Gryphon House books are available for special premiums and sales promotions as well as for fund-raising use. Special editions or book excerpts also can be created to specification. For details, contact the Director of Marketing at the address above.

 Gryphon House is a member of the Green Press Initiative, a nonprofit program dedicated to supporting publishers in their efforts to reduce their use of fiber sourced forests. For further information visit www.greenpressinitiative.org.

Table of Contents

Introduction

The Weekly Curriculum is designed to help preschool teachers solve the challenge of planning activities and learning experiences for each approaching week with 52 weekly thematic ideas—one theme for each week of the year.

Each week begins with a simple-to-prepare opening activity, reducing time-consuming preparation. Additional activities are related to the opening activity. The activities require little or no preparation; any materials are inexpensive, everyday items that can be found in your classroom, your home, your supermarket, or your library. Best of all, these child-tested themes are interesting to children as well as educational, and they stress a child-centered approach.

The Weekly Curriculum can be used by classroom teachers, daycare providers, home child care providers, home-schooling parents, education students planning for practicum work, parents and grandparents, and nannies.

How to Use This Book
Open to the beginning of any chapter, and you will find an activity perfect for introducing a theme or topic to children. The book is set up by weekly themes, but it isn't necessary to start on a Monday. Begin whenever children's interest in a previous theme begins to lag. Sometimes children's interest in a theme goes on for several weeks; at other times, for only a few days. Let the children's interest be your best guide.

With the exception of the calendar-related themes, themes can be used whenever children are interested in them. If children's free play is about princes and princesses, you might choose the themes about *Royalty*. If children begin moving the classroom furniture to create hiding places, the themes of *Hiding Places*, *Table Talk*, or *Charming Chairs* might be appropriate.

Each weekly theme contains the following components:
- An activity to introduce the weekly curriculum theme
- Weekly curriculum vocabulary
- Weekly curriculum extension activities
- Learning center ideas
- Related books

The weekly curriculum extension activities are labeled by curriculum area, including Art, Math, Science, Field Trip, Language, Movement, and Music. This will help teachers plan a well-rounded curriculum.

The methods used in activities in any one chapter might be adapted to activities in another. For example, an activity with cards ("Math Bears" in *Real Bears*, page 194) could be adapted to the *Charming Chairs* theme by having children draw chairs on small papers of several different colors, and then using those pictures for sorting, matching, or patterning by color.

One note of caution—each chapter contains ideas for theme-related snacks/cooking activities. Always be aware of children's food allergies and sensitivities to foods you are planning to use. Always plan alternate snacks for children who cannot eat or handle the food in these activities.

The author hopes that this book makes teachers' lives easier and that it brings to children the deep joys of learning.

Special Days and Holidays

The First Week of School

Introducing the Weekly Curriculum Theme

Weekly Curriculum Vocabulary

Art Area
Block Area
Dramatic Play Area
learning center
(learning area)
Library
Manipulatives Area
modeling dough
self-portrait

Materials

blocks from the Block Area

1. Welcome the children to school. Tell them they will be learning about the room and how to use items that are in different parts of the room.

2. Show the blocks to the children. Talk about a few of the things that people can do with blocks. As a group, go to the Block Area. Show the children how to take a few blocks and accessories off the shelf, safely build something simple with them, and return them to their proper place. Encourage the children, a few at a time, to practice taking items from the shelf and putting them back in their proper places.

3. Briefly discuss simple safety rules for the Block Area, such as "build structures no higher than your own head" and "take structures apart one block at a time." (This is a positive way to say, "Don't knock down structures.")

4. Demonstrate the use of another classroom area. For example, take a simple puzzle off the shelf, show the children how to put it together, and then put it away. Continue with other areas.

5. If there are two teachers, each teacher can work with half of the children, demonstrating different areas.

Using Modeling Dough

Art

Materials

modeling dough

1. Show a small group of children where to find modeling dough, and discuss any special rules for using it (for example, staying at the table).
2. Give each child a small amount of dough. Demonstrate a few ways to use the dough, such as pounding it, rolling it into a ball or snake, pinching it, or pinching off small pieces, and encourage them to try these ways with you.
3. When the children are finished, gather the dough and demonstrate how to put it away.

Note: To prevent the spread of germs, make sure children wash their hands before and after using modeling dough.

Using Crayons and Markers

Art

Materials

crayons • markers • paper

1. Show the children where the crayons, markers, and paper are located. Give supplies to each child.
2. Demonstrate ways to make a variety of marks on paper with a crayon (thin/thick lines, straight/curvy lines, outlines of items) and how to color in areas.
3. Give the children time to experiment with these techniques.
4. Repeat the demonstration using a marker. Let the children practice putting the cap on the marker when it is not in use.
5. Demonstrate how to put away the materials.

Drawing Self-Portraits

Art

Materials

crayons • paper

1. Let the children see you draw a very simple sketch of yourself. Mention the eyes, nose, mouth, arms, legs, and other parts of your body as you draw them.
2. Put your self-portrait away and then encourage each child to draw a self-portrait.
3. Label the self-portraits with their names and the date.
4. Have the children make self-portraits at the beginning of each month during the school year.
5. Save these in the children's assessment portfolios. At the end of the year, you'll have a collection that provides a visual record of their developing skills.

Using Paste

Art, Math, and Music

Materials

paste ● plastic bottle caps or paper towels ● pre-cut paper shapes ● construction paper

1. Prepare paste for each child by putting a small amount into individual bottle caps or onto paper towels.
2. Explain to the children that they are going to learn a way to stick papers together. Show them the paper shapes and a piece of construction paper and tell them that when they use the paste, the shapes will stay on the paper.
3. Ask the children to look at their thumbs, and then talk about the size of their thumbnails. Show them an amount of paste the same size as their thumbnails. Using that amount, paste several shapes to your paper and show the children that the shapes are sticking to the paper.
4. With children, sing the "I Can Paste" song below after using the paste. Sing it again.
5. Give materials to the children, and encourage them to use an amount of paste the same size as their thumbnails to stick their shapes to the construction paper. Help the children who need it.
6. Repeat the song many times during the week.

I Can Paste
Tune: *Mary Had a Little Lamb*
A little bit is all I need,
All I need, all I need.
A little bit is all I need
To make my papers stick.

The same size as my thumbnail, (children show thumbnail)
My thumbnail, my thumbnail.
The same size as my thumbnail,
To make my papers stick.

School Tour

Field Trip

1. Take a short and simple walk with small groups of children to show them how to get from the room to the bathroom, where and how to wash their hands, and where to throw away used paper towels. Show them how to return to the room.

Farmer in the Dell

Games

1. Play this simple circle game with the children. Ask one child to be the Farmer. The other children walk in a circle around the Farmer.
2. Sing the song together.
3. Repeat the game until every child has a turn to be chosen and to choose another child.

> **The Farmer in the Dell**
> *The farmer in the dell, the farmer in the dell.*
> *Heigh-ho the derry-o, the farmer in the dell.*
>
> *The farmer takes a wife/husband/friend.* (farmer brings a second child into the circle)
> *The farmer takes a wife/husband/friend.*
> *Heigh-ho the derry-o, the farmer takes a wife/husband/friend.*
>
> *The wife/husband/friend takes a child. . .* (wife chooses a third child to join in the circle)
> *The child takes a dog. . .*
> *The dog takes a cat. . .*
> *The cat takes a rat. . .*
> *The rat takes the cheese. . .*
>
> *The cheese stands alone. . .* (everyone except cheese leaves the center of the circle)

Children in Our Group

Games

1. For a variation on Farmer in the Dell, ask the children to stand in a circle. Choose one child to stand in the center, which is the "school."

2. Sing the song below. The child in the center of the circle chooses the next child to come to the center (school). Substitute the children's names for the names in the song.

> Tune: *Farmer in the Dell*
> *(Chandra) came to school.*
> *(Chandra) came to school.*
> *Heigh-ho the derry-oh!*
> *(Chandra) came to school.*
>
> *(Chandra) chooses (LeVar).*
> *(Chandra) chooses (LeVar).*
> *Heigh-ho the derry-oh!*
> *(Chandra) chooses (LeVar).*

3. Continue singing and playing until every child has been chosen and all are in the "school." Sing the final verse:

> *We all came to school.*
> *We all came to school.*
> *To work and play, it's fun all day.*
> *We all came to school.*

Getting Acquainted

Language

Materials
photos of all of the children ● copy machine or computer scanner ● glue ● paper ● hole punch ● yarn or string ● markers

1. Before doing this activity, make a computer scan or photocopy of each child's photo and glue each copy to a piece of paper, one page per child. Then, make an "Our Class" book by punching holes in the sides of each page and tying string or yarn through the holes.
2. Label each page with the child's first name.
3. Read the book with the children, having each pictured child stand when her picture is shown.
4. Read the book again, inviting the children to name each picture with you. Repeat this activity many times in the next weeks until children know each other's names.

Taking Care of Books

Language

Materials

picture books (more books than the number of children in your group)

1. Demonstrate to the children how to carefully remove a book from its location and how to hold it gently.
2. Show them how to open a book and use their eyes to look at the first page. (Some children may not yet know how to look at the book. They may turn pages while looking around the room.)
3. Demonstrate gently turning pages, using the thumb and forefinger to grasp the edge of the page. (Placing palms in the center of the page and pushing the page to turn it causes pages to buckle and wrinkle, eventually causing pages to tear.)
4. On each page, demonstrate how to look at it to get information from it. "I see a house, a girl, and a dog." Ask children what they see. Point to the items they name and repeat their words to reinforce the answers.
5. At the book's end, close the book and demonstrate taking it safely back to "its home" where you first found it. Show them how to carefully replace the book.
6. Give children the opportunity, a few at a time, to select books and practice what they've just learned.
7. Repeat this lesson daily during the first few weeks of school and as necessary after that.

Cleaning Up the Room

Music

1. Each time you demonstrate putting away items in the classroom, sing the first verse of the following song.
2. With the children, make up a verse about what they are putting away.
3. Encourage the children to sing or chant the following song at clean-up time.

   Cleaning Song
   Every day when we play at school.
   Every day when we play at school.
   Every day when we play at school,
   We help clean up the room.

   Possible additional verses:

   We pick up toys and put them away,
   We pick up toys and put them away,
   We pick up toys and put them away,
   We help clean up the room.

   We pick up trash and put it in the trash can,
   Pick up trash and put it in the trash can.
   We pick up trash and put it in the trash can,
   We help clean up the room.

4. Add any other verses that the children suggest.

Playing Chase

Outdoors

1. Many children enjoy chasing each other outdoors, but some are intimidated by this game.
2. Show all the children an outside area where it is safe to play chasing games, and show them areas where no chasing is allowed.

Easy Snacks

Snack/Cooking

Materials

various finger foods (see below) ● napkins ● beverage, such as juice ● 8-ounce, plastic measuring cups for liquids ● drinking cups ● trash can

1. To help the children learn to use the snack area and serve their own snacks, serve simple items during the first week. Show them how to get a napkin, take a serving, and bring it to the snack table. Suggested snacks for this week include pretzels, cheese crackers, animal crackers, apple wedges, and orange slices.

2. Help the children learn to pour their own beverages with a minimum of spills. Pre-pour 1-ounce servings into small, plastic measuring pitchers. Show how to pour from these into drinking cups.

3. Show children where to dispose of their napkins, cups, and any uneaten food/drink when they are finished.

Note: Always check for allergies and/or food sensitivities and preferences before serving any food.

Learning Center Ideas

1. Begin the school year with very few items in your room. This avoids overstimulation and makes it easier for children to choose which items to use.
2. Each day add a few items, showing children how to use them and how to put them away.

Related Books (Introduce popular children's books this week, too.)

The Kissing Hand by Audrey Penn

Little Cliff's First Day of School by Clifton L. Taulbert

Look Out Kindergarten, Here I Come! by Nancy L. Carlson

Miss Bindergarten Gets Ready for Kindergarten by Joseph Slate

The Night Before Kindergarten by Natasha Wing

Shawn and Keeper: Show and Tell by Jonathan London

Second Week of School

Introducing the Weekly Curriculum Theme

Weekly Curriculum Vocabulary

chase
count
serving spoon
snack
spread

Materials

tote bag ● variety of items from around the room, one or more items per child

1. Place all of the classroom items in the tote bag.
2. Ask each child to reach into the bag without looking and remove an item. Challenge the child to return it to its place in the room. If needed, allow another child to help the first child find the proper place for the item.
3. Remind children repeatedly of the importance of returning items to their appropriate places every day.

Celebrate National Playdough Day

Art

Materials

playdough ● small rolling pins or ½" diameter dowel sticks cut into 8" lengths ● birthday candles ● cookie cutters ● blunt, plastic knives

1. September 18 is National Playdough Day. Celebrate during the second week of school by adding materials to expand the children's use of playdough.
2. Show the children how to pat the playdough flat on the table, and then use the rollers to flatten it further.
3. On other days add different implements, such as candles, cookie cutters, and plastic knives, to enhance the playdough experience.

Block Pals

Blocks

Materials

clean, empty snack food cans with lids ● glue ● clear tape ● small, whole-body pictures of each child, front and back ● clear contact paper

1. Glue the lids securely onto the snack food cans.
2. Tape a front view picture of one of the children on one side of a can. Place the back view of the child on the other side of the can. Cover the surface of the can with clear contact paper to protect the picture.
3. Repeat using pictures of all of the children and of familiar adults at school.
4. Place these Block Pals in the Block Area where children can use them in block play or other dramatic play.

VIP Visitors

Classroom Visitor

1. Arrange to have adults from other classes come to your room to introduce themselves. If possible, have them stay long enough to play with a few children or read to a small group. Meeting adults in the classroom helps children feel comfortable with them.
2. Suggested visitors include the director or principal, cook, school nurse, music teacher, librarian, and any other adult who works at the school.

Around the Building

Field Trip

1. Take the children outside for a walk around the school to see the front, back, sides, playgrounds, different entrances and exits, and other parts of the school grounds.

Remembering Faces

Games

Materials

photos of each child ● photocopy machine or computer scanner ● plastic zipper-closure bag ● lids from yogurt containers, two for each child ● glue

1. Make two identical photocopies or computer scans of each child's photo.
2. Make a memory-type game by cutting each picture to fit inside the yogurt lids and gluing one inside each lid.
3. Divide the lids into groups with five pairs of pictures in each group. Put each group into separate plastic bags.
4. Place one group of lids face down. Show the children how to play the game by turning over two lids at a time, trying to make a match. They can play alone or take turns with another player.
5. Send the games home overnight with children so they can practice visual memory skills and show their families pictures of their new friends.

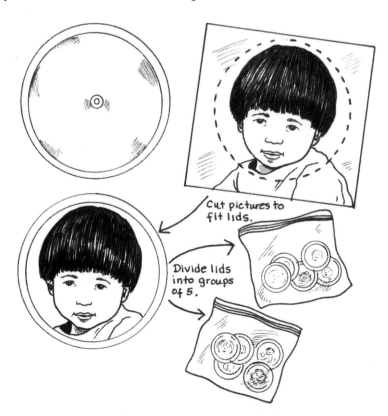

Cut pictures to fit lids.

Divide lids into groups of 5.

Chase Me!

Games and Outdoors

1. Help the children learn each other's names while you show them how to play a circle chasing game. Ask the children to sit in a circle, facing inward, with one child ("IT") walking around the outside of the circle.
2. IT walks around the outside of the circle, gently tapping each child on the head. As a child is tapped, she calls out the appropriate name.
3. When she desires, IT yells, "Chase me!" when she taps a child. The tapped child chases IT around the outside of the circle. IT attempts to get to the tapped child's empty place in the circle without being caught.
4. Children who are caught sit in the center of the circle until another child is caught. Then the child sitting in the center takes the newly caught child's place in the circle.
5. A tapped child becomes IT for the next turn.

Friends-O

Music

Materials

small stuffed animal

1. While the children are sitting in a circle, hand a stuffed animal to one child. Have the group sing the following song about that child, substituting the child's name for the name in parentheses.

> *Friends-O*
> Tune: *Bingo*
> *Oh, this is our good friend at school and*
> *(Bobby) is his name-o.*
> *(Bobby) is his name.*
> *(Bobby) is his name.*
> *(Bobby) is his name.*
> *And (Bobby) is our friend-o.*

2. The child now passes the stuffed animal to the next child and the group sings about that "friend-o." Continue until you've sung about every child. Whisper to the last child to pass the animal to you. The children will enjoy singing about you, and you'll have their attention as the game ends.

Basic Tag

Outdoors

1. Show the children how to play a simple tag game. Choose a child to be "IT." IT chases the others and when he tags another child, that child becomes IT. The first child joins those being chased.
2. Explain that some people like to play this game with an area designated as a "base," which is a "safe" place. If a runner is touching the base, IT cannot tag him. If children wish to have a base, let them designate the area (such as a fence or a tree trunk).

A Week of Do-It-Yourself Snacks

Snack/Cooking

Materials

see each day below

1. Help the children assume more responsibility for serving their own individual snacks by serving items such as those below. On each of the days, the children visit the Snack Area a few at a time to make and eat their snacks.

Monday—Applesauce and Crumbs (Using a Serving Spoon

Materials

2 serving dishes • applesauce • graham cracker crumbs • a large and a small serving spoon • small bowls or plates, 1 for each child • teaspoons

1. Fill one serving dish with applesauce and the other with graham cracker crumbs.
2. Place a large serving spoon in the applesauce and a small serving spoon in the crumbs.
3. Demonstrate how to transfer a spoonful of applesauce to an individual bowl and how to sprinkle a spoonful of graham cracker crumbs over the applesauce. Show how to stir the mixture with a teaspoon, then eat.
4. Ask the children to prepare their own snack.
5. Demonstrate clean-up procedures for the children to follow.

Tuesday—Buttered Toast (Spreading One Food on Another)

Materials

toasted bread, 1 slice for each child • paper plates • butter knives or plastic, serrated-edged knives • soft butter

1. Demonstrate using the knife to spread soft butter on toast.

Caution: Only adults use the toaster.

2. Give each child a piece of toast. Ask them to butter their toast.
3. Demonstrate clean-up procedures.
4. Remind children to keep knives away from their mouths.

Wednesday—Crazy, Mixed-Up Snack (Using Scoops)

Materials

serving bowls • 1 coffee scoop for each serving bowl • various bite-size dry foods, such as cereal pieces and cut-up dried fruits • sandwich-size zipper-closure plastic bags

1. Place one food item into each of the serving bowls.
2. Demonstrate how to take one scoop of each food and place it into a zipper-closure bag.
3. Show the children how to close the bag, shake it to mix the foods, and then open the bags to eat the snacks.
4. Ask the children to make their own snacks.

Thursday—Number Snack (Counting Snacks)

Materials

marker • large index card • pretzel twists • serving bowl • napkins

1. Use the marker to write the numeral 3 and draw three actual-size pretzel twists on the index card.
2. Demonstrate how to select the correct number of pretzels by matching pretzels from the bowl to the pretzel pictures. Demonstrate putting the pretzels in a napkin for snack.
3. Encourage the children to count out the right number of pretzels, and then eat and enjoy them!
4. Demonstrate clean-up procedures.

Friday—Crackers and Jam (Combining Techniques)

Materials
large and small serving bowl • crackers • jam • marker • large index card • paper plates • butter knives or plastic, serrated-blade knives

1. Put crackers into a large serving bowl and jam into a small serving bowl.
2. Write the numeral 4 and draw four actual-size crackers on a large index card.
3. Demonstrate how to count out four crackers and spread them with jam.
4. Encourage the children to count out the right amount of crackers and put jam on them.
5. Demonstrate clean-up procedures.

Learning Center Ideas

1. As in the first week, continue to add a few items to the room each day, showing the children how to use them and how to put them away.

Related Books
At this time of the year, choose books that are simple. Include concept books and all-time favorites.

Counting Wildflowers by Bruce McMillan

Caps for Sale by Esphyr Slobodkina

Growing Colors by Bruce McMillan

Is it Red, Is it Yellow, Is it Blue? by Tana Hoban

Inch by Inch by Leo Lionni

Lunch by Denise Fleming

Over in the Meadow by Ezra Jack Keats

October Is National Pretzel Month

Introducing the Weekly Curriculum Theme

Materials

bag of pretzels ● a chart ● marker

1. Give each child a pretzel. Encourage the children to explore their pretzels using their five senses, beginning with sight.
2. Ask the children to describe how the pretzel looks. On the chart write: "A pretzel looks…" and record children's one- or two-word answers in a list.
3. Next, ask the children to explore the aroma. On the chart write: "A pretzel smells…" and list children's one- or two-word answers.
4. Repeat with sound, feel, and taste. For sound, children might describe its sound when it breaks.
5. Review the chart lists with the children. Save the chart for the music activity on page 37.

Weekly Curriculum Vocabulary

pretzel
rod
stick
twist
words generated on the chart in the introductory activity

Pretzel Practice

Art

Materials

simple recipe for uncooked modeling dough ● ingredients for modeling dough ● mixing bowls and utensils, as needed ● rolling pins ● plastic knives

1. Ask the children to help you mix up a no-cook recipe for modeling dough (using your favorite recipe).
2. When the dough is finished, give each child a piece of it. Encourage them to roll out their dough with a rolling pin.
3. Show them how to cut off a strip of dough to make "pretzel rods" and how to twist the strips to make "pretzel twists."
4. This activity provides good practice before making bread dough pretzels (page 37).

Pretzel People

Art and Snack/Cooking

Materials

pretzels in a variety of shapes and sizes ● carrot sticks and/or carrot curls ● dark and golden raisins ● plain paper plates

1. Put out all the ingredients and challenge the children to create Pretzel People on their paper plates.
2. Display the creations so everyone can see them. Then each artist can eat his own work of art!

Can You Make a Pretzel?

Construction/Manipulatives Area

Materials

variety of materials that can or cannot be twisted into pretzel shapes, such as shoelaces, yarn, ribbons, string, snap-together blocks, wooden blocks, Styrofoam pieces, paper strips, and cardboard strips

1. Challenge the children to explore the items to see which can and which cannot be twisted into pretzel shapes.
2. Encourage the children to see which can be shaped into pretzel-like rods.

Pretzel Letters

Language

Materials

various alphabet books ● pretzel sticks and rings

1. Read any alphabet book to the children.
2. Provide the children with pretzel sticks and rings, and challenge them to use these to make letters. They may need to break some pretzels to get half circles and other shapes they need.
3. Let the children look in alphabet books if they need help remembering how letters look.
4. Encourage the children to show their creations to each other and tell what they've made.
5. Eat the letters!

Pretzel Shapes

Math

Materials

pictures of a square, a rectangle, and several kinds of triangles ● stick pretzels

1. Show the pictures and talk about each shape.
2. Give each child a handful of pretzel sticks. Challenge the children to use the pretzels to make the shapes.
3. Talk about the shapes the children made, and then everyone can eat their pretzel shapes.

Exploring Three

Math

Materials

pretzel twists, one for each child ● pattern blocks

1. Ask the children to count the number of holes in their pretzel twists (3).
2. Ask the children to each bring to the group three items that are the same (e.g., three crayons, three puppets, or three books). Help them see that all of these are ways of showing "three."
3. Let the children eat their pretzels while you show several different ways of using pattern blocks to represent the number three (e.g., a red block and two yellow blocks, three diamond shapes laid end to end, or three diamond shapes arranged in a tulip shape).
4. Provide pattern blocks, and encourage each child to make five different groupings of three blocks.
5. Have the children work in shifts, making all of their groupings on the same table. When everyone has finished, encourage the children to look at the many different ways to represent three.

Pretzel Patterns

Math

Materials

large and small pretzel twists

1. Provide large and small pretzel twists, and challenge the children to use them to make patterns (small/small/large; large/small/large/small; large/small/small).
2. Eat the pretzels when finished.

We Like Pretzels

Music

Materials

chart from opening activity

1. Using the chart from the opening activity (page 33), ask the children, in turn, to select words from the chart to insert in place of the underlined word in the song below.

> Tune: *Frère Jacques*
> *We like pretzels, we like pretzels.*
> *Yes we do. (Repeat)*
> *Pretzels feel bumpy. (Repeat)*
> *Through and through. (Repeat)*

2. Change the third line of the song as desired (e.g. Pretzels taste _____, smell _____, look _____, sound _____).

Making Pretzels

Science and Snack/Cooking

Materials

frozen bread dough ● paper plates, one for each child ● kosher salt ● baking pans ● oven or toaster oven

1. Thaw the dough according to package directions.
2. Give each child a portion of thawed dough on a paper plate. Save some of the raw dough to use in step #6.
3. Encourage the children to roll their dough into "snakes," twist their snakes into any shape, and then sprinkle kosher salt over their creations.
4. Place these shapes on baking pans and bake them according to directions on the dough package. As they bake, encourage the children to look through the glass door of the oven from time to time to see the shapes expand as the dough rises.
5. When done, remove the pretzels from the oven (adult only) and allow them to cool.
6. Distribute the pretzels and ask the children to compare their baked pretzels with a bit of raw dough you saved earlier. How did the heat change the dough?
7. Let the children eat their pretzels.

Banana and Pretzel Rolls

Snack/Cooking

Materials

pretzels ● zipper-closure plastic bags ● unit blocks ● bowls ● bananas ● knife

1. Give each child a few pretzels, a plastic bag, and a unit block. Ask the children to place their pretzels into their bags, seal them closed, and use a block to pound the pretzels into crumbs.
2. Ask the children to pour their crumbs into individual bowls.
3. Cut unpeeled bananas into fourths (adult only).
4. Give each child a banana piece to peel and then roll in the crumbs. Let the children eat their banana snacks and remaining crumbs.

Cold, Crunchy, and Salty

Snack/Cooking

Materials

small cups of soft vanilla ice cream, one for each child ● pretzel rods

1. Give each child a cup of ice cream and a pretzel rod to dip into the ice cream. Encourage them to eat this cold, crunchy, and salty treat!

Learning Center Ideas

Dramatic Play Area

Materials

aprons and chef's hat(s) • mixing spoons and bowls • rolling pins • yarn •
scissors • tape • paper (for menus) and pads of paper (for order pads) • pencils

1. Encourage the children to use the materials to create a pretzel bakery in the
   Dramatic Play Area.
2. Show them how to cut lengths of yarn for pretzel rods and how to tape twists of
   yarn for pretzel twists.

Related Books

Chicka Chicka Boom Boom by John Archambault and Bill Martin, Jr.
Counting Kisses by Karen Katz
Dr. Seuss's ABC by Dr. Seuss
I Spy Two Eyes: Numbers in Art by Lucy Micklethwait
Pretzel by Margret Rey
Pretzels: One of the World's Oldest Snack Foods by Elaine Landau
The Very Hungry Caterpillar by Eric Carle
Walter the Baker by Eric Carle

Third Week in November—
Children's Book Week

Introducing the Weekly Curriculum Theme

Weekly Curriculum Vocabulary

create
writing
writer
author
illustrator
illustrations
pages
words
story
idea
read

Materials

children's books in a variety of formats such as:

- hardcover books
- paperback books
- pop-up books
- board books
- lift-the-flap books
- shape books
- recorded books
- big books
- tiny, hand-sized books

1. Show the books to the children, talking about the many different kinds of books. Also call attention to the variety of illustrations.

2. Tell the children that an "author" writes the words for every book and an "illustrator" draws or paints the pictures.

3. Ask if any of the children are authors or illustrators. Remind them of (and show them) books they have made in school this year. Help them conclude that they are authors and illustrators. Explain that they will be exploring, writing, and illustrating books this week.

4. During the week, read books in a variety of formats.

Point of View—Big Book

Art and Language

Materials

any favorite storybook

1. This activity helps children understand a story's point of view. (In many children's books, the story is told from the narrator's point of view.)
2. Read any favorite book to the children and briefly discuss the story.
3. Ask the children how the story might be different if one of the characters told the story. For example, how would the Troll tell the story of *The Three Billy Goats Gruff*? How would one of the lazy animals tell the story of *The Little Red Hen*?
4. Repeat the activity at other times using other favorite stories.
5. Read *The True Story of the Three Little Pigs by A. Wolf* by Jon Scieszka. This is a funny book that tells the story from the wolf's point of view.

Circle Book

Art and Math

Materials

drawing paper ● scissors ● variety of items that are circles (coin, clock face, compact disc) ● crayons ● 2 identical paper plates ● stapler

1. Beforehand, cut drawing paper into circles slightly smaller than the plates.
2. Show the circular items and talk about things that are circles. Ask the children to name other items that are circles.
3. Give each child a pre-cut paper circle. Challenge the children to draw a picture of something that is a circle.
4. Offer to write the names of their items on their papers. Ask the children to sign their names, as illustrators, on their pages.
5. Gather the pages and staple them into a book, using the two paper plates as covers.
6. Read the book to the group, identifying the author/illustrator of each page.

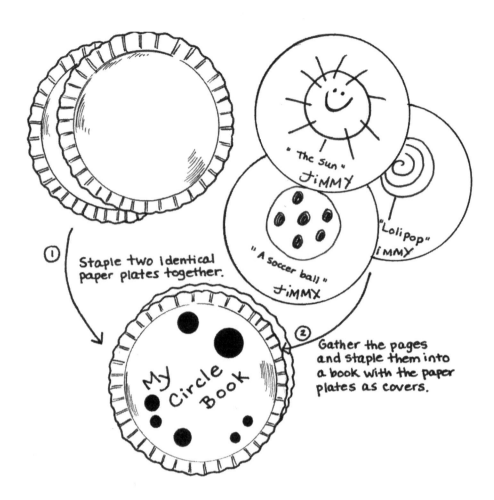

① Staple two identical paper plates together.

"The Sun" JiMMY

"A soccer ball" JiMMX

"LoliPop" JiMMY

My Circle Book

② Gather the pages and staple them into a book with the paper plates as covers.

Bookmobile

Field Trip

1. Call your local library and ask them to schedule a bookmobile to make a stop at your location.
2. When the bookmobile arrives, let the children tour this "library on wheels" and let them each check out a book (on your library card) to keep in the classroom for a week.
3. Publicize this bookmobile visit, and invite parents to tour and use the vehicle, also.
4. If possible, ask the bookmobile to make a return trip so children can return their books. Otherwise, return the children's books to the library for them.

Visit a Local Bookstore

Field Trip

1. Visit a local bookstore where children can be surrounded by books. In advance, request that the store provide story time for the children.

Who Said That?

Games and Language

1. To play this game, quote a character from a familiar storybook and ask the children to identify the character. Suggestions include:
   - "Who's that tramping across my bridge?"—the troll in *Three Billy Goats Gruff*
   - "Who will help me plant the wheat?"—the little red hen in the book of the same name
   - "This porridge is too hot!"—Goldilocks in *Goldilocks and the Three Bears*

Real and Make-Believe

Language

Materials

non-fiction books

1. Always include non-fiction books in your class library and read them at story time. Choose books with clear illustrations.
2. Young children especially enjoy non-fiction picture books about transportation, toys, spiders, snakes, motorcycles, gardens, art and great paintings, dolls, concepts, and pets.
3. Help children understand the difference between fiction (make-believe) and non-fiction (things that are real).
4. After reading any book, ask the children if they think the book is about something real or if it is make-believe.

Estimation Activities

Language and Math

Materials

any picture book ● chart paper ● marker

1. Before reading a book to the class, ask the children to estimate how many pages are in the book. Before estimating, decide if you will count each paper as one total page or two back-and-front pages.
2. As a group, count the pages to see whose estimate was closest.
3. Record the book's name and its number of pages on chart paper.
4. Repeat the activity on other days, keeping a written record of book titles and the number of pages in each book.
5. Do the children notice any similarities?

How Do They Move?

Movement

1. Encourage the children to move like characters in some of their favorite stories.
2. Begin by giving suggestions; later, let the children suggest characters. Suggestions include:
    ● the wild things in *Where the Wild Things Are*
    ● Goldilocks when she wakes up in Baby Bear's bed

Our Favorite Songs

Music

Materials

drawing paper, 1 sheet per child ● crayons or markers ● stapler ● construction paper ● copy machine, optional ● computer, printer, and computer paper, optional

1. Ask the children to think of all the songs they've learned at school. What are their favorite songs?
2. Provide paper, markers, and crayons and encourage each child to draw a picture of her favorite song and sign the page, as illustrator.
3. Ask the children to write the song's name on their paper or dictate this for you to write.
4. Staple the pages together between two pieces of construction paper. Title it "Our Favorite Songs."

5. Use this book for future music activities.
6. If desired, make several copies of this book, and use the computer to write the words of each song, one song per page.
7. Compile several books with a song picture on one page and the song's lyrics on the facing page.
8. Children can take turns taking the copies home so they can sing favorite songs with their families.

Outdoor Story Time

Outdoors

1. Have story time outdoors.
2. Take books outside at outdoor play time so children who wish to can read.

Exploring Same and Different

Science

Materials

chart paper ● marker ● two books that have similarities and differences (e.g., *The Mixed-Up Chameleon* by Eric Carle and *A Color of His Own* by Leo Lionni)

1. Use favorite books to explore similarities and differences.
2. On the chart paper, make two columns. Title one "Same" and the other "Different."
3. Read both books to the group.
4. Discuss the two books and ask the children to tell you what was the same and what was different about the books. Place their answers in the correct column.
5. During the year, repeat the activity with other similar books.

Same	Different

Story Time Snacks

Snack/Cooking

1. Serve snacks that are related to the children's favorite books, such as:
   - bread and jam (*Bread and Jam for Frances*)
   - oatmeal (porridge) (*The Three Bears*)
   - gingerbread men cookies (*The Gingerbread Man*)
   - vegetable soup (*Growing Vegetable Soup*)
   - pizza (*Hello, Pizza Man*)

Making Books

Writing

Materials

drawing paper • markers, crayons, and pencils • construction paper • stapler (adult only)

1. Provide a variety of materials so children can make an assortment of books.
2. Assist children in stapling their books together.

Learning Center Ideas

Literacy Area

Materials

books from the Introductory Activity

1. Place the books in the class library and encourage the children to explore the various types of books.

Related Books

Any book is appropriate for this week that celebrates children's books. Let the children choose their favorites. Remember to include non-fiction selections, too.

December 6—
Mitten Tree Day

Materials

mittens (use either the children's or bring in a supply) ● any version of the story, *The Mitten* (see Related Books list on page 53) ● bedspread or sheet

1. Ask the children to wear their mittens for this activity.
2. Read *The Mitten* and discuss it. Ask the children if they think it is real or make-believe.
3. Encourage the children to choose parts to act out the story. If several children want to be the same animal, that's fine.
4. Spread the bedspread on the floor. Pretend this is the mitten. As you re-tell the story, children crawl under the bedspread when their animal crawls into the mitten.
5. At the appropriate time, they toss the blanket in the air and tumble out from underneath.

Weekly Curriculum Vocabulary

cold
estimate
mittens
protect
stretch
warm

Story Props for Retelling *The Mitten*

Art and Language

Materials

8" x 11" tagboard ● scissors ● stapler ● hole punch ● 18" lengths of yarn, one for each child ● staple remover ● markers ● construction paper and plain paper

1. Before presenting the activity, cut out identical mitten shapes from 8" x 11" tagboard, two for each child (see mitten pattern). Staple each pair of mitten shapes together in three places to keep the shapes from sliding. Then, punch holes 1" apart along the edges of each stapled pair of mittens and tie one end of a yarn piece to the hole that is under the thumb and closest to the wrist of the tagboard mitten. Repeat for all mittens.

2. Give each child one of these double mittens and ask them to sew the mitten closed by sewing along the edge with the attached yarn. Show them how to sew by putting yarn into each hole from the top and pulling it out the bottom.

3. Help the children tie off the end of the yarn when they have finished sewing.

4. Help them remove the staples with a staple remover.

5. Encourage the children to use markers to decorate their mittens as desired.

6. They can use paper, markers, and scissors to make any animals they want to fit into their mittens. Remind them the animals must be small enough to fit inside. This mitten will not stretch!

7. Encourage the children to use these props to retell the mitten story in their own way.

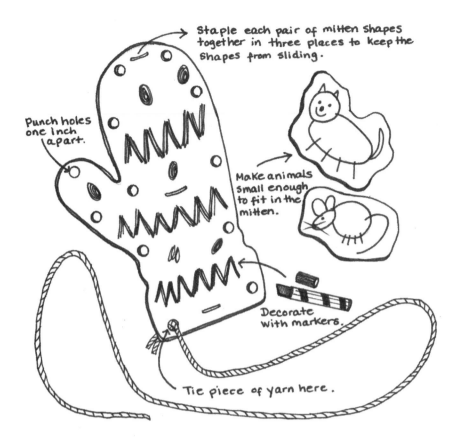

Staple each pair of mitten shapes together in three places to keep the shapes from sliding.

Punch holes one inch apart.

Make animals small enough to fit in the mitten.

Decorate with markers.

Tie piece of yarn here.

Mitten Tree

Language

Materials

small branch ● bucket ● sand ● vinyl-clad paper clips ● children's mittens (from previous activity) ● paper and pen

1. Put a branch, large end down, into a bucket. Hold it as you fill the bucket with sand to keep the branch in place.
2. Help the children use the paper clips to hang their decorated mittens on the "tree."
3. Encourage the children to dictate two- or three-sentence stories about the tree, or ask all the children to contribute to one longer class-composed story.
4. Write down the children's story.

Mitten Tree Song

Language

Materials

mitten tree (see previous activity)

1. To help enhance children's use of descriptive language, encourage them to sing about the mittens on their mitten tree using the song below.

> Tune: *Mary Had a Little Lamb*
> *Once there was a mitten tree,*
> *Mitten tree, mitten tree.*
> *Once there was a mitten tree,*
> *It grew so very tall.*
>
> *On it were (green) mittens,*
> *(Green) mittens, (green) mittens.*
> *On it were (green) mittens.*
> *For some hands, so small.*
>
> *On it were (striped) mittens,*
> *(Striped) mittens, (striped) mittens.*
> *On it were (striped) mittens.*
> *For some hands, so small.*

Animals and Mittens

Math

Materials

mittens of different sizes ● small animal counters

1. Put mittens and small animal counters in the math center.
2. Children can count animals while filling the mittens with them, or they can sort the animals by color, size, or type and put them into separate mittens.

How Many?

Math

Materials

one mitten ● small animal counters ● chart paper and marker

1. Encourage the children to estimate how many animal counters the mitten will hold. Record the guesses on a piece of chart paper.
2. Add animals to the mitten until it is full.
3. Count the animals as a child removes them, and then check the children's estimation. Was it the same as, higher, or lower than the actual number?
4. On other days, repeat with mittens of other sizes.

I Like Mittens

Music

1. Sing the following song with the children.

   Tune: *Are You Sleeping?*
   I like mittens.
   I like mittens.
   Yes, I do.
   Yes, I do.
   Mittens keep my hands warm.
   Mittens keep my hands warm,
   Through and through,
   Through and through.

   I like mittens.
   I like mittens.
   Yes, I do.
   Yes, I do.
   They are soft and fuzzy.
   They are soft and fuzzy,
   Through and through,
   Through and through.

Str-e-e-e-tching a Mitten

Science

Materials

The Mitten (any version) • a pair of old mittens • small animal counters (or small classroom items) • fabric samples

1. Read the book *The Mitten* to the children again.
2. Discuss what happened to the mitten as more animals squeezed in.
3. Ask each child to add a small animal to one of the mittens. Encourage them to observe how it stretches as more and more animals are added.
4. Fill the mitten as full as possible without letting it burst. Empty it and compare it to its mate. Did it change in any way, or did it return to normal size?
5. Provide many small samples of fabric for children to explore. Do any of the fabrics stretch like the mitten?

Oven Mitts and Mittens—What Do They Do?

Science

Materials

several oven mitts • children's mittens • ice cubes • paper towels

1. Ask the children to hold their own mittens. Discuss what mittens are used for—protecting hands from the cold.
2. Show oven mitts to the children. Discuss their use—protecting hands from hot items. Do the children think the oven mitts can also protect their hands from cold? Discuss this.
3. Give each child, in turn, an oven mitt, two ice cubes, and a paper towel. Have them put the mitt on one hand, then hold an ice cube in each hand for as long as is comfortable. When necessary, they should put the cubes on the paper towel.
4. What do they observe? Can an oven mitt protect hands from the cold?

Insulation and Layers

Science

Materials

ice cubes • mittens • paper plates

1. Discuss again the idea that mittens keep our hands warm. Ask the children if they think mittens can keep things cold.
2. Have the children place some ice cubes into one mitten, and then some ice cubes in several layers of mittens stuffed inside each other. Place each on a paper plate.
3. Place these items side by side in a visible place in the room.
4. Check the mittens every hour. What do the children observe? Help them understand that while one mitten keeps the ice insulated from the classroom's warm air, several layers of mittens provide still more insulation. Mittens keep our hands warm in the same way. Our hands are warmer than the outdoor air, and mittens keep the cold air from our hands.

More About Insulation and Layers

Science

Materials

an old mitten • 8" lengths of yarn, one for each child

1. Unravel part of an old mitten so the children can see that it is made of one long piece of yarn.
2. Give each child an 8" piece of yarn and challenge him to take it apart. They will discover that it is made from many small yarn pieces layered and twisted together. Remind them of the earlier experiment with layering. The many layers within the yarn help insulate warm hands from the cold air.

Learning Center Ideas

Dramatic Play Area

Materials

mittens of various sizes • shopping bags • play money

1. Add the items to the Dramatic Play Area so the children can create a mitten store.

Related Books

The Missing Mitten Mystery by Stephen Kellogg
The Mitten by Jan Brett
The Mitten: An Old Ukrainian Folktale by Alvin R. Tresselt
Mushroom in the Rain by Mirra Ginsburg (This is a twist on the theme that there is always room for one more. It's a good story to compare with *The Mitten*.)

January 21—
Hugging Day

Introducing the Weekly Curriculum Theme

Weekly Curriculum Vocabulary

bear hug
cooperate
cooperation
friend
gentle
hug
rigatoni

1. Tell the children that National Hugging Day occurs this week.
2. Give each child a big, gentle hug and encourage the children to give gentle hugs to each other.
3. Hugging Day is near the time for observing Martin Luther King, Jr.'s birthday, and some of this week's activities can also be used for that observance because they emphasize cooperation and treating others with dignity, kindness, and respect.
4. Talk about Hugging Day and how it is a time to hug people we care about. Discuss how we also show our love by treating each other kindly and gently. Remind children that not everyone likes to be hugged and touched, and it is important to ask before you hug a friend.
5. Discuss additional ways to show caring, such as taking turns cheerfully, helping those who need our help, comforting friends who are upset, and so on.

Hugs on the Ceiling—A Mural

Art

Materials
large piece of bulletin board paper ● markers ● masking tape

1. On a large piece of bulletin board paper, ask the children to draw pictures of people and things they like to hug (trees, dolls, stuffed animals). They can draw these in any direction.
2. Make loops of masking tape with the sticky side out. Stick these to the back of the mural, and then attach the mural flat against the ceiling so the children can see it while lying on their backs and looking up.

A Hug for You

Art

Materials
bulletin board paper ● markers ● scissors

1. The children take turns lying down with just their head, shoulders, and outstretched arms on the bulletin board paper. Trace an outline around each child.
2. Encourage the children to color in their facial features on the outline. Then give them child-safe scissors to cut around their outlines, except for the hands.
3. Cut around each child's outlined hands. On the arms, write "My Hug Is for You!"

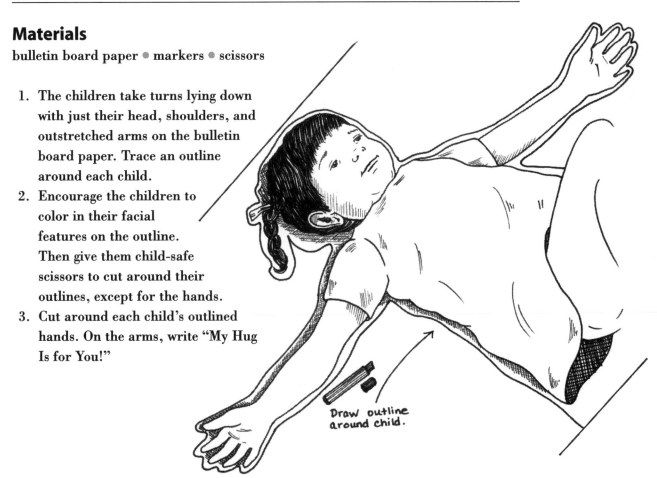

Draw outline around child.

Hugging Book
Language

Materials
paper ● stapler ● markers

1. Beforehand, make a four-page blank book for each child by stapling together white paper.
2. Discuss hugs, including who the children like to hug, and who hugs them.
3. Give each child a blank book.
4. Encourage the children to draw on each page someone who hugs them. Encourage them to draw each person showing something distinctive about him or her. Perhaps Aunt Marie has long curly hair, or perhaps baby sister wears her purple dress.
5. Encourage the children to show and "read" their books to each other or, in turn, to a small group of friends.

Communicating Without Words
Language

1. Show the children how to give tiny hugs by hooking their own index finger around the index finger of another. Both children then gently squeeze their fingers for the tiny hug.
2. To quiet the group, give a tiny hug to a child and place your hugging finger across your mouth to signal the need to be quiet.
3. Ask that child to give a tiny hug and then a quiet signal to three people within her reach. Each child who is hugged passes it to others until all are quiet.
4. Practice this a few times each day to remind the children of the procedure.

The "Ug" Family
Language

Materials
sentence strips ● marker ● pocket chart

1. Use the hug theme to investigate and learn about the "ug" family of words. Write __ug on a sentence strip. On small pieces of strip, write individual consonants.
2. Place the __ug in a pocket chart.

3. Ask each child to select a consonant to place in the blank to form words such as *hug, rug, bug, mug, dug, tug*, and so on. They can also form nonsense words such as *kug* and *nug*.
4. Ask the group to read each word that is formed.

My Hug Is This Big

Math

Materials

yarn ● scissors ● masking tape ● fine-tip permanent marker ● clear cellophane tape

1. Each child takes a turn standing with his arms outstretched to the sides, as if about to give a hug.
2. Use yarn to measure the child's hug from fingertip to fingertip. Cut the yarn and put a strip of masking tape at one end. Write the child's name on the masking tape. Repeat with all the children.
3. With the children, compare the lengths of yarn. Whose hug is longest? Shortest?
4. If desired, stretch out the yarn lengths on a bulletin board with the caption "My Hug Is THIS BIG!"

Variation: Attach all of the lengths of yarn end to end, making one long piece of yarn. Tape one end to a classroom wall, then string it around and around the room, taping it at 3' intervals. Show the children how far all of their hugs reach when put together.

Estimating Kisses and Hugs

Math

Materials

transparent plastic jars, several sizes ● chocolate candy kisses and hugs ● paper and pencil

1. At the beginning of the week, fill a small transparent jar with chocolate candy kisses and hugs. Replace the lid.
2. Display the jar on a table along with a piece of paper and a pencil for children to write their names and the numeral that represents how many candy pieces they think are in the jar. (If necessary, help the children write with their names and their number guesses.)
3. After all the children have estimated a number, empty the jar and count the contents with the group.
4. The child with the number closest to the correct number distributes a piece of candy to each child, and then fills a different jar for the next day's activity.
5. Repeat the activity each day, changing the number of candy pieces or the size of the jar.

Hugging Song

Music

1. Sing the song below, substituting other names for the ones in parentheses.

    Tune: *Here We Go 'Round the Mulberry Bush*
    I like to hug (my Mommy),
    (My Mommy), (my Mommy).
    I like to hug (my Mommy),
    Because I love (her) so.

    I like to hug (my Teddy bear),
    (My Teddy bear), (my Teddy bear).
    I like to hug (my Teddy bear),
    Because I love (it) so.

Hugging Roll-'Em-Ups

Snack/Cooking

Materials

thin slices of ham or turkey ● lettuce leaves ● individual cups of ranch dressing

1. Show the children how to place a meat slice on top of a lettuce leaf and then roll the two together so the lettuce (on the outside) is hugging the meat (on the inside).
2. Let each child repeat the process.
3. Provide cups of ranch dressing to use as a dip.

Rigatoni Hugs

Snack/Cooking

Materials

rigatoni, 2 pieces per child ● string cheese ● mild salad dressing in small cups, 1 per child

1. Precook and cool rigatoni. Cut the string cheese in half, crosswise, and into fourths, lengthwise.
2. Give each child two pieces each of rigatoni and cheese. Demonstrate how to slide the cheese into the rigatoni.
3. Provide individual cups of dressing for children to use as a dip.

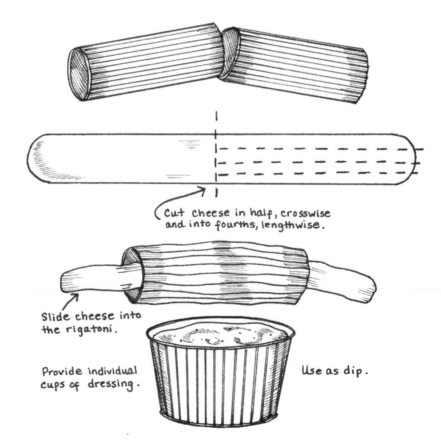

Cut cheese in half, crosswise and into fourths, lengthwise.

Slide cheese into the rigatoni.

Provide individual cups of dressing.

Use as dip.

Learning Center Ideas

Reading Area

Materials

stuffed animals • baby dolls and rag dolls • books about friendship and hugging (see below)

1. Emphasize hugging in the Reading Area. Encourage the children to hug and read to a doll or stuffed animal.

Related Books

Ask Mr. Bear by Marjorie Flack
A Book of Hugs by Dave Ross
Coco the Koala by Vera De Backker
Hug by Jez Alborough
Hugs and Kisses by Christophe Loupy
I Love You Like Crazy Cakes by Rose A. Lewis
Pass the Fritters, Critters by Cheryl Chapman
The Relatives Came by Cynthia Rylant
The Runaway Rice Cake by Ying Chang Compestine
So Much by Trish Cooke

4th Week of January—
Think Warm Thoughts Week

Materials

any book about summer and hot weather activities (see suggestions on page 66)

1. Warm up the winter days with a week of warm weather activities.
2. Read a book about summertime.
3. Tell the children they will be pretending that the weather is hot. Encourage them to remember things they like to do on hot summer days and nights.
4. Ask them about things they do or places they go with their families in the summer.

Weekly Curriculum Vocabulary

buried (in the sand)
cone
different
float
plant (noun, verb)
same
shop (noun, verb)
sink

Summer Clouds

Art

Materials

white construction paper ● pencils ● child-safe scissors

1. Give each child a sheet of white construction paper. Help them fold their papers in half horizontally.
2. Ask the children to draw a large cloud shape on the outside of their folded papers, encouraging them to make their own individual cloud shapes.
3. Help them hold their papers closed and cut out their shape on the lines, forming two identical cloud shapes.
4. Help them write their names on their shapes.
5. Gather the clouds and mix them up.
6. Challenge the children to find matching pairs. Some will do so by matching shapes; others will match names. Remind the children that some clouds will need to be flipped over in order to find their match.
7. Place the activity in the Manipulatives Area for children to use independently.

Ice Cream Parlor

Dramatic Play and Language

Materials

cardboard box ● scissors ● brown construction paper ● tape ● Koosh balls, yarn balls, or cotton balls (for ice cream balls) ● clean empty ice cream containers ● ice cream scoops ● aprons ● cash register ● coin purses and wallets ● various art supplies, as needed

1. Suggest that the children make an ice cream shop for "summer customers."
2. Cut holes in the bottom of a cardboard box (adult only). Then turn the box upside down, with the holes on top to hold "ice cream cones."
3. Show the children how to make brown paper cones by rolling them into a cone shape and taping them along the seam. Put the cones into the cone holder.
4. Provide the remaining materials and let the children use their imaginations to set up their shop.
5. Support their efforts to make signs, menus, money, and more with items from the Art Area.

Roll brown paper into cone shape and tape along seam.

Summer and Winter Items: Same and Different

Language

Materials

items used in summer (beach pail and shovel, swim tube, paper fan) • items used in winter (coat, mittens, snow shovel) • items used year-round (sweater, towel, teddy bear)

1. Display the summer, winter, and year-round items.
2. Ask the children to identify items used in winter. Then ask them to identify items used in summer.
3. Talk about the items that fit into both categories.
4. Select a child to choose any two items and encourage him or her to tell the group two ways the items are the same and two ways they are different. Repeat so that everyone has a turn.

Seasonal Sports

Language

Materials (if desired)

items (or pictures of items) used in summer sports (baseball bat, bathing suit, roller skates) • items (or pictures of items) used in winter sports (football, snowshoes, hockey puck, ice skates)

1. Talk about the items and their associated sports. Discuss reasons why they are enjoyed at a particular time of year.
2. Discuss how some sports are adapted to be played year-round. (For example, indoor ice skating rinks allow skating in summer, and indoor pools allow swimming and diving in winter.)

Summer Flowers

Math

Materials

permanent marker ● 11 plastic flowerpots ● florist's foam or Styrofoam ● variety of artificial flowers, some with one blossom and some with many blossoms

1. With the marker, write one numeral, 0-10, on each flowerpot.
2. Tightly fill each pot with florist's foam.
3. Encourage the children to count the blossoms on each flower to find ones that match the numeral on each pot, using one or more flower stems to match the correct total.
4. Ask them to "plant" the flowers in the matching pots.
5. Encourage the children to find a friend to check their work, providing counting practice for another child.
6. Challenge the children to put the pots in order from 0-10.

Jumping Frogs

Movement

1. Encourage the children to sing and act out the following song:

> Tune: *Old MacDonald Had a Farm*
> *Five frogs were at the pond one day,*
> *Jump, frogs, jump.*
> *They thought they'd play and play all day,*
> *Jump, frogs, jump.*
> *Jumping here, jumping there,*
> *Frogs jumping everywhere.*
> *One frog jumped high and jumped away,*
> *Jump, frogs, jump.*

2. Repeat with four frogs, then three, and so on until you get to zero.

January Picnic

Outdoors

Materials

picnic basket ● easily-eaten snack such as sandwich halves or apple wedges ● napkins ● shower curtain liners ● blankets ● plastic ants, if desired

1. Help everyone bundle up to go outdoors to enjoy a quick picnic.
2. Pack the picnic basket with a snack and napkins.
3. Once outside, place the shower curtain liners on top of the cold ground or snow and cover with blankets. If desired, toss some plastic ants on the blanket, just for fun.
4. Enjoy the outdoor picnic. If the weather is too bitter for an outdoor picnic, have the picnic on your classroom floor.

Summer at the Pond

Science

Materials

water table or large, plastic storage containers ● sanitized Styrofoam trays ● scissors ● variety of items that do not float including plastic frogs, plastic fishing worms, and plastic fishing lures with hooks removed ● laminated signs "float" and "sink" ● aquarium-size fishing nets

1. Make pond creatures by cutting out shapes such as fish, bugs, and snakes from sanitized Styrofoam trays. These items will float in water.
2. Place several inches of water in the water table.
3. Put the Styrofoam shapes and the items that do not float next to the water table and encourage the children to explore.

Caution: Closely supervise water play.

4. Support the children's discoveries as they explore.
5. The following day, place the signs and fishing nets nearby. Encourage the children to catch items with the nets and place them on the appropriate sign.

Fruit Ice

Snack/Cooking

Materials

permanent marker * small waxed paper cups * orange or grape juice * freezer

1. Write each child's name on a separate paper cup.
2. Ask each child to pour juice into his cup.
3. Put the cups in the freezer.
4. When the juice is frozen, the children peel the cups away from their frozen juice, a little at a time, so they can eat the frozen treat.

Learning Center Ideas

Sensory Area

Sand Table—Summer at the Beach

Materials

sand table or large, plastic storage bin(s) * sand * plastic bugs * assorted seashells or river rocks * beach pails and shovels * beach towel

1. Place sand in the sand table or storage bin.
2. Bury some of the plastic bugs in the sand. Add other items and encourage the children to pretend they are playing at water's edge on a hot, summery day.

Related Books

Anansi Goes Fishing by Eric A. Kimmel
Frogs by Gail Gibbons
Grandma Summer by Harley Jessup
Grandpa and Bo by Kevin Henkes
Harry by the Sea by Gene Zion
Henry and Mudge in the Green Time by Cynthia Rylant
How I Spent My Summer Vacation by Mark Teague
Ice Cream by Elisha Cooper
The Icky Sticky Frog by Dawn Bentley
In the Small, Small Pond by Denise Fleming
In the Tall, Tall Grass by Denise Fleming
Jump, Frog, Jump! by Robert Kalan
One Hot Summer Day by Nina Crews
Simply Delicious by Margaret Mahy
Tuesday by David Wiesner

February Is Friendship Month

Introducing the Weekly Curriculum Theme

Materials

any book about friendship (see list of books on page 73)

1. Read a book about friendship.
2. With the children, talk about friendship, focusing on what friends do with each other and how they show they care about each other.

Weekly Curriculum Vocabulary

autograph
different
estimate
friend
friendship
same

Painting With a Friend

Art

Materials

easels and easel paper ● paints

1. Set up easels, side by side, so the children can paint with their friends.

Friendship Drawings

Art

Materials

paper ● crayons

1. Pair up the children and have each pair stand up and look at each other.
2. Instruct each child to look closely at her friend, noticing the style and colors of clothing and shoes, hair and eye color, hair length and style, and so on.
3. Ask each child to draw the other child in the pair, and then sign her work with the word "by" preceding her name. (Help those children who need assistance writing their name.)
4. Then the children trade pictures so the child who is depicted in the pictures can also write his name on the portrait.
5. Display the portraits where everyone can enjoy them.

Good Friends Bulletin Board

Bulletin Board

Materials

camera

1. Take pictures of the children throughout the day, indoors and out, while they are interacting with each other.
2. Get the film developed overnight.
3. The next day, hang the photos in a casual arrangement on a bulletin board titled "Good Friends."
4. Invite families to look at the display.

Friendship Carpets

Cooperation

Materials

carpet squares ● manipulatives, such as Duplos or Legos, puzzles, board games, patterning materials, small magnets, and magnetic items

1. To provide opportunities for cooperation and friendship, occasionally put carpet squares on the floor with manipulatives on them.
2. Encourage a pair of children to sit at each carpet and play together with the materials that are there.

Friend, May We?

Games and Outdoors

1. This group game is a variation of "Mother, May I?"
2. Choose a child to be IT (the "Friend"). He stands with his back to the children, who stand behind a line a good distance from him.
3. The group sings the following:

> Tune: *Twinkle, Twinkle Little Star*
> *Friend, oh, friend, how do you do?*
> *How many steps may we take to you?*

4. The Friend answers and the children take that many steps. The game continues in this manner.
5. The Friend will be able to determine how close the children are by the sounds of their voices.
6. When desired, the Friend answers, "None!" The children run back to the starting line with the Friend in pursuit. The child caught by the Friend becomes the Friend for the next game.

Autograph/Phone Books

Language

Materials

blank books, 1 for each child ● pencils

1. This activity gives children practice writing their own names and reading their friends' names.

2. Explain that an autograph book is a place to collect signatures (a person's name written by that person).

3. Give each child a blank book.

Note: Purchase blank books or make them by stapling sheets of paper together.

4. Encourage the children to gather signatures from their friends and also sign their friends' books.

5. To provide practice writing and reading numerals, encourage (and help, if necessary) the children to use the blank books as telephone books. Each child can write her name and telephone number in each other's books.

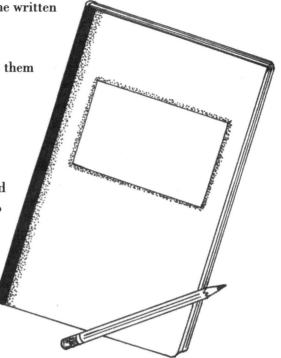

Note: Be sure to get parents' permission before allowing children to trade phone numbers.

Best Friends—Q and U

Language

Materials

chart paper • marker • A-B-C picture books • pencils and crayons • children's journals

1. Ask the children to name words that begin with the letter "Q."

2. Print these words on the chart paper.

3. After you have written several words, ask if anyone notices something special about the words. If nobody responds, show the children that the letter Q is always followed by the letter U. Tell them that Q has a best friend. Ask if anyone can guess the friend's name.

4. Continue adding to the list of words and, with the children, check to see if Q is always followed by its friend U.

5. Look in several A-B-C books, noticing the words the author uses for Q. Do all of these items begin with Q-U?

6. Challenge the children to copy a few of the words into their journals and to illustrate them.

How Many?

Math and Cooperation

Materials

large appliance boxes in several sizes

1. Before the children arrive, remove or open both ends of the boxes.
2. Ask the children to estimate how many friends can fit into one of the boxes.
3. Place the box on its side and let the children enter one at a time.

Caution: Supervise closely to ensure safety.

4. Was their estimate too few, too many, or just right?
5. Repeat with boxes that are different sizes.

Friendship Dance

Movement

1. Ask the children to move in pairs, dancing while holding hands, crawling together through a maze, and jumping together.
2. Encourage them to suggest other ways they can move together.

Friendship Song

Music

1. Ask the children to sing the first verse of the following song. Then, in turn, sing about each child in the group.
2. End the song by repeating the first verse.

> Tune: *The Farmer in the Dell*
> *We are all good friends.*
> *We are all good friends.*
> *I like you and you like me.*
> *We are all good friends.*
>
> *_____ is our friend.*
> *_____ is our friend.*
> *We work and play at school all day.*
> *_____ is our friend.*

Hello, Friends

Music

1. Help the children learn about taking turns, listening for their turns, and waiting patiently for others to formulate ideas while singing the following call-and-response song.

2. Divide the children into two groups who sing, back and forth, to each other.

> Tune: *Skip to My Lou*
> *(Group 1): Hello, friends, how are you?*
> *(Group 2:) We're just fine. How are you?*
> *(Group 1): We're fine, too. Hey, what's new?*
> *(Everyone): Let's all have a good day.*

3. Repeat the verse, with the groups changing the parts they sing.

Friend's Fingerprints

Science

Materials

ink pad ● paper ● marker ● magnifying glasses ● computer scanner and printer, optional

1. Fingerprints provide an opportunity to talk about how friends are the same and how they are different. Explain that everyone has fingerprints, and while some fingerprints are similar, no two people have identical prints.

2. On several pieces of paper, write every child's name on every sheet.

3. Encourage each child to press an index finger onto the ink pad, and then press the finger beside her name on each of the papers.

4. Provide magnifying glasses so the children can examine the prints, looking for similarities and differences.

5. If possible, scan the fingerprints, enlarge them, and print them so they are easier to compare.

6. If desired, use these as a border on the "Good Friends" bulletin board.

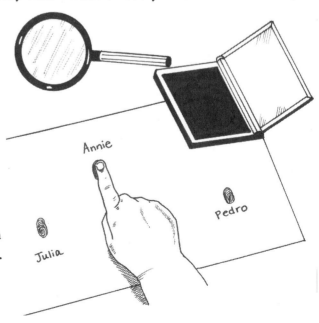

Friendship Snack Mix

Snack/Cooking

Materials

variety of snack items (such as raisins, cereal squares and circles, slivered almonds, and dried banana slices) ● serving bowl and serving spoon ● small cups

1. Ask each child to add a small amount of a snack item to a large bowl. Mix well.
2. Each child fills a cup with mix and serves it to a friend.

Learning Center Ideas

Writing Area

Materials

recycled envelopes and postage stamps ● paper ● pens and pencils

1. Place these items in the Writing Area so the children can write notes and deliver them to their friends.

Related Books

Best Friends by Steven Kellogg
Brianna, Jamaica, and the Dance of Spring by Juanita Havill
Bruno the Baker by Lars Klinting
Corduroy by Don Freeman
The Friendship Tree by Kathy Caple
Frog and Toad Are Friends by Arnold Lobel
George and Martha (any in the series) by James Marshall
Jamaica and Brianna by Juanita Havill
Miss Spider's Tea Party by David Kirk
Moonbear's Friend by Frank Asch
The Rainbow Fish by Marcus Pfister
Rainbow Fish to the Rescue by Marcus Pfister

February Is
Dental
Health
Month

Introducing the Weekly Curriculum Theme

Weekly Curriculum Vocabulary

baby teeth
dental
dentist
floss
germs
hygiene
permanent teeth
stains
tooth
tooth decay
toothbrush

Materials

toothbrush and toothpaste ● small bag ● stuffed animal

1. Before the children arrive, put the toothbrush and toothpaste in the bag.
2. Show the stuffed animal to the children. Tell them that the animal isn't feeling too well today. His tooth had been hurting very badly, so he went to the dentist. Make up a story about the dentist finding a sick tooth, treating the tooth, and then talking with the animal about taking care of its teeth. Ask the children what the dentist might have said.
3. Ask a child to reach into the bag and remove the toothbrush and toothpaste. Discuss tooth care and how brushing removes sticky foods from teeth. When germs get in the sticky foods, the germs also stick to the teeth and hurt them. Keeping teeth clean keeps germs from sticking. Flossing helps to clean teeth, too.

Floss Painting

Art

Materials

3 small bowls ● tempera paint, 3 colors ● 8 ½" x 11" white paper, 2 sheets per child ● dental floss ● glue stick ● 18" x 24" sheets of construction paper in matching colors

1. Pour a small amount of paint into each bowl.
2. In turn, give each child three 18" pieces of floss. Remind each child that floss is for painting, not for putting in their mouths or around their necks.
3. Ask the children to put one piece of floss into each paint color, leaving a few inches unpainted.
4. Show the children how to drop one piece of floss onto one sheet of paper with the unpainted end off the paper, and then cover the paper with the second sheet.
5. Help the child hold the top sheet in place with the palm of one hand while she pulls the floss sideways from between the paper sheets.
6. Repeat with the other two colors.
7. The children will each have two floss paintings. Help them use a glue stick to mount their papers side by side on a piece of construction paper.

Painting With Toothbrushes

Art

Materials

cardboard egg cartons ● paint ● toothbrushes

1. Ask the children to pretend that the egg cartons are teeth.
2. Challenge them to "brush the teeth" with toothbrushes and paint. The paint will show how thoroughly they brushed.

I Brushed My Teeth Today

Language

Materials

markers ● chart paper

1. Make two columns on the chart paper. Label one "I Brushed My Teeth Today." Label the other "I Forgot to Brush My Teeth Today."
2. Children write their names (or make a mark) in the correct column. (This provides motivation to brush and provides practice in writing names.)
3. Repeat the activity every day for the week, providing motivation to build a healthy habit.

I Brushed My Teeth Today	I Forgot to Brush My Teeth Today

Baby Teeth and Permanent Teeth

Language and Science

Materials

Little Rabbit's Loose Tooth by Lucy Bate

1. Read the book, and then talk about baby teeth and the permanent teeth that grow in to replace them.
2. Emphasize that no more teeth grow in if permanent teeth are damaged or destroyed. That's why we need to take good care of our teeth.
3. With the children, review how to care for baby teeth and permanent teeth.

I Like This Toothpaste Best

Math

Materials

construction paper ● scissors ● markers ● small paper plates and napkins ● small cups of water ● 3 different brands or flavors of toothpaste ● chart paper ● tape ● glue sticks

1. Cut out toothpaste tube shapes from construction paper and give one to each child. Ask each child to write his name on his toothpaste tube shape.
2. Give each child a paper plate, a napkin, and a cup of water.
3. Put a tiny amount of toothpaste onto each plate. Show the toothpaste tube to the children so they will know which brand or flavor they are sampling. Ask them to taste a tiny amount of their sample. Have them clean their tongues with their napkins, and then swish and swallow a bit of water.
4. In turn, repeat #3 with the other two toothpastes.
5. Make a graph on a piece of chart paper with 3 columns, each labeled "I Like This Toothpaste." With tape, attach one toothpaste tube to the top of each column on the graph.
6. Ask the children to glue their paper toothpaste-tube shapes in the column headed by the tube that indicates the taste they prefer.
7. Discuss results. Which toothpaste was most popular? Which was the least popular? Use the graph to explore the concepts *more, less, greater than, less than, the same as, most, least,* and so on.

I Like This Toothpaste	I Like This Toothpaste	I Like This Toothpaste

Germ, Germ, Toothbrush

Movement

1. This circle game is played like Duck, Duck, Goose.
2. Select one child to be IT. All the other children sit on the ground in a circle, facing the center of the circle.
3. IT walks around the outside of the circle, tapping each child gently on the head as she says, "Germ," "germ," "germ" as she touches each head. Finally she says, "Toothbrush" when touching one child's head. That child gets up and chases IT around the circle.
4. If the second child catches the first, IT must sit in the center of the circle until another child is caught and placed in the center.

5. If IT makes it around the circle and back to the second child's place without being caught, she now sits in that place.
6. Either way, the second child becomes IT and the game continues.

I Brushed My Teeth Today
Music

1. Sing the following to the tune of "The Farmer in the Dell."

   I brushed my teeth today.
   I brushed my teeth today.
   They're sparkling white
   And clean and bright.
   I brushed my teeth today.

   My teeth feel very clean.
   My teeth feel very clean.
   They're sparkling white
   And clean and bright.
   My teeth feel very clean.

Stained Eggs
Science

Materials
hard-boiled eggs with white shells, 1 for each child plus a few extra ●
permanent fine-tip marker ● clear plastic cups ● cola, any brand, regular or diet ●
clear bowl ● toothbrushes and toothpaste

1. Use the permanent marker to write each child's name on a hard-boiled egg.
2. Review the importance of brushing teeth, explaining that many foods stain our teeth and that brushing regularly can prevent stain build-up.
3. Discuss cola drinks. Are they good for teeth? Tell the children they will be scientists, exploring how cola affects teeth. They will pretend that the white eggs are their white teeth.
4. Give each child a plastic cup. Ask them to place their eggs into their cups. Pour some cola into each cup, covering the egg. Place any extra eggs in the bowl. Do not cover these with cola.

5. Let the eggs soak for 45 minutes. Ask the children to check them after 20 minutes by briefly taking them out of their cups. What do they notice?

6. After 45 minutes, ask the children to remove their eggs and compare them with the eggs in the bowl. What do they notice? How did the cola change their eggs?

7. Let the children brush their eggs with toothpaste. What do they observe? Can they brush long enough to return the eggs to their original color?

8. DO NOT allow children to eat these eggs.

What Snacks Are Healthy for My Teeth?

Snack/Cooking

Materials

chocolate cookies with cream filling ● hand mirrors ● apple wedges (⅛ apple for each child)

1. Give each child a chocolate cookie (and no beverage) to eat. Remind them to chew slowly.

2. After they have eaten, ask the children to look in mirrors to see what's on their teeth. (Chocolate crumbs will stick to their teeth and gums.)

3. Next, serve apple wedges to the children and remind them to chew slowly. Ask them to look again in the mirrors. What do they notice? (Apples will begin cleaning the crumbs from their teeth.)

4. Repeat #3 and observe that teeth appear even cleaner. Discuss their observations; lead children to conclude that sweet cookies stick to their teeth while apples help clean their teeth and leave no sticky remains on their teeth.

5. Keep a mirror near the Snack Area so the children can inspect their teeth after other snacks.

Learning Center Ideas

Dramatic Play Area

Dentist's Office

Materials

small unbreakable mirrors ● an appointment book and pen ● scraps of paper (to make appointment reminder cards) ● pictures of smiles ● toothbrushes and toothpaste

1. Help the children set up a dentist's office in the Dramatic Play Area.
2. Provide the materials above, as well as any other materials they request.

Related Books

The Bear's Toothache by David M. McPhail
How Many Teeth (Let's-Read-And-Find-Out-Book) by Paul Showers
Little Rabbit's Loose Tooth by Lucy Bate
Those Icky Sticky Smelly Cavity-Causing But...Invisible Germs by Julie Stricklin
The Tooth Book by Theo LeSieg
The Tooth Fairy Book by Deborah Kovacs

February 2—
Groundhog Day

Materials
chart paper ● marker

Begin this activity before Groundhog Day.
1. Groundhog Day is February 2 every year. On the Monday before Groundhog Day (or the week before, if Groundhog Day falls on a Monday), write the following note to the class on chart paper:

February 2 will be Groundhog Day.
The groundhog will come out of its burrow.
If it sees its shadow, it will hurry back inside and we will have six more weeks of cold weather.
If it doesn't see its shadow, it will stay out, and warm weather will come soon.

Weekly Curriculum Vocabulary

burrow
groundhog
hibernate
hibernation
shadow
Spring

2. Read the note to the children and explain to them about Groundhog Day. If weather permits, go outside so everyone can see their shadows. If not, shine a flashlight or projection light on the children's hands and on several objects to show their shadows.

3. Every day until Groundhog Day, discuss the present day's weather and ask the children if they think the groundhog would be able to see its shadow today. Record the children's decision, and on February 1 ask the children to look at the record and predict whether the animal will see its shadow the next day.

4. On February 2 write on the chart whether or not the groundhog saw its shadow. Also write: "Was the groundhog right?"

5. For the next six weeks, have the children record daily whether the weather is warm or cold. At the end of the six weeks compare the results—more warm days or more cold days? Decide if the groundhog was correct.

Weekly Curriculum Extension Activities

Groundhogs and Their Burrows

Art

Materials

small, white, lightweight paper plates, 1 for each child ● sponges ● scissors ● spring-type clothespins ● brown paint in a shallow dish ● crayons and markers ● child-safe scissors ● scraps of construction paper in brown and white ● stapler and glue ● duct tape ● paint stirrers (from a paint supply store) ● brown mailing envelopes

1. Give each child a paper plate to make a groundhog stick puppet that comes out of its burrow.

2. Cut sponges into pieces and clip a clothespin onto each sponge piece. Encourage the children to dip a sponge into brown paint and then press it onto their paper plates to create brown fur on their groundhog's face (the paper plate).

3. When the paint dries, they can use crayons and markers to add eyes, a nose, and whiskers to the face.

4. Encourage them to cut out brown ears and white teeth from construction paper. Demonstrate how to staple on the ears and glue the teeth in place.

5. Give each child a paint stirrer. Show them how to tape their groundhog faces onto the ends of their paint stirrers.

6. Cut brown mailing envelopes in half crosswise. Slit the end of each envelope half and give one to each child. Demonstrate how to slide the puppet into either open end. The groundhog is now asleep in its home! When the child pushes the stick, the groundhog emerges.

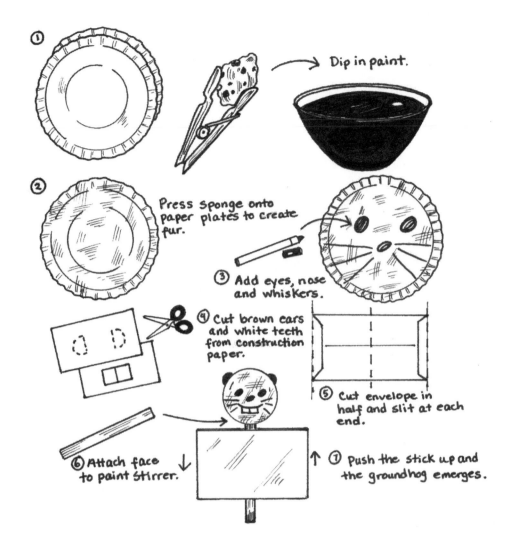

① Dip in paint.

② Press sponge onto paper plates to create fur.

③ Add eyes, nose and whiskers.

④ Cut brown ears and white teeth from construction paper.

⑤ Cut envelope in half and slit at each end.

⑥ Attach face to paint stirrer.

⑦ Push the stick up and the groundhog emerges.

Groundhog Poem

Language

Materials

markers ● chart paper ● index card ● scissors ● drinking straw ● tape

1. Write the poem below on a piece of chart paper.
2. Cut out a small circle from an index card. Make a groundhog-face stick puppet by taping the circle to a drinking straw and decorating it to look like a groundhog. Use this as a pointer while you read the poem with the children.
3. Ask the children to hold their puppets that they made in the "Groundhogs and their Burrows" activity (page 82). Tell them to keep their puppets in their "burrows" until the poem's final line, and then they can manipulate their puppets out of the burrows.

In a burrow under the hill,
Groundhog is sleeping
Quiet and still.
On Groundhog Day
He'll come out to see
If there's a shadow.
What will it be?

Six cold weeks
Or an early spring?
We're as curious as anything.
On Groundhog Day
We'll wait to see,
Will he come out?
Yes! One, two, three! (children push groundhogs out of their burrows)

Groundhogs and Burrows Matching Game

Math

Materials

six 5" squares of white felt ● scissors (adult only) ● fine-tip permanent marker ● dark brown felt

1. Cut out a burrow shape from each square of white felt. These become snow-covered groundhog burrows.
2. Write a numeral, 0-5, on each burrow.
3. Cut out fifteen 2" tall "blob" shapes from brown felt for groundhogs. Draw dots for eyes and a nose. Draw two teeth.
4. Challenge the children to place the burrows in numerical order and "hide" the correct number of groundhogs behind each burrow.
5. Have the children ask a friend to check their work. This also provides counting practice for the child who is checking.

Passage of Time

Math

Materials

marker ● calendar

1. Children will notice and experience the passage of time while you chart the weather for the six weeks following Groundhog Day (see opening activity).

Mark these days on a calendar, noticing how many days have passed and how many more days you will observe the weather before the six weeks end.

Groundhog Patterns

Math

Materials
dark and light brown construction paper ● scissors ● crayons or markers

1. Cut out 3" squares from dark brown and light brown construction paper.
2. Give each child a light brown square and a dark brown square. Encourage them to draw one groundhog on each paper square.
3. Gather all of the pictures and let the children use them for patterning activities.

Groundhog's Home

Movement—Indoors or Outdoors

Materials
several large appliance boxes ● duct tape ● blanket ● flashlights

1. Gather several empty appliance boxes. Open both ends of all but one.
2. Use heavy duct tape to tape the open boxes end-to-end to form a tunnel.
3. Open the remaining box at one end only. Attach this end to the tunnel. This is the groundhog's home.
4. Put a blanket in this final box to add comfort to the groundhog's home.
5. Place flashlights near the tunnel's open end.
6. Let the children pretend to be groundhogs who crawl down an earthen tunnel into the burrow. When they are ready, they can crawl back out through the tunnel to look for their shadows.
7. When a groundhog emerges, a child with a flashlight may shine a light on him. If so, he goes back into his burrow.
8. If no sun shines on him, he comes out of the tunnel and may choose to become the sun.

9. To allow more children to play with less waiting time, set up several tunnels and use several flashlights.

Groundhog Song
Music

1. Sing the following song with the children.

> Tune: *The Farmer in the Dell*
> *When cold weather comes around,*
> *The groundhog sleeps in the ground.*
> *If he's scared by his shadow on Groundhog Day,*
> *He goes back in the ground.*

Hibernation
Science

Materials
books about animals that hibernate

1. Talk about and read books about animals that hibernate like the groundhog. Discuss hibernation.

Groundhogs in the Ground
Snack/Cooking

Materials
wax paper ● refrigerated biscuits, one for each child ● low-fat hot dogs, one for every four children ● knife (adult only) ● toaster oven

1. Have the children work in small groups. Place a sheet of wax paper in front of each child to provide a clean work surface.
2. Give each child a refrigerated biscuit and ask the children to flatten them by patting them.
3. Cut the hot dogs into fourths and give one piece to each child. Tell the children that the hot dogs are groundhogs. Ask the children to place their groundhogs in the center of their biscuits and pull the biscuit dough up and over the groundhogs, crimping the biscuit closed at the top.

4. Bake these according to directions on the biscuit can.

5. Allow them to cool thoroughly before eating. Some biscuits may not close completely, allowing the child to see the groundhog inside.

Edible Groundhogs
Snack/Cooking

Materials for each child
plastic knife • round crackers • peanut butter • miniature round crackers • raisins (or brown M&M's) • miniature marshmallows, cut in half • napkins

1. Make groundhog snacks with the children. Start by giving each child a large cracker. Ask the children to spread peanut butter on their crackers.

Note: Check for food allergies and food sensitivities before serving any food to children. Plan an alternate snack for those children who cannot eat peanut butter.

2. Encourage the children to make groundhog faces. They can use the two miniature crackers for ears, three raisins for eyes and a nose, and marshmallow halves for teeth.

3. The children can hide their animals under napkins. When it's time to eat, the groundhogs can pop out, ready to "burrow" into the chefs' mouths!

Learning Center Ideas
Science Area

Materials
pictures of groundhogs and other animals that hibernate • books about groundhogs and other animals that hibernate • plastic animals • stretchy socks (for animals to burrow into and hibernate)

1. Add the materials to the Science Area to help children learn about groundhogs and hibernation.

Related Books
Four Stories for Four Seasons by Tomie dePaola
How Do Bears Sleep? by E. J. Bird
Little Groundhog's Shadow by Janet Craig
Time to Sleep by Denise Fleming
The Valentine Bears by Eve Bunting
Wake Me in Spring by James Preller

March 2nd—
Dr. Seuss's Birthday

Introducing the Weekly Curriculum Theme

Weekly Curriculum Vocabulary

doctor
Dr. Seuss
emergency
magnifying glass
opposite
pattern
rhyme
speck
top

Materials

any books by Dr. Seuss

1. Read one book by Dr. Seuss to the children. Show them the cover and a few pages of several others, too.
2. Tell the children that Dr. Seuss's birthday is this week. Explain that his many rhyming books show that he likes pretending and he likes rhyming words.
3. Ask one child to suggest a pretend present he or she might give Dr. Seuss. Then ask another child to make up a nonsense word that rhymes with the present's name.
4. Now ask the second child to think up a pretend present, and the next child, in turn, to make up a rhyming nonsense word. Continue until each child has a turn.
5. Encourage the group to help children who have difficulty finding a rhyming word.
6. Read one or more of Dr. Seuss's books each day this week.

The Cat's Hat

Art

Materials

The Cat in the Hat by Dr. Seuss ● sentence strips long enough to become headbands ● red crayons ● white construction paper ● stapler

1. Read *The Cat in the Hat* by Dr. Seuss to the children.
2. Provide all of the materials and tell the children that they will be making Cat Hats.
3. Encourage the children to color horizontal red stripes on the white paper.
4. Show them how to staple the white paper onto the sentence strip's center.
5. Place the strip around the child's head to fit it as a headband. Staple it to fit.

① Color white paper with red horizontal stripes.

— Staple

Staple

② Then staple colored paper to sentence strip headband.

Dr. Seuss's Birthday

Bulletin Board and Language

Materials

Dr. Seuss books ● drawing paper ● drawing materials ● bulletin board covered with paper ● large picture of a birthday cake

1. To conclude the week's activities, review some of the Dr. Seuss books you have read and encourage the children to discuss them.
2. Provide drawing materials so each child can draw a picture of their favorite book. Ask each child to dictate to you why this book is their favorite.
3. Hang the picture of a birthday cake in the middle of the bulletin board. Arrange the children's pictures around the birthday cake picture. Title the board: "Happy Birthday, Dr. Seuss!"

Seussville

Dramatic Play

Materials

(see below)

1. Put items from any of the Dr. Seuss books you've read in the Dramatic Play Area. For example:
   - *Cat in the Hat* hats made from white paper bags or bags painted with red and white stripes
   - plastic apples or apple-shaped erasers
   - plastic fish or fish-shaped erasers
   - magnifying glasses
   - cotton balls (for dust bunnies) with a black speck on them
   - plastic eggs
   - plastic foxes
   - socks
   - alphabet cards

Fish Tic-Tac-Toe

Games

Materials

permanent marker ● 18" square of white felt ● red and blue felt ● scissors

1. With the marker, draw a large Tic-Tac-Toe grid on the square of white felt.
2. Cut out five fish shapes from red felt and five from blue felt.
3. Show the children how to use the fish in place of X's and O's to play a Tic-Tac-Toe game.

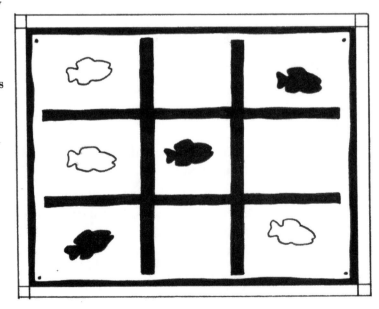

When We Need Help

Language

Materials

The Cat in the Hat by Dr. Seuss • sentence strip • marker • discarded telephones • index cards

1. Read *The Cat in the Hat* to the group.
2. Discuss some of the trouble that occurred in the story.
3. Discuss what to do if there really is trouble at home: Call 9-1-1. Write 9-1-1 on a sentence strip and show it to the children.
4. Show the children how to use a telephone to call the emergency number. Let them role play calling for help. Be certain they understand that they should only call that number if they really do need help.
5. Work individually with children to help them learn their addresses. Write each child's address on a separate index card. With them, role play calling 9-1-1 for help and telling emergency workers where they live.

Opposites

Language

Materials

Dr. Seuss's Wacky Book of Opposites

1. Read the book to the children to expose them to the concept of opposites. Some may understand the concept of opposites, but most will not be familiar with that word. Repetition of activities like this one help children learn what the word "opposite" means.
2. Play a game about opposites by asking the children to fill in the word at the end of sentences like these:

    Not old, but _____.
    Not wet, but _____.
    Not up, but _____.

3. Encourage the children to help each other with the answers.

Rhyming Names

Language

1. Any time of the day, focus on rhyming sounds like the words in the books by Dr. Seuss. For example, when calling children to line up, call out nonsense words that rhyme with their first names, such as:

   Zarry, tarry, first comes Larry.
   Mair-ed, dair-ed, next is Jarred.

How Many Apples?

Math

Materials

white paper ● stapler ● *Ten Apples Up on Top* by Dr. Seuss ● crayons

1. Prepare blank books by stapling five sheets of paper together. Make one for each child.
2. Read *Ten Apples Up on Top* to the children.
3. Give each child a blank book with the following sentence written on the bottom of each page:

   _____ *apples up on top.*

4. Encourage the children to draw a Seuss-like, silly character on each page and their choice of the number of apples atop the characters.
5. Help them count the apples on each character and write that numeral in the blank.
6. Encourage them to read each other's books.

Fish Patterns

Math

Materials

One Fish, Two Fish, Red Fish, Blue Fish by Dr. Seuss ● red and blue construction paper ● scissors ● 3' long strips of adding machine paper (from a roll) ● glue

1. Read the book to the children.
2. Pre-cut red and blue fish shapes using the red and blue construction paper (see fish pattern).

3. Give each child a strip of adding machine paper. Encourage them to form a repeating pattern of one red fish, two blue fish, one red fish, two blue fish on their strips of papers.
4. Ask them to glue their patterns to their papers.
5. Encourage children who are interested to create additional patterns with the materials.

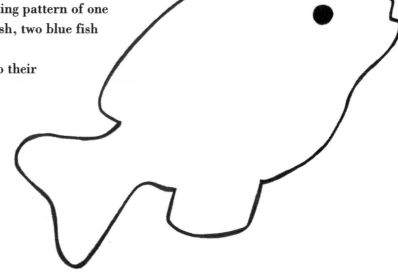

Counting Apples

Math

Materials

60 apple-shaped erasers ● markers ● index cards

1. Use a marker to write the numerals 0-10 on blank index cards.
2. Show the children how to spread out the cards and count the appropriate number of apple erasers onto each card.
3. Have the children ask a friend to check their work.

Apple Seeds

Math and Snack/Cooking

Materials

Ten Apples Up On Top! by Dr. Seuss ● 10 fresh apples ● knife (adult only) ● teaspoon ● plain paper plates

1. Read *Ten Apples Up On Top!* to the children.
2. Show the children an apple and ask them to estimate how many seeds are inside.
3. Cut the apple in half (adult only), scoop out the seeds, and count them.
4. Ask the children to estimate how many seeds will be in 10 apples.
5. Cut the apples in half, one at a time, scooping and counting the seeds as above.
6. Count the seeds again, this time putting 10 seeds on each plate and any left over on another plate.
7. Count the seeds by tens. Were the children's estimates low, high, or correct?
8. Serve the apples for snack.

Green Eggs and Ham

Music

1. Sing the song below. Let each child, in turn, suggest what he doesn't like to eat. Substitute those words for "green eggs and ham" and substitute the child's name for "Sam-I-am."

> Tune: *Mary Had a Little Lamb*
> *I do not like green eggs and ham,*
> *Eggs and ham, eggs and ham.*
> *I do not like green eggs and ham.*
> *I do not like them, Sam-I-am.*
>
> *I do not like blue potatoes and peas,*
> *Potatoes and peas, potatoes and peas.*
> *I do not like blue potatoes and peas.*
> *I do not like them, [Laura]-I-am.*

Exploring Small Things

Science

Materials

Horton Hears a Who by Dr. Seuss ● magnifying glasses ● items to explore, such as woven fabric, onion skin, picture books, wooden block, salt, and newspaper ● photographs

1. Read *Horton Hears a Who* to the children. Talk about how a magnifying glass can help us see small items and their details more easily.
2. Demonstrate safe and proper use of the magnifying glasses.
3. Make materials available for children to explore.

Ten Apples Applesauce

Snack/Cooking

Materials

Ten Apples Up on Top! by Dr. Seuss • applesauce • serving spoon • bowls and spoons

1. On the day that you read *Ten Apples Up on Top!*, serve applesauce for snack.
2. Let the children serve themselves applesauce.

Learning Center Ideas

Art and Writing Areas

Dr. Seuss books • paper • markers

1. Encourage the children to explore the Dr. Seuss books, focusing on the illustrations.
2. Challenge them to draw Seuss-like characters and give them Seuss-like names.

Related Books

More than two dozen of Dr. Seuss's books are currently in print, and out-of-print favorites are still available at many libraries. This list merely suggests a few.

The Cat in the Hat
The Cat in the Hat Comes Back
The Cat in the Hat Songbook
Dr. Seuss's ABC
Dr. Seuss's Wacky Book of Opposites
The Foot Book: Dr. Seuss's Wacky Book of Opposites
Fox in Socks
Green Eggs and Ham
Horton Hears a Who
One Fish Two Fish Red Fish Blue Fish
Ten Apples Up on Top! by Theo LeSieg
There's a Wocket in My Pocket! Dr. Seuss's Book of Ridiculous Rhymes

March 25— National Pancake Day

Introducing the Weekly Curriculum Theme

Weekly Curriculum Vocabulary

apple
gooey
jam
jelly
liquid
pancake
pear
potato
round
solid
squash
syrup
zucchini

Materials

box of pancake mix ● calendar (showing the month of March)

1. Hold up the box of pancake mix and ask the children if they know what it is. Let them share memories of times when they have eaten pancakes.
2. Tell the children that March 25 is National Pancake Day, and that this week they will be learning about and eating pancakes.
3. Together, find March 25 on the calendar. Count the days until Pancake Day. Mark the calendar in some way so the children can find Pancake Day.
4. Celebrate this day all week long!

Funny Faces

Art and Snack/Cooking

Materials

ingredients to make faces, such as banana slices drizzled with lemon juice, raisins, sliced strawberries, canned pineapple chunks cut into fourths, and coconut ● small bowls and serving spoons ● paper plates ● thawed and warmed frozen pancakes, 1 for each child ● forks

1. Place the "face-making" ingredients into small bowls. Place a spoon in each bowl.
2. Serve pancakes, one on each paper plate.
3. Each child takes a plate with a pancake and a fork.
4. Encourage the children to use the ingredients in the bowls to turn their pancakes into Funny Faces. Encourage their creativity!
5. Enjoy the giggles as the Funny Faces disappear.

Note: Check for food allergies and food sensitivities before serving any food to children. Plan an alternate snack for those children who cannot eat pancakes or fresh fruit.

Pancake Restaurant

Field Trip

Take a field trip to a local pancake restaurant or to a restaurant that serves pancakes. When arranging the trip, ask if the children can tour the kitchen, where they will be able to see large appliances and cooking utensils. If possible, arrange for the children to watch the cook make small pancakes that they can eat.

What Is Round?

Language

Materials

paper ● stapler ● *Round Is a Pancake* by Joan Baranski, optional ● chart paper ● marker ● pocket chart ● sentence strips ● 4-page blank books with the sentence frame (below) on each page, 1 book for each child ● index cards

1. Make blank books by stapling together four sheets of paper.
2. If available, read *Round Is a Pancake*. If you don't have the book, skip to the next step.
3. Discuss the round shape of a pancake. Talk about other things that are round. Write the names of these items on the chart as the children name them.
4. In a pocket chart, place a sentence strip with the following sentence:
   A pancake is round.
5. Below that, place a sentence strip with the following sentence:
   A _____ is round.
6. Make smaller, individual sentence strips for each word in the first sentence. Let each child take a turn putting these in the blank space of the second sentence. Each time, read the resulting sentence with the children.
7. Give the children the blank books and ask them to draw on each page something that is round. Have them fill in the blanks by copying words from the chart. If the item they drew isn't on the chart, write the word on an index card for them to copy.

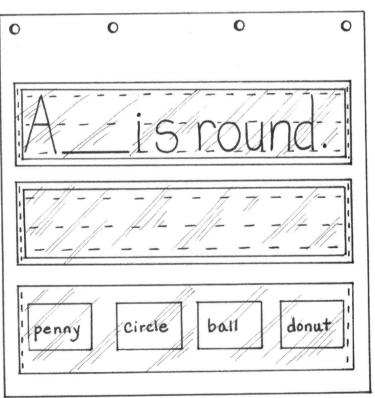

Measuring and Mixing

Math and Snack/Cooking

Materials

Pancakes, Pancakes! by Eric Carle, optional • tablespoon measuring spoons, 3 of these • 3 bowls for ingredients • pancake mix or plain flour • several eggs, beaten • milk • small plastic bowls and measuring tablespoons • teaspoons, 1 for each child, for mixing ingredients • butter • frying pan • spatula • paper plates • strawberry jam and maple syrup

1. Read *Pancakes, Pancakes!* to the children. This book is about making pancakes, from gathering the ingredients to making the cakes. It helps the reader understand the original source of every ingredient. If you don't have the book, discuss pancake making and pancake ingredients with the children.

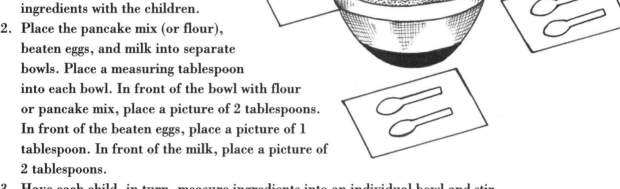

2. Place the pancake mix (or flour), beaten eggs, and milk into separate bowls. Place a measuring tablespoon into each bowl. In front of the bowl with flour or pancake mix, place a picture of 2 tablespoons. In front of the beaten eggs, place a picture of 1 tablespoon. In front of the milk, place a picture of 2 tablespoons.

3. Have each child, in turn, measure ingredients into an individual bowl and stir until well mixed.

4. Pour this mixture into the buttered frying pan (adult only) and cook it until the underside is brown. Flip the pancake and cook the other side. Place this on a paper plate until cool.

Caution: Keep children at a distance while you pour the pancake mixture into the hot frying pan. Make sure children wash their hands after mixing the batter that contains raw eggs.

5. Serve the cool pancakes with a choice of strawberry jam or maple syrup.

Note: Check for food allergies and plan an alternate snack for those who cannot eat their creations.

Number Book

Math

Materials

paper ● stapler ● *Blueberries for Sal* by Robert McCloskey, optional ● hole punch ● dark blue construction paper ● crayons ● glue sticks

1. Make a blank book for each child by stapling five sheets of paper together.
2. Read *Blueberries for Sal*, if available.
3. Explain that some people like to eat pancakes with blueberries cooked into them, and that they will be making a book with pictures of blueberry pancakes.
4. Ask the children to punch holes in the blue paper. These will be the "blueberries."
5. Encourage the children to draw a pancake on each page of their blank books. Then they can glue any number of "blueberries" on each pancake.
6. Help the children count the number of berries on each page, and help them write that numeral on each page.

Another Point of View

Movement

1. Tell the following story and ask the children to act out making pancakes from the ingredients' point of view.
2. Assign one "hungry child" and one child each for flour, eggs, milk, serving plate, and spoon. Assign four children to hold hands as the mixing bowl, and four children to hold hands as the frying pan.

   Once there was a hungry child who wanted to have pancakes for breakfast. First he gathered the flour, the eggs, and the milk.

3. Ask the children to say what happens next and act out the parts as the story progresses. Be prepared for lots of giggles and lots of fun!

I Like Pancakes

Music

1. Sing the following song with the children. After the second verse, ask the children to suggest other verses, naming and singing about other items that can go with pancakes.

Tune: *Frère Jacques*
I like pancakes; I like pancakes.
Yes, I do; yes, I do.
Some with maple syrup, some with maple syrup.
How 'bout you? How 'bout you?

I like pancakes; I like pancakes.
Yes, I do; yes, I do.
Some with gooey jam, some with gooey jam.
How 'bout you? How 'bout you?

Changes and More Changes

Science

1. When the children are mixing pancake batter (Measuring and Mixing on page 99), suggest that they observe and discuss the changes that occur when they mix the ingredients together.
2. While you are cooking their pancakes, let them observe from a safe distance. Together, discuss how heat changes the liquid batter. Use the words "liquid" and "solid."

Jams, Jellies, and Preserves

Science

Materials
variety of jams, jellies, and preserves ● teaspoons ● small dishes ● small coffee stirrers ● napkins

1. Place a spoonful of jam, jelly, or preserves into each small dish. Include a variety of flavors and at least two varieties of each flavor. For example, grape jelly and grape jam; strawberry preserves and strawberry jam.
2. Provide plenty of stirrers and napkins, and encourage the children to taste and compare just a bit of each item. Help them focus on taste and texture.
3. Encourage them to discuss which tastes and textures they prefer.

Still More Pancakes

Science and Snack/Cooking

Materials

basic pancake ingredients ● minced apple ● mashed banana ● zucchini or yellow squash and sour cream ● potatoes and applesauce

1. Using the pancake recipe on page 99, enjoy a variety of pancakes during the week.
2. Mix minced apple into pancake batter and cook pancakes as usual. Serve with applesauce.
3. Mix one mashed banana into each batch of pancake batter. Cook pancakes as usual. Serve with a light dusting of cinnamon and banana slices on top.
4. For savory pancakes, puree any amount of drained, cooked zucchini or yellow squash, add to pancake batter, and cook as usual. Serve with a dollop of sour cream for spreading on top.
5. For potato pancakes, grate or shred one large potato, drain, and add to one recipe of pancake mix batter. Cook as usual. Serve with applesauce for spreading on top.

Learning Center Ideas

Dramatic Play Area

Materials

aprons ● frying pans ● spatulas ● plates ● forks ● poster board (for signs) ● markers ● empty boxes from pancake mix and frozen pancakes ● empty syrup bottles and jam/jelly jars ● discarded CDs (pancakes) ● strips of corrugated paper (bacon) ● small Styrofoam packing cylinders (sausage) ● file folders (menus) ● small memo pads for taking restaurant orders ● pencils

1. Add a few of the props above to the Dramatic Play Area so children can create their own pancake restaurant.

Related Books

Blueberries for Sal by Robert McCloskey
The Great Pancake Escape by Paul Many
If You Give a Pig a Pancake by Laura Joffe Numeroff
Pancakes for Breakfast by Tomie dePaola
Pancakes, Pancakes! by Eric Carle
Penelope Penguin's Pancake Party by Debbie Pollard
Piggy's Pancake Parlor by David M. McPhail
Round Is a Pancake by Joan Baranski

April 22— Earth Day

Introducing the Weekly Curriculum Theme

Materials

poster board ● marker ● current calendar

1. Make a sign on a piece of poster board that says: "April 22 Is Earth Day." Show the children the sign and help them read it.
2. Talk about Earth Day, which is a day to think about taking care of our planet—Earth. Compare this to taking care of our homes. We keep our homes clean and tidy, and make needed repairs. Since we all live on Earth, we must work together to keep Earth clean and tidy, and to prevent damage to it.
3. Talk briefly about litter, air pollution, and water pollution, which are ways that the Earth is "dirty."
4. Talk briefly about recycling and reducing waste as ways we can help Earth. For example, conserving art supplies and using paper scraps instead of throwing them away helps Earth.
5. Hang the sign beside your calendar display.

Weekly Curriculum Vocabulary

conserving
Earth
pollution
recycle
reduce
re-use
tidy
use up

Is This the Earth?

Art

Materials

duct tape ● 15" length of bubble wrap ● variety of brushes and sponges ● 2 shades of blue paint, 2 shades of green paint, and brown paint ● white construction paper ● scissors ● 8" x 11" sheets of black construction paper

1. Tape the bubble wrap to a table. Pour each color of paint into a separate shallow container.
2. Encourage the children to brush and sponge paint over the bubble wrap's surface, trying to avoid covering one color of paint with another.
3. Cut out 7" diameter circles from white construction paper. Each child presses a white circle onto the bubble wrap and then lifts it straight up. It will look something like pictures of Earth.
4. When their circles dry, the children glue them to the center of their black paper to represent Earth in space.

County Extension Office

Class Visitor

1. In many areas, the County Extension Office provides classroom programs for Earth Day. Call a County Agent for information. (Find the telephone number in the government section of a telephone book.)

A Walk in the Neighborhood

Field Trip

1. Any walk in the neighborhood can be a simple field trip. Decide on a purpose for your walk and talk about that before leaving. For an Earth Day walk, look for signs of new, spring growth.

Writing With Water

Language

Materials

index cards • marker • chalkboard • cotton swabs • small containers of water

1. After talking about Earth Day, ask the children to tell you words that relate to this day (for example, water, Earth, pollution, and so on).
2. Write each word on a separate index card and display the words near the chalkboard.
3. Provide cotton swabs and containers of water.
4. Ask the children to take turns choosing a word card and writing their word on the chalkboard with a wet swab.
5. Repeat as often as children are interested.

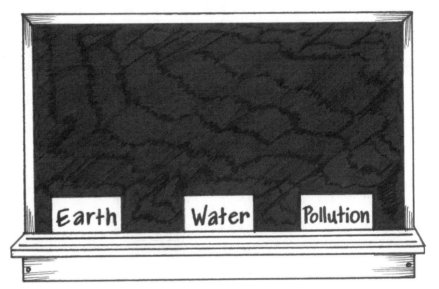

Countdown to Earth Day

Math

Materials

current calendar • construction paper • scissors • small staplers

1. With the children, find the current date on the calendar. Then find April 22. Count the days until Earth Day.
2. Cut construction paper into strips. Encourage each child to count out and take that number of construction paper strips.
3. Show the children how to join their paper strips into a chain. Staple the links together.
4. Count the links in the resulting chain. There will be as many links as the number of days until Earth Day.
5. Ask one child to make an extra chain to hang by the calendar at school. Every day, cut off one link of the chain. When all links are gone, it will be Earth Day.
6. The children can take home their chains so they can count the number of days until Earth Day with their family. Remind children to remove one link of chain when they wake up each morning.

Recycling Song

Music

1. Ask each child, in turn, to name something she can re-use or recycle and tell how she can do it. For example, "I can use a plastic food container to hold my rock collection."
2. After each child's turn, sing the song below. Continue until each child has a turn.

> Tune: *Row, Row, Row Your Boat*
> *Take good care of Earth.*
> *Recycle when you can.*
> *Let's reduce our garbage.*
> *That's a good, good plan.*

Polluted Water

Science

Materials

letter to parents • sensory table • water • various pollutants brought from home

1. Send a letter to parents telling them their children will be learning about water pollution as part of your study of Earth Day. In the letter, ask them to send in one item that could pollute a river or lake, such as paper and junk mail (one of the largest trash problems), soda cans, orange and banana peels, eggshells, coffee grounds, empty plastic bottles, and so on.
2. Put several inches of water in the sensory table and ask the children to add their pollutants. Ask them to stir the water with their hands.
3. Ask the children to look at the water. Would they want to drink it or swim in it? Why or why not? Remind them that people who are careless about trash pollute rivers and lakes.
4. Talk about how polluted water affects thirsty animals that need to drink from rivers and lakes.
5. Make sure the children wash hands thoroughly after they play in this water.
6. Save some of this water for the Watering Plants activity on the next page.

Note: Thoroughly clean the sensory table and sanitize it after this activity.

Watering Plants

Science

Materials

small plants • clean water • water saved from Polluted Water activity (previous page) • permanent marker

1. Review what the children have learned about water pollution in the Polluted Water activity.
2. Display the plants. Ask the children to divide these into two groups: one to be watered with clean water; the other to be watered with polluted water. Label the plants.
3. Let the children take turns watering the plants over the next month. Check them daily to see if there are changes.
4. Discuss the children's observations.

Recycling for Animal Friends

Science

Materials

newspapers

1. Ask the children to collect newspapers.
2. Take a field trip to a local animal shelter or veterinarian's office to donate the newspapers and to see how they are used with the animals.

Products of the Earth

Snack/Cooking

Materials

fresh fruit and vegetables

1. Serve fresh fruits and vegetables, reminding the children that these are products of our Earth.

Learning Center Ideas

Art and Construction Areas

Materials

variety of disposable items, such as plastic jugs, food packages, toiletry packages, scrap paper, magazines, aluminum pans, and wrapping paper ● glue ● masking tape and duct tape ● paint and paintbrushes

1. Place these and other items in the Art Area/Construction Area for children to recycle into new items.

Related Books

Crinkleroot's Guide to Knowing Animal Habitats by Jim Arnosky (also, any others in the Crinkleroot series)

Every Day Is Earth Day: A Craft Book by Kathy Ross

Field Trips: Bug Hunting, Animal Tracking, Bird-Watching, Shore Walking by Jim Arnosky

The Great Kapok Tree: A Tale of the Amazon Rain Forest by Lynne Cherry

Over in the Meadow by John Langstaff

Over in the Meadow: An Old Nursery Counting Rhyme by Paul Galdone

Where Once There Was a Wood by Denise Fleming

Wonderful Worms by Linda Glaser

Second Sunday in May— Mother's Day

Introducing the Weekly Curriculum Theme

Materials
any story book with a "mother" character (suggestions on page 114) •
chart paper • marker

1. Read a book with a mother character to the children.
2. Talk about the mother in the story, then talk about the mothers that the children know.

Note: Throughout the week, be sensitive to children who do not have a mother or mother figure in their lives. Encourage them to think about their grandmothers, aunts, sisters, or any woman who plays a significant role in their lives.

3. As children talk about things mothers do, list these on a chart page titled "What Mothers Do."

Weekly Curriculum Vocabulary

grandmother
great grandmother
Mommy
mother
Mother
Mother's Day
words from the list
  in the opening
  activity, describing
  things mothers do

Picture of My Mom

Art

Materials

drawing paper ● crayons

1. Ask the children to close their eyes and think about their mothers—their hair color, hair length, eye color, and favorite clothes.
2. Give children paper and crayons and encourage each child to make a picture of her mother or any significant woman in her life.
3. Save these and use them with the All About Mom activity (below) to make a Mother's Day present.

Remembering Mama

Games

Materials

5" squares of drawing paper ● crayons

1. Give each child a 5" square of paper. Ask them to draw a picture of their Mom.
2. Help them write their names on the papers.
3. Spread five of these drawings in front of the children and identify each one.
4. While all of the children close their eyes, remove one picture and put it where the children cannot see it.
5. Then the children open their eyes.
6. Select a child to tell whose picture is missing. Let the group help, if necessary.
7. Continue while interest lasts using different pictures each time. Repeat the game at other times.

All About Mom

Language

Materials

scrap paper ● pen ● 8 ½" x 11" drawing paper ● 12" x 18" construction paper ● glue ● child-drawn pictures of their mothers (see Picture of My Mom activity above) ● clear contact paper or laminate

1. Working with one child at a time, ask the child to tell you some things about her mother (or significant woman). Record these on scrap paper.

2. If the child needs help, ask her:

   - What does she look like?
   - What color is her hair?
   - What are her favorite clothes?
   - What does she do most of the time?
   - What is her favorite food?
   - What is her favorite restaurant?
   - What does she like to do with you?
   - What do you like to do with her?

3. Write down each child's answers onto the drawing paper.

4. Give a sheet of 12" x 18" construction paper to the child. Ask her to turn it so the long edge is horizontal.

5. Help the child place her mother's picture and her dictated words side-by-side on the construction paper, and help her glue these in place.

6. Laminate the finished gift so it will last for many years.

7. The children can take these home as Mother's Day gifts. Encourage them to keep this gift a surprise until Mother's Day.

"She has short hair."

"Her favorite food is pizza."

"She likes to read to me."

"I like to play blocks with her."

Laminate

My Mother's Mother

Language

1. Discuss with the children that even mothers (mommies) have mothers. Help them understand that their grandmothers are the parents of the children's mothers (and fathers). For children who have great grandmothers that they know, help them understand that these women are also mothers—the mothers of the children's grandparents.

Storybook Seriation

Math

Materials

5 storybooks about mothers (see suggestions on page 114)

1. Ask several children to select storybooks about mothers from the class library.
2. Place five of these that are quite different in size in front of the children. Select a child to place them in order from smallest to largest.
3. Ask the child to explain his selections. (Some children might arrange the books by height, some by width, and some by thickness.)
4. Mix up the books, and then select another child to place them in order from largest to smallest.
5. Encourage the children to play this game together.

How Mothers Move

Movement

1. Ask each child, in turn, to say something that mothers do.
2. After each response, challenge the rest of the children to pantomime how mothers move while they are doing that thing.

Variation: One child moves as a mother would move, and the other children guess what the child is doing.

Mother's Day Song

Music

1. Help the children learn the following song.
2. Encourage them to sing the song to their mothers on Mother's Day.

> Tune: *Old MacDonald Had a Farm*
> *I've a present for my Mom*
> *It's for Mother's Day.*
> *It's a present that she'll love*
> *In a very special way.*
> *It's a hug, and a kiss.*
> *It's a smile that looks just like this.* (point to smile)
> *I've a present for my Mom*
> *It's for Mother's Day.*

I Love Mommy

Music

1. After discussing the things mothers do (see Introducing the Weekly Curriculum Theme), sing the following song with the children, substituting words from the chart in the second verse.
2. Encourage the children to sing the song to their mothers on Mother's Day.

> Tune: *The Wheels on the Bus*
> *I love Mommy, yes I do.*
> *Yes I do; yes I do.*
> *I love Mommy, yes I do.*
> *I love Mom.*
>
> *My Mommy (cooks my favorite foods).*
> *(Favorite foods); (favorite foods).*
> *My Mommy (cooks my favorite foods).*
> *I love Mom.*

Mother's Day Dinner

Snack/Cooking

Materials

hot dogs ● plastic, serrated-blade knives ● baked beans ● microwave-safe pan ● green beans, coleslaw, and milk

1. Help the children learn to prepare a simple meal (with adult supervision). **Note:** After the children have practiced with you, send home a note to parents explaining that the child wishes to help prepare a Mother's Day Meal. Send full directions and a menu in the note.
2. Cut the hot dogs into quarters. Give each child ¼ of a hot dog.
3. Ask the children to use plastic serrated knives to cut the hot dogs into tiny chunks. Supervise closely.
4. Open a can of baked beans (adult only).
5. If necessary, help the children pour the beans into the pan, add the hot dog chunks, and stir.
6. Heat in the microwave oven (adult only).
7. Serve with heated green beans, coleslaw, and milk.

Learning Center Ideas

Dramatic Play Area

Materials

camera • briefcase or small suitcase • lunch box • magazines • purse • shoes • scarf • newspaper • calendars and appointment books.

1. Add some fresh items to the Dramatic Play Area to encourage play about mothers.

Related Books

Are You My Mother? by P.D. Eastman

Ask Mr. Bear by Marjorie Flack

Clifford's Happy Mother's Day by Norman Bridwell

Come On, Rain! by Karen Hesse

Mama, Do You Love Me? by Barbara M. Joosse

The Mother's Day Mice by Eve Bunting

My Mama Had a Dancing Heart by Libba Moore Gray

On Mother's Lap by Ann Herbert Scott

Present for Mom by Vivian French

A Ride on Mother's Back: A Day of Baby Carrying Around the World by Emery Bernhard

Wake Up, Emily, It's Mother's Day by Patricia Reilly Giff

What Mommies Do Best by Laura Joffe Numeroff

What Moms Can't Do by Douglas Wood

Third Sunday in June—
Father's Day

Introducing the Weekly Curriculum Theme

Materials

What Daddies Do Best by Lynn Munsinger (or any other book about fathers—see
suggestions on page 120) ● chart paper ● marker

1. Read *What Daddies Do Best* or any other book about fathers.
2. Talk about the daddy in the story, and then talk about real dads the
   children know.

Note: Throughout the week be sensitive to children who do not have a father or
father figure in their lives. Encourage them to think about their grandfathers,
uncles, brothers, or any man who plays a significant role in their lives.

3. On the chart, make a list of things that dads do.

Weekly Curriculum Vocabulary

daddy (any dad)
Daddy (my own dad)
father
Father's Day
grandfather
great grandfather
words from the list
  in the opening
  activity, describing
  things fathers do

What Dads Can Do
Art and Language

Materials
drawing paper ● construction paper ● stapler ● crayons ● pen

1. Make blank books by stapling together five sheets of drawing paper between two sheets of construction paper. Make one for each child.
2. Review the chart from the opening activity.
3. Using one page each day, each child makes a "How To..." book of things his dad does.
4. Each day, ask the children to draw pictures of their father doing something he can do. Write their dictated words telling what their dad is doing and how he does it (e.g., cook dinner, drive a car, and wash dishes).
5. On the book's last page, the children draw something they do together with their dads. Add their dictated words.
6. If the children have no father or father figure in their lives, suggest that they make a book about a man who is important to them, such as an uncle, grandfather, friend, neighbor, or male teacher at school.

My Father's Father
Language

1. Discuss with the children that even fathers (daddies) have fathers. Help them understand that their grandfathers are the parents of the children's fathers (and mothers). For children who have great grandfathers that they know, help them understand that these men are also fathers—the fathers of the children's grandparents.

My Dad Drives
Math

Materials
large paper graph ● marker ● pencils

1. Make a five column graph with one of the following words at the top of each column: car, truck, van, bus, other. Title it "What Does Your Dad Drive?" (See sample graph on page 120.)

2. Discuss the graph with the children.

3. Ask the children to sign their names or make a mark in the appropriate column. If their dad drives more than one of the vehicles, ask them to choose the one that he likes best.

Note: If the dads (or other males in their lives) of the children don't drive, change the graph to one about their dads' favorite color or favorite food.

4. Use the graph to explore concepts of more/less, more than/fewer than, the same as, how many more/less, and so on.

Moving Like Dad

Movement

Materials

chart "Things That Dads Do" from the opening activity (page 115)

1. Use the chart from the opening activity and, as a group, pantomime how a dad moves when he is doing those things.

2. Ask the children for suggestions of other ways to move like dads. Suggestions might include when he is tired, when he is exercising, in the morning when he wakes up, and when he is playing with the child.

A Song for Dad

Music

1. Help the children learn this song.

2. Encourage them to sing the song to their fathers on Father's Day.

> Tune: *Old MacDonald Had a Farm*
> *I've a present for my Dad;*
> *It's for Father's Day.*
> *It's a present that he'll love*
> *In a very special way.*
> *It's a hug, and a kiss.*
> *It's a smile that looks just like this.* (point to smile)
> *I've a present for my Dad;*
> *It's for Father's Day.*

I Love Daddy

Music

1. After discussing the things daddies do (Introducing the Weekly Curriculum Theme), sing this song with the children, substituting words from the chart in the second verse.
2. Encourage children to sing the song to their fathers on Father's Day.

> Tune: *The Wheels on the Bus*
> *I love Daddy, yes I do.*
> *Yes I do; yes I do.*
> *I love Daddy, yes I do.*
> *I love Dad.*
>
> *My daddy (cooks my favorite foods).*
> *(Favorite foods); (favorite foods).*
> *My Daddy (cooks my favorite foods).*
> *I love Dad.*

Backrubs

Science

1. Talk about how backrubs help us relax.
2. The children work in pairs, taking turns rubbing each other's backs.
3. Give pointers on rubbing gently up and down either side of the spine, but never directly on the spine.
4. Show children how to gently knead the muscles between the neck and shoulders. Let them practice every day.
5. Suggest to children that they surprise their dad with a gentle backrub on Father's Day.

Dad's Favorite: P-B-&-J

Snack/Cooking

Materials

bread ● serrated-blade, plastic knives ● peanut butter ● jelly or fruit spread

1. Provide materials for children to make peanut butter and jelly sandwiches. **Note:** Always check for allergies and food sensitivities and preferences before serving any food.
2. Remind children they can make these at home for their dads.

Pineapple Cream Cheese and Crackers

Snack/Cooking

Materials

bowl of crushed pineapple, drained • tablespoon • card with picture of one tablespoon • whipped cream cheese • serrated-blade, plastic knives • card with picture of two knives • small paper cups • crackers

1. Place the tablespoon and the card with the picture of one tablespoon in front of the pineapple bowl. In front of the cream cheese, place a plastic knife and the card with the picture of two knives.

2. Explain to the children that they will make a pineapple-cream cheese spread by putting one spoonful of pineapple and two knives full of cream cheese into their cup.
3. Show them how to mix this with a knife and spread it on crackers for their snack.
4. Tell them that some dads might like to eat this for a snack.
5. Send the recipe home with the children so they can make this for their families and for their dad on Father's Day.

Special Visitors

1. Designate a morning for dads to come to school with their children. They can play together indoors and out, read together, and draw pictures of each other. Children can fix and serve a simple snack. Children who don't have fathers in their lives (or whose dads can't come) can invite a grandfather, uncle, neighbor, or another significant male.

Learning Center Ideas

Dramatic Play Area

Materials

camera • briefcase • lunchbox • calculator • men's athletic shoes • newspaper • eyeglass frames • magazines • calendars and appointment books • wallet • baseball cap

1. Add fresh items to the Dramatic Play area to encourage play about fathers.

car	truck	van	bus	other

Related Books

Hush, Little Alien by Daniel Kirk

I Love My Daddy Because by Laurel Porter-Gaylord

Just Like My Dad by Tricia Gardella

My Dad by Anthony Brown

One Round Moon and a Star for Me by Ingrid Mennen

A Perfect Fathers' Day by Eve Bunting

What Daddies Do Best by Lynn Munsinger

What Dads Can't Do by Douglas Wood

What Mary Jo Shared by Janice May Udry

Third Week of July—
Chill Out Week

Introducing the Weekly Curriculum Theme

Materials

large stack of newspapers (Ask parents, friends, and neighbors to save and donate newspapers. Newspaper ink can be messy; ask for plain paper, if desired.)

1. Pretend it's snowing to escape the summer's heat! For several days before beginning this week of activities, tell the children that it is going to snow. When they tell you it is too hot, state with confidence that it will soon snow.
2. On Monday, tell the children that it will begin snowing very soon.
3. Sit on the floor with the children and give each child a small stack of newspaper and show them how to open the papers into individual sheets. Show them how to tear these into smaller and smaller pieces, with the final pieces no larger than the size of their little fingers. Have them place this pile on the floor in front of where they are sitting.
4. Tear your own stack of paper with them.
5. When a large amount of paper has been torn, say you know it is going to snow. Begin throwing your torn paper "snowflakes" in the air, shouting, "Look! It's snowing! I knew it would snow!" Encourage the children to join in the fun.

Weekly Curriculum Vocabulary

br-r-r-r-r
cold
frosty
mitten
shiver
snow
snowball

6. When children are through playing in this snow, ask them to shovel it (with brooms, dustpans, and hands) into several grocery bags or boxes. Use this later for children to make snowmen on blue bulletin board paper.

7. Display this where the cold scene can cool all who see it.

Note: Be sure to wash hands after this activity to remove all the newspaper ink.

Weekly Curriculum Extension Activities

Painting With Snowballs

Art

Materials

tempera paint ● bowls ● tongs ● tweezers ● cotton balls ● paper

1. Pour paint into bowls.
2. Show the children how to use tongs or tweezers to hold the cotton balls.
3. Demonstrate how to dab the cotton balls into the paint and then onto paper.
4. Encourage all methods of painting—dabbing, dragging, swirling, dropping cotton balls, and more.

Merry Mittens

Art

Materials

wallpaper sample pages (or construction paper), 1 sheet per child ● washable markers ● child-safe scissors ● hole punch ● 18" lengths of yarn ● bulletin board ● pushpins

1. Give each child a wallpaper sample page or piece of construction paper. Help each child, in turn, fold her paper in half.
2. Ask the child to hold a marker in her drawing hand while she holds her thumb out and fingers together on her other hand.
3. Help her trace the hand that has the thumb out and fingers together, avoiding the folded edge of the paper.
4. Help her hold both layers of paper together while she cuts out the resulting mitten shapes.
5. Ask the child to punch a hole at the "wrist" of each mitten and tie each end of the yarn to a separate mitten.
6. Help children hang their mittens with pushpins on a bulletin board with the caption: "On a Cold, Cold Day We Wore Our Mittens."

On a Cold, Cold Day

Language

Materials

bulletin board (see previous activity) • paper • pen • crayons • stapler • construction paper

1. After the children have completed the bulletin board (see Merry Mittens, page 122), talk about other things the children remember doing, or wish they could do, on a cold, cold day.
2. Write "Once upon a time on a cold, cold day..." on sheets of paper (one for each child). Give one sheet to each child and encourage the children to draw a picture of something they have done or wish they could do on a cold, cold day.
3. Write the children's dictated words on their papers.
4. Compile the pages into a class-made book with a construction paper cover.

Snowflakes

Math

Materials

wax paper • white glue • ⅛ teaspoon measuring spoons • silver glitter in a shallow dish • cotton swabs, 6 for each child • white thread

1. Talk about snowflakes. Tell the children that each flake has six sides or six points, and that each flake is unique.
2. Working with small groups of children at a time, give each child a square of wax paper.
3. Ask the children to sprinkle ⅛ teaspoon of glitter in the center of their wax paper and then cover that with a 2" diameter (or more) puddle of glue.

Caution: Make sure the children wash their hands after using glitter so they won't rub any into their eyes.

4. Encourage the children to arrange their cotton swabs in the glue to form a snowflake. If necessary, add more glue so the swabs will be secure when the glue dries.
5. Ask the children to sprinkle another ⅛ teaspoon of glitter on top of all the glue. Allow it to dry. (This may take more than one day.)
6. Peel off the wax paper.
7. Help the children attach a length of string to the flake. Hang the flakes from the ceiling for an instant snow palace effect.

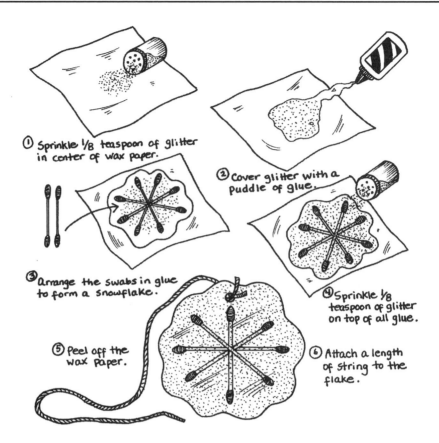

1. Sprinkle 1/8 teaspoon of glitter in center of wax paper.
2. Cover glitter with a puddle of glue.
3. Arrange the swabs in glue to form a snowflake.
4. Sprinkle 1/8 teaspoon of glitter on top of all glue.
5. Peel off the wax paper.
6. Attach a length of string to the flake.

Snowball Fight

Movement

Materials

newspaper ● masking tape

1. Encourage the children to make small "snowballs" by rolling up newspaper and covering the outside with enough masking tape to hold in a ball shape.
2. Let them have a gentle snowball fight, cautioning them to aim all snowballs below the neck.

Summer Snow Song

Music

1. Sing the following song with children.

   Tune: ***London Bridge Is Falling Down***
   We're pretending it is cold.
   It is cold. It is cold.
   We're pretending it is cold,
   In the summertime.

   Summer snow is falling down,
   Falling down, falling down.
   Summer snow is falling down,
   In the summertime.

Summer Snow People and Their Pets

Outdoors

Materials

newspaper, large amounts ● masking tape, large amounts ● child-safe scissors ● construction paper ● glue

1. Ask parents, friends, and neighbors to save and donate newspapers.
2. Show the children how to roll a ball of newspaper and to keep adding more paper to make the ball larger.
3. Help the children wrap masking tape around the balls to give them shape and hold them together.
4. Help the children build the newspaper balls into snow people and snow animals. Encourage the children's creative ideas about making non-traditional shapes for these.
5. Children can cut out features from construction paper and glue them on their creations.

Exploring Ice

Science

Materials

large block of ice • water table • salt • squirting bottles, turkey basters, and funnels • water • tempera paint thinned with water • paintbrushes • terry towels • mop • camera

1. Put a large block of ice in the water table.

Note: Freeze water in a dishpan, or have a large block of ice delivered from an ice company.

2. Encourage the children to explore the block of ice as they wish.
3. Challenge them to find ways to melt the ice, and provide squirting bottles, turkey basters, funnels and any other materials they request.
4. Provide paint and paintbrushes so the children can paint the ice, inside and out.
5. Take lots of pictures to share with families and others.
6. Keep towels and a mop handy for clean up!

Snow Scene

Sensory

Materials

sensory table • white flour • toy cars and trucks • building blocks • flour sifters

1. Put a few inches of white flour in the sensory table.
2. Add the remaining materials and let children build a wintry scene in the flour.
3. Encourage the children to drive the cars through snowy roads and sift flour over it all to create a snowstorm.

Caution: Don't let children create flour dust in the air. Inhaled dust could create breathing problems for some children.

Frosty's Frosty Treat

Snack/Cooking

Materials

blender • unsweetened fruit juice • crushed ice • ¼ cup plastic measuring cups • drinking cups

1. Working with four children at a time, ask each child to put ¼ cup of juice and ¼ cup of crushed ice into the blender.

Caution: Supervise closely.

2. Blend these together to make a sugar-free frosty treat that will serve the four who cooperated to make it.

Snowman's Icy Icicle

Snack/Cooking

Materials

blender • strawberry-banana yogurt • orange juice • 5-oz. wax paper drinking cups

1. Blend equal amounts of yogurt and juice.

Caution: Supervise closely.

2. Help the children pour about four ounces of the mixture into each cup.
3. Freeze until frozen hard.
4. Give a frozen treat to each child. Show them how to peel back the cup, a little at a time, to eat the frozen treats.

Learning Center Ideas

Dramatic Play Area

Materials

winter sports equipment • gloves and mittens • jackets • sweaters • knitted hats • boots • Styrofoam balls or paper balls (for snowballs) • empty cocoa mix container • cups for pretend cocoa

1. Add a few of these and other winter materials to the Dramatic Play Area to encourage "cold weather" play.

Related Books

Animals in Winter (Let's-Read-And-Find-Out Science) by Henrietta Bancroft

Dream Snow by Eric Carle

Elmer in the Snow by David McKee

Flannel Kisses by Linda Crotta Brennan

The First Snowfall by Anne F. Rockwell

Grandmother Winter by Phyllis Root

Over and Over by Charlotte Zolotow

Snow Dance by Lezlie Evans

Snow Family by Daniel Kirk

Snow Is Falling (Let's-Read-And-Find-Out Science) by Franklyn Mansfield Branley

Snowie Rolie by William Joyce

The Snowman by Raymond Briggs (a wordless book)

The Snowy Day by Ezra Jack Keats

When It Starts to Snow by Phillis Gershator

August 6—
Wiggle
Your Toes Day

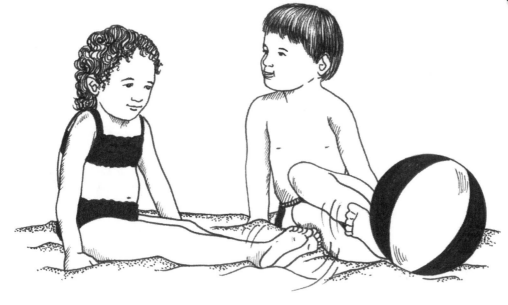

Introducing the Weekly Curriculum Theme

Materials
Hello Toes! Hello Feet! by Ann Whitford Paul (optional) ● chart paper ● marker ●
sentence strips, optional

1. Read the book to the children. In the story, a small child talks about all the things her toes and feet do in a day, from being the first part of her that touches the floor each morning, to squishing in wet mud, to jumping, tiptoeing, marching, and more.
2. Ask the children how their feet help them move.
3. List their responses on the chart paper, using the sentence strips if desired.
4. Read the chart several times with the children.

Weekly Curriculum Vocabulary

feet
jump
jumping
squish
squishing
tiptoe
tiptoeing
toes
words from the
chart the
children generate

Shoe Rubbings

Art

Materials

children's shoes • plain paper • tape • peeled crayons

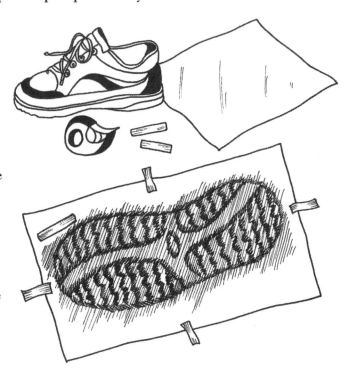

1. Ask each child to remove one shoe.
2. Help the child cover the shoe's sole with paper and tape the paper in place so it won't slip.
3. The child rubs the side of a peeled crayon over the paper. This will reproduce the sole's pattern.
4. Display the rubbings where children can see and compare them.

To the Shoe Store

Field Trip

1. Call ahead and set up a visit to a shoe store. Ask the proprietor to be ready to show the children different kinds of shoes—big, small, high-heeled, flat, open-toed, dance shoes, athletic shoes, and so on.

Writing About Feet

Language

Materials

marker ● sentence strips ● light blue construction paper strips ● pocket chart ●
chart from opening activity ● paper ● pencils

1. Copy the composition frame below using sentence strips and place these in the
    pocket chart. Use a blue strip for each blank.

    > *Smart Feet*
    > *I have smart feet.*
    > *Smart feet are neat.*
    > *My feet can _____*
    > *and _____ and ____.*
    > *I have smart feet.*

2. Read the composition to the children and ask them what words could go in the
    blanks. (Some will refer to the opening chart for ideas.)
3. Write their suggested words on sentence strips, inserting their words in the
    blanks. Repeat several times, making new word cards each time.
4. Write the composition frame on pieces of paper, one for each child. Give the
    papers to the children and ask them to dictate how they want to fill in their
    blanks, or, with those who can, let them copy words from the chart.
5. Help them read their compositions to each other.

Counting by Twos

Math

1. Help the children count all of the feet in your group.
2. Introduce the word "pair" and discuss its meaning. Count feet again, this time
    counting by twos.

Our Feet

Math

Materials

markers ● poster board ● scissors

1. Trace each child's feet on a piece of poster board. Cut out the resulting shapes (adult only).
2. Place these where children can explore them. Suggest they use them for matching or measuring. Challenge them to find other ways to use the foot outlines.

Wiggling and Using Our Toes

Movement

Materials

soft balls made of socks or pantyhose (twice as many balls as children) ● clothes hamper or other plastic container ● small stuffed animals, scarves, and ribbons

1. Ask the children to take off their shoes and socks and sit on the floor in a circle.
2. Scatter the soft balls on the floor and put the hamper in the center of the circle.
3. Challenge the children to move while seated and use only their feet and toes to pick up the balls and put them in the hamper.
4. As the children drop balls in the hamper, remove the balls and scatter them again on the floor.
5. On other days, use small stuffed animals, scarves, or ribbon instead of the balls.

Left Foot, Right Foot

Movement

Materials

stickers, 1 for each child

1. Place a sticker on the toe of each child's right shoe.
2. Talk with the children about "right" and "left."

3. Play movement games where the leader gives directions such as, "Stand on your left foot," or "Put your right foot on your left knee."
4. Extend this to directions about the right/left leg, then the right/left arm and hand.

My Happy Feet

Music

1. Sing the song below, letting each child, in turn, name a way that feet can move. Substitute that word for "run" in the second verse. Repeat the first verse to end the song.
2. Encourage the children to move their feet to match the words they are singing.

Tune: *The Wheels on the Bus*
I can move so many ways,
Many ways, many ways.
I can move so many ways,
On my happy feet.

I can _____ on my feet,
On my feet, on my feet.
I can _____ on my feet,
On my happy feet.

One-Foot Tag

Outdoors

1. Suggest that the children play One-Foot Tag outdoors.
2. To play this game of Tag, any child who is balanced on one foot cannot be tagged by IT. All other rules of Tag are the same.
3. Explain that IT cannot touch a child who is balanced on one foot to cause that child to lose balance.

What Do Toes Do?

Science

Materials

children's shoes and socks

1. Ask the children to remove their shoes and socks. Ask them why they have toes. What do toes do?
2. Select a child to move in various ways (such as hop, jump, walk, or run) while the others pay particular attention to his toes.
3. Guide them to discover that toes help with balance and with propelling the foot forward or off the ground.
4. Let the children move around the room with bare feet, paying attention to the work their toes are doing.

Dirty Toes

Snack/Cooking

Materials

thick, rod-shaped pretzels • peanut butter or cheese spread • small cups, 1 for each child

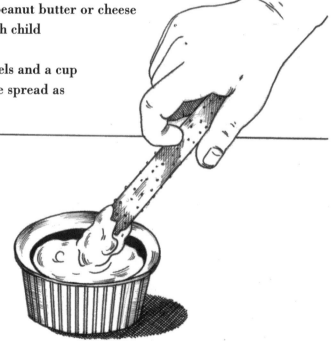

1. Give each child two pretzels and a cup of peanut butter or cheese spread as a dip.

Caution: Check for peanut allergies!

2. Tell the children to pretend that the pretzels are somebody's big toes.
3. Ask them to dip the big toe pretzels into their dip, making a delicious snack of "dirty toes."

Learning Center Ideas

Dramatic Play Area

Materials

rulers (for measuring feet) ● pair of shoelaces ● pair of shoes ● cooking pot ●
spoon ● chart page ● marker ● note to parents

1. Show the children the materials and ask which ones they would need to begin
   setting up a shoe store in the Dramatic Play Area.
2. Encourage them to brainstorm other items they might need. Write their
   suggestions on a chart page.
3. Send a note home asking parents to donate or lend the needed items.
4. Encourage the children to set up the shoe store.

More Learning Center Ideas

Manipulatives

Materials

two different-colored long shoelaces ● scissors ● adult-size, lace-up shoe

1. Cut off one end of each shoelace and tie the cut ends together, forming one long
   lace of two different colors.
2. Lace the adult shoe and ask a child slip one foot inside.
3. Show the child how to tie a bow by making two "bunny ear" loops and then
   tying those loops in a knot.

Related Books

The Foot Book by Dr. Seuss
Hello Toes! Hello Feet! by Ann Whitford Paul
My Feet by Aliki
My Two Hands/My Two Feet by Rick Walton
Red Dancing Shoes by Denise Lewis Patrick
Whose Feet? by Jeannette Rowe
Whose Shoe? by Margaret Miller

Science Themes

Caterpillars and Butterflies

Introducing the Weekly Curriculum Theme

Weekly Curriculum Vocabulary

butterfly

caterpillar

chrysalis

egg

hatch

laboratory

lepidopterist

life cycle

specimen

Materials

The Very Hungry Caterpillar by Eric Carle and *From Caterpillar to Butterfly (Let's-Read-and-Find-Out-Science)* by Deborah Heiligman

1. Read *The Very Hungry Caterpillar* to the children.
2. Discuss the story. Is it real or make-believe? (Some of it is accurate, but caterpillars don't eat the foods depicted in the book.)
3. Read *From Caterpillar to Butterfly* or any other simple, non-fiction description of a caterpillar's change into a butterfly.
4. Encourage the children to pretend they are tiny caterpillar eggs hatching into caterpillars, eating and growing, becoming a chrysalis, and emerging as a butterfly.

Painted Butterflies

Art

Materials

easel paper ● scissors ● paint and paintbrushes

1. Cut easel paper into butterfly shapes for the children to paint at the easel. Tell the children not to be concerned about whether both sides of their butterflies are mirror images of each other.

Crawling Caterpillar Puppet

Art

Materials

white construction paper ● scissors and child-safe scissors ● glue ●
black construction paper ● books about caterpillars and butterflies ●
crayons or markers ● drinking straws ● clear tape

1. Cut out 2" diameter circles from white construction paper, 13 for each child.
2. Help each child count out 13 circles.
3. Encourage the children to glue their circles together, slightly overlapping on the sides, to form a caterpillar.
4. Ask each child to cut out six strips from black paper and glue these to the caterpillar for legs. Let the caterpillars dry overnight.
5. Encourage the children to look in books to see what real caterpillars look like and what their colors are, and then use crayons or markers to color their caterpillars.
6. Help the children accordion fold their caterpillars, and then unfold them. Help them tape one drinking straw to each end of their caterpillars, with the straws hanging down for puppet handles.
7. The children can make their caterpillars "crawl" by holding one straw in each hand and manipulating the straws.

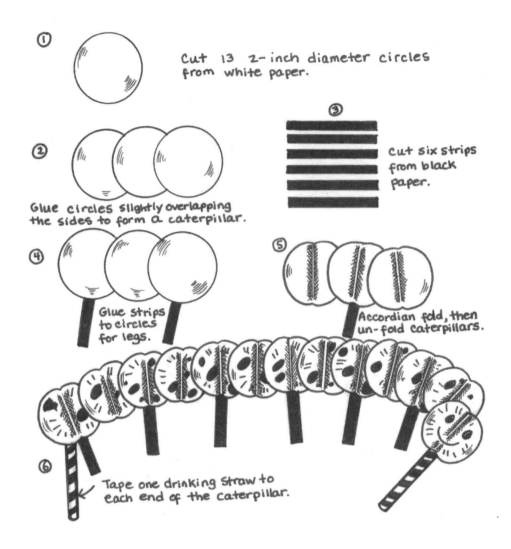

① Cut 13 2-inch diameter circles from white paper.

② Glue circles slightly overlapping the sides to form a caterpillar.

③ Cut six strips from black paper.

④ Glue strips to circles for legs.

⑤ Accordian fold, then un-fold caterpillars.

⑥ Tape one drinking straw to each end of the caterpillar.

Flying Butterfly Puppet

Art

Materials

construction paper • scissors • crayons or markers • paper clips • child-safe scissors • clear tape • drinking straws, 1 for each child

1. Cut out 4" squares from construction paper, one for each child.
2. Give each child a construction paper square and help him fold the square in half, placing the fold on the left and the open side on the right.
3. Help each child use a crayon to draw just the rounded parts of a large B on the folded paper as though the straight edge of the B is along the paper's fold. Do NOT draw the straight edge of the B.

Note: For some children you might need to hold their hand as they draw the B.

4. Slide two paper clips onto the paper's fold to hold the paper closed. Help each child cut along the crayoned shape through both layers of paper.

5. Remove the paper clips and open the paper to find a butterfly.

6. The children can use crayons or markers to color their butterflies.

7. Tape the butterfly's body to the end of a drinking straw.

8. Gently wave the straw back and forth and the butterfly will appear to be flying.

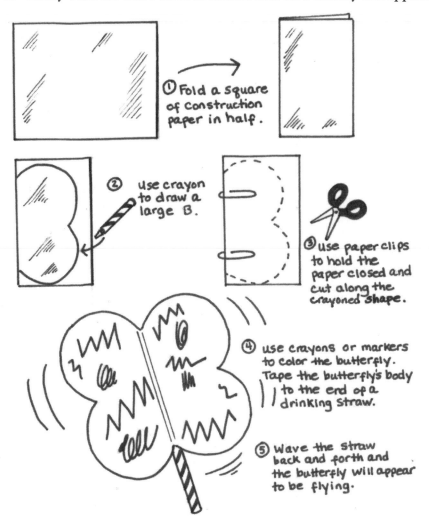

Drawing Butterflies

Art and Science

Materials

various non-fiction books with pictures of real butterflies ● art materials, such as paper, markers, and crayons

1. Place the books and art materials at the art table so the children can choose to draw pictures of real butterflies.

Visit a Butterfly House

Field Trip

1. Visit a butterfly house or butterfly garden. Arrange in advance for a guide to show items of particular interest to children.

Puppet Show

Language

Materials

child-made caterpillar and butterfly puppets (see Crawling Caterpillar Puppet on page 139 and Flying Butterfly Puppet on page 140)

1. Challenge the children to create spontaneous stories or sing made-up songs for their puppets to act out.
2. The children can use the puppets when they sing "The Life Cycle Song" (see next page).

Ordinal Numbers

Math

1. While talking about the life cycle of a caterpillar and butterfly, use ordinal numbers—first, second, third, fourth, and so on.

I'm a Caterpillar; I'm a Butterfly

Movement

Materials

small bath towels or head scarfs, 1 for each child

1. With the children, act out the life cycle of the butterfly.
2. Give each child a head scarf or small bath towel.
3. Ask them to crouch on the floor under their bath towel. They are the eggs and should begin hatching.
4. Then they become caterpillars pretending to eat leaves (their towels are the pretend leaves). As the caterpillars grow and grow, the children extend their bodies.

5. The caterpillars begin to form a chrysalis by wrapping the towel around their bodies. Remind the children that they must stay very still and quiet.

6. The butterflies begin to crawl out of the chrysalis. They wrap the discarded towel around their back, grab one corner of each end in opposite hands, and stretch out their arms. The towel becomes the butterfly wings, and the butterflies fly away to begin the life cycle again.

The Life Cycle Song

Music

1. With the children, sing the song below.

2. Help the children see that this is a circular song. The butterfly lays an egg in the last verse. After that verse, the children could begin the song again with the caterpillar hatching from the egg.

3. Ask the children if they can think of any books that are circular in this way (for example, *If You Give a Mouse a Cookie*).

> Tune: *Wheels on the Bus* (The tune is close to this, but you will need to add some notes so everything fits.)
> *A caterpillar hatched from an egg one day.*
> *(Repeat 2 times)*
> *And it ate and it ate and it ate.*
>
> *It ate leaves all night and day.*
> *(Repeat 2 times)*
> *And it grew and it grew and it grew.*
>
> *It grew and it grew and it shed its skin.*
> *(Repeat 2 times)*
> *Then it hung upside-down on a leaf.*
>
> *It made a chrysalis and it stayed inside.*
> *(Repeat 2 times)*
> *Then it came out—a butterfly.*
>
> *The butterfly flew from flower to flower.*
> *(Repeat 2 times)*
> *Then it laid an egg on a leaf.*

Butterflies and Caterpillars

Science

1. Order a kit that allows children to watch caterpillars grow and become butterflies. These kits are available through school supply catalogs and on the Internet (search: live butterfly school kit).
2. Avoid ordering just before a school holiday. The life cycle is short and the butterflies may hatch before school starts again.

Life Cycle Cards

Science

Materials

several sets of commercially available or teacher-made cards of the butterfly's life cycle

1. With the children, arrange the cards in order starting with either the egg or with the adult butterfly.
2. Talk about each stage of the cycle and how each stage leads to the next.
3. Discuss the way the cycle repeats and repeats and repeats.
4. Sing the "Life Cycle Song" (page 143).

Very Hungry Caterpillar Food

Snack/Cooking

Materials

The Very Hungry Caterpillar by Eric Carle

1. Serve any of the items eaten by the caterpillar in the book, such as pears, strawberries, or watermelon.

Butterfly Crackers

Snack/Cooking

Materials

rectangular crackers • spreadable fruit or jelly • blunt, plastic knife • paper plates • round crackers • whipped cream cheese • diced dried fruit, such as raisins, apples, and pineapple • pretzel sticks

1. Encourage the children to put spreadable fruit on a rectangular cracker and place it in the center of their plates for the butterfly's body.
2. Ask them to spread whipped cream cheese on two round crackers and place one on each side of the rectangle to form the butterfly's wings.
3. The children can decorate the wings with diced, dried fruit and add pretzel stick halves for butterfly antennae.
4. Display the finished butterflies so the children can admire each other's creations, then let the artists eat their handiwork.

Learning Center Ideas

Dramatic Play Area

Materials

plastic butterflies and caterpillars • butterfly/caterpillar field guides • butterfly nets • paper and pencils • magnifying glasses • small containers for the "specimens"

1. Provide these materials and any other related items the children request so they can pretend to be *lepidopterists* (people who study butterflies).

Related Books

Butterfly by Rebecca Stefoff
The Butterfly Alphabet by Brian Cassie and Jerry Pallotta
Butterfly House by Eve Bunting
An Extraordinary Life: The Story of a Monarch Butterfly by Laurence Pringle
    (text is for older children, but the book contains excellent pictures including the
    lifecycle)
Eyewitness Explorers Butterflies and Moths by John Feltwell
From Caterpillar to Butterfly by Deborah Heiligman
The Very Hungry Caterpillar by Eric Carle
Waiting for Wings by Lois Ehlert
Where Butterflies Grow by Joanne Ryder
Where Does the Butterfly Go When It Rains? by May Garelick

Exploring Warm and Cold

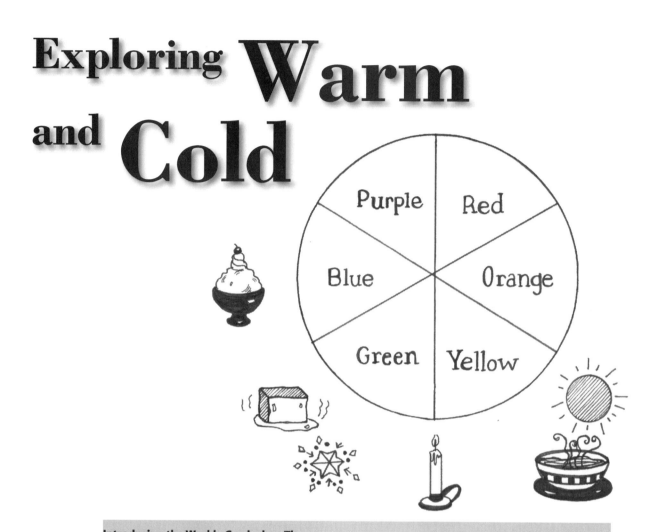

Weekly Curriculum Vocabulary

baby
cool
elephant
pool
splash
squirt
warm

Materials

SPLASH! by Flora McDonnell

1. This book features animals in India. In the story, it is HOT, and all the animals are hot. Baby elephant has an idea. The other animals follow him to the water hole where they drink and play, splashing and squirting. Finally, they are cool.

2. Read the book with the children.

3. Read the book again, stopping to point out the warm colors (yellow, orange, red) used when the animals are hot. Show how the author introduces the cooler colors (blue, aqua, white) when the animals reach the water, and how the proportions of cool and warm colors change as the animals become cooler. Compare the "hottest" and "coolest" pages.

4. Talk about why yellow, orange, and red might be "warm" colors. They are colors we associate with the sun and with fire.

5. Talk about why blue, aqua, and white might be considered "cool" colors. They are colors we associate with water and with snow.

Warm and Cool

Art and Language

Materials

SPLASH! by Flora McDonnell ● plain paper ● crayons and markers in warm and cool colors

1. After reading *SPLASH!*, encourage the children to use warm colors to draw a picture about a thing or a place that is warm or hot. Write the children's dictated descriptions on their pictures. Show the pictures to the group, then save the pictures.
2. On another day, read the book again. Challenge the children to use cool colors to draw pictures of cool or cold subjects. Write children's dictated descriptions on their pictures.
3. Let the children show their pictures.
4. Divide a bulletin board in half vertically. Label one half "Warm" and the other half "Cool." Display the children's art in the appropriate section on this board.

The Listening Hunter

Games and Language

Materials

small toy stuffed animal

1. Choose a small toy animal to hide during this game.
2. Select one child (the hunter) and ask him to leave the room and close the door.
3. Select another child to hide the stuffed animal while the group watches.
4. Ask the hunter to return to the room and begin to look for the hidden item.
5. As the hunter explores the room looking for the animal, the children say "warm" as he nears the hidden item and "cool" as he moves away from the item. They may also say "hot" or "cold" as the hunter gets very near to or far from the item.
6. When the hunter finds the object, he chooses the next hunter. Play continues each day until every child has had a turn to be the hunter.

The "Ool" Family

Language

Materials

sentence strips ● marker ● pocket chart

1. Use the warm/cold theme to investigate and learn about the "ool" family of words. Write __ool on a sentence strip. On small pieces of sentence strips, write individual consonants.
2. Place the __ool sentence strip in a pocket chart. Ask the children, in turn, to select a consonant to place in the blank to form words such as *cool, fool, tool* and *pool*. They can also form nonsense words such as *lool* and *sool*.
3. Ask the group to read each word that is formed.

Acting Out a Poem

Language and Movement

Materials

"Walking to the Water Hole" by Barbara Backer

1. Using the rhyme "Walking to the Water Hole" below, act out the story from *SPLASH!*
2. Let the children decide which animals they want to be. Having several of each animal is just fine.
3. Designate an area of the room as the pool of water.
4. Have all of the animals say, "I'm hot! I'm so hot!"
5. The children who are the baby elephant(s) begin walking as you read the rhyme.
6. In turn, the children act out their parts, following the baby elephant(s).
7. As the children learn the rhyme, encourage them to say it with you.

> **Walking to the Water Hole**
> *Walking to the water hole;*
> *Walking to the pool.*
> *Follow baby elephant,*
> *Soon you will be cool.*
>
> *Come on, mother elephant,*
> *I'm going to the pool.* (baby elephant beckons mother)
> *Follow baby elephant,*
> *Soon you will be cool.*

Come on, orange tiger,
We're going to the pool. (baby and mother beckon tiger)
Follow baby elephant,
Soon you will be cool.

Come on, big rhinoceros,
We're going to the pool. (animals beckon rhinoceros)
Follow baby elephant,
Soon you will be cool.

Come on all you flying birds,
We're going to the pool. (animals beckon birds)
Follow baby elephant,
Soon you will be cool.

Splash! Splosh! (animals make splashing motions)
Whoosh! Sploosh!
Squirt, squirt, squirt.

Splash! Splosh!
Whoosh! Sploosh!
Squirt, squirt, squirt.

Now we're cool, we are not hot.
We're very, very cool.
Thank you, baby elephant, (animals nod at baby)
For leading us to the pool.

Ordinal Numbers

Math

1. Ordinal numbers tell about the order of things.
2. Use ordinal numbers to talk about the animals in the story. Who went first, second, third, and so on?

How Many Legs?

Math

Materials

bulletin board paper ● marker

1. Divide a piece of bulletin board paper in half vertically. On one half write "Two Legs," and on the other half write "Four Legs."
2. Talk about each animal in *SPLASH!*
3. With the children, decide in which column you should write each animal's name.
4. Count the animals in each group. Compare the two groups using words such as *more, less,* and *same as.*

Explore Warm and Cold Outdoors

Outdoors and Science

Materials

plastic dishpans ● cool water and ice ● sweatbands/headbands ●
wading pool ● turkey basters ● squirt bottles (from ketchup or liquid dish
detergent) ● change of clothing for each child

1. On a warm day, place dishpans of cool water in a shady outdoor place. If desired, add ice to the water.
2. As children play and become warm, encourage them to immerse their hands and forearms into the water. Does this help them feel cooler all over?
3. Immerse some sweatbands or headbands in the cool water, wring out the water, and offer the bands to the children. Do the cool bands help them feel cooler all over?
4. Place several of the basins in the direct sun. Ask the children to check on these from time to time. Is their temperature different from the shaded basins? Encourage discussion about why this might be. What warmed the water?
5. Extend the fun and learning: In hot weather, fill a wading pool with cool water. Add turkey basters and squirt bottles, and have splashing and squirting games. Children can wear bathing suits, or summer clothes if a complete change of clothing is available.

Comparing Warm and Cold Foods

Snack/Cooking

Materials

raw carrot cut into thin strips ● sharp knife (adult only) ●
microwave oven (adult only) ● orange juice ●
small waxed paper cups ●
baking sheet ● freezer

1. Explore the differences between warm and cold foods.
2. Cut a cold, raw carrot into thin strips. Heat some of the carrot in a microwave oven (adult only). Serve the children tastes of cold, raw carrot and warm, cooked carrot. Discuss how the carrots are the same and how they are different.
3. Pour orange juice into small paper cups. Place some of the cups on a baking sheet and put them into the freezer. Leave the rest of the cups out. Serve the room temperature orange juice and cups of frozen juice. Discuss the children's observations.

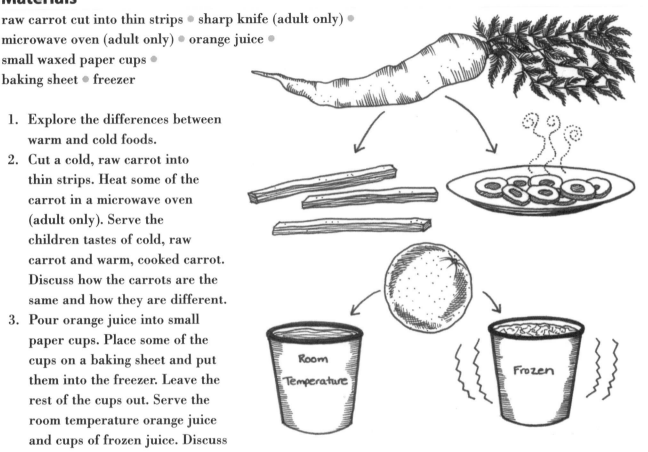

Learning Center Ideas

Science Area

Materials

books with vivid, artistic pictures that make use of warm and cool colors ● pictures of paintings by the "Great Masters" ● samples of paint colors

1. Place the materials in the Science Area and encourage the children to talk about warm and cool colors while they explore the items.
2. Encourage the children to sort the samples of paint colors into warm and cool colors.

Related Books

Explore warm and cool colors in these books:

Before & After: A Book of Nature Timescapes by Jan Thornhill

Heckedy Peg by Audrey Wood

King Bidgood's in the Bathtub by Audrey Wood

Where the Wild Things Are by Maurice Sendak

Five Senses—First Week—
Seeing, Hearing, and Touching

Introducing the Weekly Curriculum Theme

Materials
any book about the five senses (see suggestions on page 159)

1. Read one of the books and introduce the five senses—seeing, hearing, touching, smelling, and tasting. Tell the children that our senses are five ways to gather information and learn about things.
2. Ask the children to be silent for 30 seconds and listen to the sounds around them. Then ask them to say what they learned using their sense of hearing. (For example, "There is a bird in the play yard," or "The garbage truck is here.")
3. Repeat, sitting quietly and paying attention to smells. Then ask the children what they learned using their sense of smelling. (For example, "The cook is making spaghetti.")
4. Repeat this for touching, tasting, and, finally, for seeing.
5. Let the children tell about things they like to see and things they hate to see. (Children are usually discouraged from using the word "hate." Let them use it in this safe context of hating a thing, not a person.)
6. Follow this activity by beginning the Five Senses Book (on the next page). Children will add to this book during the two-week study of the five senses.

Weekly Curriculum Vocabulary

different

ears

eyes

fingers

hands

hear

loud

quiet

same

see

texture

touch

All Five Senses—Five Senses Book

Art and Language

Materials

drawing paper ● crayons or markers ● pen

1. After the opening activity (see above), give each child a sheet of paper. Ask them to draw something they like to see.
2. When they bring you their finished paper, write: "I like to see ____." Then fill in the blank with the object the child drew.
3. Give them a second sheet of paper and ask them to draw something they don't like to see. Repeat step number two, replacing "like" with "don't like."
4. Repeat the activity on other days discussing what children like and don't like to hear and what they like and don't like to touch/feel.
5. Save the papers. When the children have completed pictures for all five senses (at the end of week number two), compile the drawings in individual books to send home to families.
6. Encourage the children to read these books to their families.

Touching—Textured Dough

Art

Materials

modeling dough ● birdseed

1. Sprinkle birdseed onto the table when children are playing with modeling dough.
2. Give no instructions; let them explore, discover, and talk with each other about what is happening.

Touching—Textured Fingerpainting

Art and Language

Materials

fingerpaint, one color ● several cafeteria trays ● sand ● cornstarch

1. Spread fingerpaint on the trays. Add sand to some of the trays and cornstarch to others. Leave some trays with only paint on them.
2. Invite the children to fingerpaint at the various trays, changing from one tray to another after a few minutes. Encourage them to discuss how the substances feel the same and how they feel different.
3. Be certain that children wash their hands well both before and after this activity. Washing before fingerpainting helps prevent the spread of germs through the paint.

Touching—Textures From Home

Bulletin Board and Language

Materials

note to families (see below) ● variety of textured materials from children's homes ● several sheets of poster board ● glue ● index cards ● marker

1. Send a note home to families explaining that their children are learning about the five senses. Ask them to send in non-returnable items that have textures, such as feathers, ribbon, buttons, fabric scraps, egg cartons, bumpy paper, bubble wrap, Styrofoam chips, cotton balls, sequins, aquarium gravel, shells, yarn, sandpaper, and any other clean, textured items.
2. Provide these materials to the children and encourage them to glue as much as possible to the poster board. Let dry.
3. On the index cards, write the children's one-word descriptions of their favorite textures on the poster board.
4. Display the finished work where children can easily reach it, touch it, and compare textures.
5. Hang the word cards around the display where children can read them to their families and to each other.

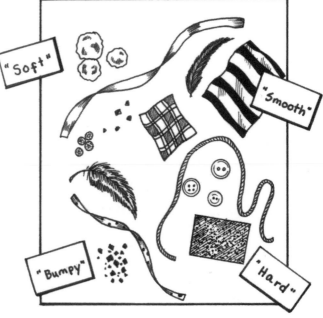

Seeing—Red Means Stop, Green Means Go

Games and Movement

Materials

green and red construction paper ● scissors ● recorded music

1. Cut out a circle from green construction paper and a circle from red construction paper.
2. Tell the children that they will be playing "Red Means Stop, Green Means Go." Explain that they will be dancing with partners, and will use their sense of "seeing" to tell them when to dance and when to stop.
3. Show the circles to the children. Explain that when they see you holding up the green circle, they should dance. When they see you holding up a red one, they should stop. They should not tell their partners to stop or go.
4. Play recorded music throughout as a background for children's dancing. Do not stop the music. This is a "looking and seeing" game, not a listening game.

Guess Who?

Games and Music

Materials

a child-size chair

1. Place the chair in front of the group so that a child sitting in the chair will have her back to the group.
2. Choose a child to sit in the chair. Ask her to cover her eyes with her hands.
3. Sing the song below, and then choose one child to ask, "Who can it be?" in a silly voice.
4. The child in the chair has three chances to guess the speaker. The speaker repeats the phrase after any incorrect guess. After a third incorrect guess, the speaker uses her own tone of voice.

> Tune: *This Old Man*
> *Listen now, one, two, three.*
> *Can you guess who this might be?*
> *Listen very carefully,*
> *Can you guess who this might be?*

5. The speaker becomes the next guesser, sitting in the chair, and another child is chosen to be the new speaker.

Letter Hunt

Language

Materials

newspapers and magazines ● pencils or markers ● index cards

1. Encourage the children to use their sense of sight while looking for familiar letters in newspapers and magazines.
2. Print a letter, both upper- and lower-case, on an index card. Show the letter to the children and help them identify it.
3. Ask the children to look for the letter in newspapers or magazines, and circle the letter every time they find it.
4. Have them show their results to each other.

Our Senses Outdoors

Outdoors

1. Remind the children to explore actively with their eyes, ears, and fingers while they are playing outdoors.

Hearing—An Earful of Information

Science

Materials

jingle bells or other "gentle" noisemaker

1. Ask the children if their sense of hearing can tell them when someone is approaching, leaving, or nearby.
2. Ask the children to spread out in the area. Have them close their eyes and listen while you walk slowly around the entire area, quietly jingling the bells.
3. Walk completely around each child so all the children can hear the change in direction of the bells.
4. Ask the children to open their eyes. Discuss whether they could tell where you were just by listening.

Touching—Feeling With Our Feet

Science

Materials

dishpans • ice water and ice • warm water • several terry cloth towels • a variety of textured items, such as bathtub mat with suction cups on the back, plastic shower curtain, woven rattan placemat, pillow, bubble wrap, carpet sample, or door mat • hand lotion

1. Pour warm water and ice water into separate dishpans. Lay out a "walking path" of textures, using items from the materials list or any other textured items. (Place the bathtub mat upside down so its suction cups are up). Include the pans of water, placing a towel after each of these.
2. Help the children remove their shoes and socks. Encourage them to take turns walking the path, stepping on each item as they go. Ask them to notice if their feet can feel the different textures.
3. Ask the children to describe how different items feel.
4. End the activity by massaging the children's feet with hand lotion before they put on their socks and shoes.

The Sounds of Snack

Snack/Cooking

Materials

celery stuffed with pineapple cream cheese • pretzels and ice cream • pudding and vanilla wafers

1. Serve a snack that combines two or more items that sound different when you bite and chew them. Choose from the selections above.
2. Ask the children to focus on their sounds of biting and chewing. Talk about which are "quiet" foods and which are "noisy" foods.

Learning Center Ideas

Science Area

Materials

eyeglass frames ● magnifying glasses ● binoculars ● music boxes ● rhythm instruments ● items with a variety of textures, such as cotton balls, modeling dough, rubber gloves, oven mitts, knitted gloves and mittens, nylon net, plastic kitchen scrubbing pads, sponges, and stuffed animals

1. Put an assortment of the materials in the Science Area for the children to explore.

Related Books

Brown Bear, Brown Bear, What Do You See? by Bill Martin, Jr. and Eric Carle
Clang, Boom, Bang by Jane Belk Moncure
Fish Eyes: A Book You Can Count On by Lois Ehlert
Forest Friends Five Senses by Cristina Garelli
Look Book by Tana Hoban
My Eyes Are for Seeing by Jane Belk Moncure
My Fingers Are for Touching by Jane Belk Moncure
My Five Senses by Margaret Miller
My Five Senses by Aliki
Open Your Eyes: Discover Your Sense of Sight by Vicki Cobb
Perk Up Your Ears: Discover Your Sense of Hearing by Vicki Cobb
Polar Bear, Polar Bear, What Do You Hear? by Bill Martin, Jr. and Eric Carle
The Very Busy Spider by Eric Carle
The Very Quiet Cricket by Eric Carle
Who Am I: A Book to Touch and Feel by Alice Wilder

Five Senses—Second Week— Smelling and Tasting

Introducing the Weekly Curriculum Theme

Weekly Curriculum Vocabulary

mouth
nose
smell
taste
tongue

Materials

chewing gum

1. With the children, talk about the senses of smell and taste. Ask the children if they think their nose helps them taste things. Tell them they will be investigating to find the answer.

2. Working with one child at a time, ask the child to hold his nose while you put ¼ piece of gum in his mouth.

3. Have the child begin chewing, while he continues holding his nose. Let him chew about 15 seconds.

4. Count to three with the children, and then ask the child to let go of his nose. He will notice a burst of flavor when he smells the aroma of the gum.

5. Repeat with all of the children and discuss their observations.

6. Ask them again if they think their nose helps them taste things.

A Smelly Picture

Art

Materials

paper • markers • white glue • fruit-flavored gelatin powder • shaker for grated cheese

1. Give each child a piece of paper. Ask them to draw a picture on their papers.
2. Ask them to spread glue over the picture.
3. Put gelatin powder into the shaker. Encourage the children to sprinkle the gelatin over the wet glue.
4. Let dry, and then the children can sniff their sweet-smelling pictures.

A Nosy Picture

Art

Materials

scissors • magazines • glue • drawing paper • crayons

1. Cut out noses from magazine advertising pictures. Glue one of these just below the center of each piece of paper (one for each child).
2. Let each child choose one of these papers.
3. Ask the children to look at the pictures and talk about them. What might be missing?
4. Give the children crayons so they can add whatever features are missing from their picture.

What Smells Like This?

Art and Language

Materials

white paper • stapler • construction paper • scratch-and-sniff stickers • markers • pen

1. Make a four-page blank book for each child by stapling two pieces of white paper between two pieces of construction paper. Give one to each child.
2. Give each child four different scratch-and-sniff stickers. It's best if children don't have the same four stickers as everyone else.
3. Ask the children to stick one sticker on each page of their books.
4. Ask each child to scratch and sniff the sticker on the first page of her book.
5. When they determine the smell of their sticker, they can draw a picture on that page of the item that smells like the sticker.
6. Repeat with the remaining stickers and pages.
7. Write the children's dictated words on their pages or encourage them to write about their pictures.

Five Senses Book

Language

Materials

five senses book from the first week about senses (see All Five Senses—Five Senses Book, page 154) • drawing paper • crayons • construction paper • stapler

1. Have the children continue adding to the five senses book they began in the first week of learning about senses. Ask them to add the following pages:

    I like to smell ____.
    I don't like to smell ____.
    I like to taste ____.
    I don't like to taste ____.

2. When the children have completed all the pages, gather each child's pages into a book. Staple them together using construction paper for a front and back cover.
3. Ask the children to read these books to three friends. Make sure that the children who are read to sign their names on the back cover.
4. Encourage the children to take home the books so they can read them to their families.

Most Popular Aroma

Math

Materials
unsweetened powdered drink mix in lemon, grape, and strawberry ● water ●
chart paper ● yellow, purple, and red markers

1. Open the drink mix packages and add just enough water to each pouch to
   dampen the mix and keep the mix from floating out.
2. On a piece of chart paper, make a graph titled "Our Favorite Aroma." Divide it
   into three columns labeled lemon, grape, strawberry. Show the graph to the
   children and discuss the activity.
3. Let each child smell all three packages of drink mix.
4. Ask each child to sign the graph in the column labeled with the smell she liked
   best. The children should use the yellow marker to sign under lemon, purple
   for grape, and red for strawberry.
5. Compare the results, exploring the concepts of *more, less, equal to, greater
   than, less than,* and other mathematical terms.

Smelling and Tasting

Music

1. Ask the children to sing the song below. (If desired, concentrate on only
   one verse.)
2. Ask one child at a time to say the words he would like to insert in the blank
   spaces, and then have the group sing that child's version.

> Tune: *Mulberry Bush*
> ____ *smells so very good, very good, very good.*
> ____ *smells so very good, but _____ smells awful.*
>
> ____ *tastes so very good, very good, very good.*
> ____ *tastes so very good, but _____ tastes awful.*

Looks the Same, Smells Different

Science

Materials

2 clear plastic cups • white vinegar • water

1. Pour water into one cup and vinegar into the other. Cover each with a napkin to mask the vinegar smell.
2. Show the cups to the children. Tell them that one cup holds water and the other holds something sour. Ask if anyone knows a way they could find out, without tasting, which one is good to drink. Can they see the difference? Feel it? Lead them to suggest smelling the items.
3. Let each child smell both cups and tell you which contains water.

Smells the Same, Tastes Different

Science

Materials

2 clear plastic cups • salt • sugar • teaspoon

1. Put a teaspoon of salt into one cup and a teaspoon of sugar in the other. Show the cups to the children and tell them that both are things that people eat. Ask them to suggest ways to identify the contents. Can they see a difference? Smell it? Feel it? Try each of these.
2. Spoon a tiny amount of each substance into the children's palms, one in each palm. Let them taste the items. Remind them that they used the sense of taste to do this.

Looks the Same, Tastes Different

Science

Materials

1 clear plastic bottle of cola with label removed • 1 clear plastic bottle of root beer with label removed • small cups, 2 for each child

1. Show the children the bottles of soda with the labels removed. Ask if they think both bottles have the same contents.
2. Make sure the children watch while you pour a small amount from each bottle into their cups. Do they sound different when you pour them? How do they look?

3. Ask them to touch the liquids. Do they feel different?
4. Let the children taste the sodas. Can they identify them?

Tasting the Difference
Snack/Cooking

Materials
foods that look similar but taste different

1. Throughout the week, serve pairs of snacks that look similar but taste different such as a peeled sweet apple/peeled tart apple; vanilla ice cream/vanilla yogurt; and so on.

Learning Center Ideas
Manipulatives Area

Materials
scratch-and-sniff stickers

1. Place the stickers where the children can use them at will.
2. Do not add tasting items to the classroom for children to explore at will.

Related Books
Busy Bunnies' Five Senses by Teddy Slater
Follow Your Nose: Discover Your Sense of Smell by Vicki Cobb
I Smell Honey by Andrea Pinkney
Little Red Hen by Byron Barton
My Five Senses by Aliki
The Relatives Came by Cynthia Rylant
Thunder Cake by Patricia Polacco
Today Is Monday by Eric Carle
What's That Smell?: A Lift and Sniff Book by Janelle Cherrington and
   Mitchell Kriegman
You Smell: and Taste and Feel and See and Hear by Mary Murphy
Your Tongue Can Tell: Discover Your Sense of Taste by Vicki Cobb

Giant Pandas

Introducing the Weekly Curriculum Theme

Weekly Curriculum Vocabulary

Materials

any non-fiction book about pandas (see list on page 172) ● chart paper ● scissors ● marker

baby
bamboo
black
Giant Panda
pouch
white

1. Read any non-fiction book about giant pandas.
2. Cut a piece of chart paper into a giant panda shape. Ask the children to recall facts about pandas, and list these on the panda-shaped paper. Be certain that children understand that pandas are not bears.
3. As children learn more about pandas during the week, add what they have learned to the chart.

Paper Plate Giant Pandas

Art

Materials

pictures of giant pandas ● large white paper plates ● small white paper plates ● stapler ● black construction paper ● pencils ● child-safe scissors ● glue

1. Show the children pictures of giant pandas.
2. Give each child a large paper plate and a small paper plate. Help each child staple together the rims of a large and small plate. This will be their giant panda's body and head.
3. Encourage the children to use the remaining materials to make the giant panda's legs, ears, and facial features.
4. Use the giant pandas on the bulletin board (see Panda Board on page 169).

Bamboo

Art

Materials

bamboo, or pictures of bamboo • newspaper • masking tape • paintbrushes • yellow, light brown, and light green tempera paint • child-safe scissors • green construction paper • glue

1. Giant pandas eat a plant called bamboo. With the children, look at real bamboo or pictures of bamboo. Discuss its long stalks and thin, pointed leaves.
2. Help the children roll the newspaper into long, skinny rolls to resemble bamboo stalks. Use masking tape to hold the rolls closed.
3. Ask the children to paint these stalks with the yellow, brown, and green paint.
4. When the paint is dry, ask the children to cut out long, thin, pointed leaves from the green paper. Have them glue these to their bamboo stalks.
5. If children desire, they can make short bamboo stalks for their pandas to hold.
6. Use the bamboo with the pandas on the bulletin board (see Panda Board on next page).

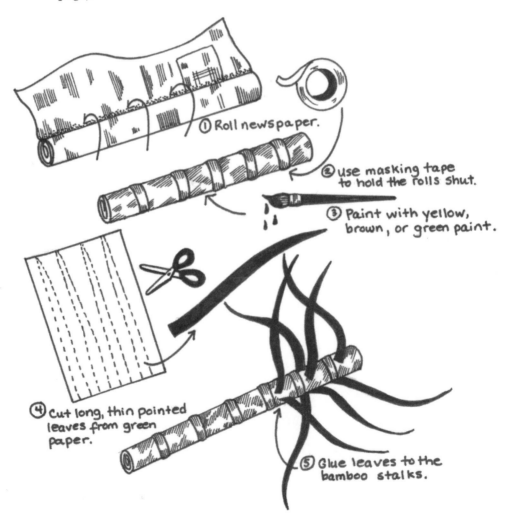

① Roll newspaper.

② Use masking tape to hold the rolls shut.

③ Paint with yellow, brown, or green paint.

④ Cut long, thin pointed leaves from green paper.

⑤ Glue leaves to the bamboo stalks.

Panda Board

Bulletin Board

Materials

paper plate giant pandas (see Paper Plate Giant Pandas on page 167) ● bamboo
(see Bamboo on previous page) ● bulletin board paper in a solid color

1. Ask the children to help you attach the bamboo and the paper plate pandas to a
   bulletin board with a solid color background. Some of the pandas can be
   behind the bamboo looking through it, and others can be in front of it.
2. Children who desire can place small bamboo stalks in their pandas' paws,
   making it appear as if they are eating the bamboo.

Playing Pandas

Dramatic Play

Materials

adults' black socks

1. Put many pairs of black socks in the Dramatic Play Area. Children can pull
   these on over their shoes and over their hands and arms, helping them look
   like pandas.

Writing About Pandas

Language

Materials

paper ● pencils ● crayons ● construction paper

1. After children learn the song about pandas (see "Panda Song" page 171), if
   appropriate, ask them to write the word "panda" using the song to help them
   remember the letters. (Help them if they need assistance spelling out the word.)
2. On a separate piece of paper, encourage them to draw a picture to illustrate
   their word.
3. Tape each child's pages to each other, and then tape all the pairs together, side
   by side. Fold these accordion-style to make an accordion-fold book. Use a sheet
   of construction paper for the cover page.

How Pandas Grow

Math and Science

Materials

stick of margarine ● books and other reference materials about pandas ●
masking tape

1. A newborn giant panda is about the size of a stick of margarine! It is 6 inches long and weighs approximately 4 ½ ounces. An adult giant panda measures about 6 feet tall and weighs between 250 and 300 pounds.
2. To demonstrate these size differences, show the children a wrapped stick of margarine, and let them hold it to feel its weight.
3. Put two strips of masking tape on the floor 6 feet apart to show the length of an adult giant panda. Place another strip 6 inches from one of the "adult" strips, to show the length of the newborn giant panda. Help the children understand that the baby will grow and grow until it is an adult.
4. To demonstrate the adult's weight, simply tell the children that the adult panda weighs more than you.

Caution: Do not allow them to attempt to lift you.

More About Giant Pandas

Math and Science

Materials

4 ½ ounces of birdseed for each "panda baby" ● knee-high stockings and
pantyhose ● scissors

1. Pour 4 ½ ounces of birdseed into the stocking and tie a knot close to the stuffing. Cut off any excess stocking. The resulting creation is the weight of a newborn panda.
2. Explain to the children that for the first month of her baby's life, the giant panda mother holds her baby constantly. Let the children take turns holding the pantyhose "panda baby" while playing and/or working. Would they want to hold this baby all of the time for a month?
3. Make several of these so all the children can have many opportunities to carry the "panda baby."

Panda Song

Music

1. Sing the following song with the children.

> Tune: *Bingo*
> *There is an animal in the zoo*
> *And panda is its name, oh!*
> *P-A-N-D-A, P-A-N-D-A,*
> *P-A-N-D-A*
> *And panda is its name, oh!*
>
> *This animal is white and black,*
> *And panda is its name, oh! (continue as in verse 1)*
>
> *This animal eats bamboo shoots,*
> *And panda is its name, oh! (continue as in verse 1)*

Pandas in Zoos

Science

1. View live pictures of pandas at the zoo by searching online for Smithsonian National Zoological Park, the San Diego Zoo, or the Atlanta Zoo.

Giant Panda Cookies

Snack/Cooking

Materials
commercially prepared, round sugar cookies • commercially prepared white frosting • blunt knives • regular and miniature chocolate chips • commercially-prepared red gel (for cake decorating) in small tube • fresh celery leaves

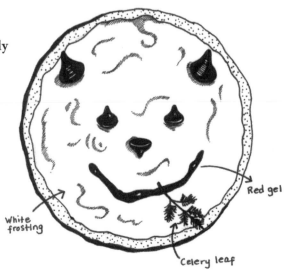

1. Working with small groups of children, help them make giant panda faces for their snack.
2. Give each child a cookie and ask them to spread white frosting on it. Next they use chocolate chips for ears, eyes, and a nose. A squeeze of red gel makes the mouth.

3. Show the children how to place a celery leaf across the mouth so the panda appears to be eating bamboo. The children can eat the leaf or remove it before eating the snack.

Learning Center Ideas
Dramatic Play Area

Materials
clipboards • pencils and pens • eyeglass frames, with no lenses (from optical shop) • science magazines with pictures of giant pandas • pictures of giant pandas from the Internet • discarded cell phones • name badges

1. Place a few of these items in the Dramatic Play Area so the children can pretend they are scientists studying giant pandas.

Related Books
I Am a Little Panda by Francois Crozat
Little Panda: The World Welcomes Hua Mei at the San Diego Zoo by Joanne Ryder
Pi-Shu, the Little Panda by John Butler

How Things Change

Introducing the Weekly Curriculum Theme

Materials
unit blocks ● grocery bags ● camera

1. For each pair of children, place 12 unit blocks in a grocery bag, making certain that each bag's blocks are identical.
2. Give a bag to each pair of children and ask them to place the blocks on the floor. Help the children discover that each pair has identical blocks.
3. Encourage the pairs to build using all of the blocks in their bag. After a few minutes, stop the building and let each pair show what they have built and describe it. Remind the children that the same number and shapes of blocks made each of these structures.
4. Take photos of the structures and display all of them together, so the children can remember and compare their structures.
5. Repeat steps three and four so the children experience building several different items with the same blocks.

Weekly Curriculum Vocabulary

change
clean
different
dirty
mud
pair
same
soil

Changing Rainbows

Art and Science

Materials

jar lids ● small pitchers of water ● red, blue, and yellow food coloring ● eyedroppers ● paper towels ● scissors

1. Work with groups of three children at a time. Give each child a jar lid to fill with water. Ask each child to add a different color of food coloring to his water. Put an eyedropper into each container of colored water.
2. Pre-cut paper towels into rainbow shapes. Give one to each child, and let the children drip one color of water onto their rainbows.
3. Have the children trade colors and drip again. Repeat with the third color. Encourage the children to observe and discuss what happens when one color drips or spreads onto another.
4. Repeat with all the children and display the rainbows together.

Building With Blocks

Blocks

Materials

Changes, Changes by Pat Hutchins ● table blocks, see description below* ● camera ● Lucite picture frames

1. Place the book *Changes, Changes* and the table blocks in the Block Area.
2. Encourage the children to look at the book and build structures with the blocks.
3. Take pictures of the structures that the children build with the blocks.
4. Display these in the Block Area in Lucite, stand-up picture frames.

* Table blocks are small blocks that are used to build on a table instead of on the floor. They look exactly like the blocks in *Changes, Changes* by Pat Hutchins.

Simple Word Families

Language

Materials
sentence strips ● markers ● pocket chart

1. Write ___*at* on a sentence strip. On small pieces of sentence strips, write one consonant per strip.
2. Place the ___*at* strip in a pocket chart and help the children read it.
3. Take turns asking each child to select a consonant to place in the blank to form words such as *cat*, *hat*, *pat*, and so on. They can also form nonsense words like *zat* and *wat*.
4. Help the children read the resulting word. Call attention to the unchanging final two letters of each word.
5. On other days, repeat with other simple word families.

How Our Blocks Changed

Language

Materials
photos from the opening activity ● construction paper ● marker

1. Use photos from the opening activity to make a book titled "How Our Blocks Changed."
2. If desired, write each pair's dictated words on the picture of their block creation.

Some Changing Things Remain the Same

Math

Materials

Changes, Changes by Pat Hutchins ● table blocks

1. Before the activity, find blocks that exactly match the blocks on any two-page spread of this book *Changes, Changes*. (Every structure built by the block people in the story is made from these same blocks.)
2. *Changes, Changes* is a wordless picture book. "Read" the book by letting the children tell what's happening in the story as you show the pictures.
3. Show the table blocks to the children. Page through the book again, matching the real table blocks with those in any picture in the book.
4. Turn to another page and see if the blocks also match the blocks in that picture. Help the children understand that any of the structures in the book can be built with this particular group of blocks.
5. If you don't have the blocks, point out that every page has identical blocks, just as each pair of children had identical blocks in the opening activity.

Change-O

Movement

1. Ask the children to move like any animal of their choice. Ask each child to tell what animal she is pretending to be.
2. Say, "Bing-O, bang-O, now it's time to change-O," and ask the children to change into something that moves with wheels. Again, let the children tell what they are pretending to be.
3. Repeat several times, suggesting that the change be the children moving like something at home, something in the air, something outside, or an idea that they suggest.
4. Use the opportunity to talk about changes.

Muddy Changes

Outdoors and Science

Materials

plastic dishpans ● soil/dirt from different areas ● buckets of water ● ladles

1. Put soil or dirt into plastic dishpans. Ask the children to add water to the dishpans of soil/dirt.
2. Discuss how the dirt changes.
3. Encourage the children to play with the resulting mud.
4. Leave the dishpans outdoors where the contents will dry from evaporation or will get wet from rain.
5. Talk about the changes from day to day.

Bubble and Fizz

Science

Materials

baking soda ● clear bowl ● plain vinegar ● plastic-top tables ● damp cleaning cloths

1. Put a small amount of baking soda into the see-through bowl. Slowly pour a small amount of vinegar onto the baking soda and watch the change. Repeat the pouring until the reaction stops. Help the children understand that vinegar alone and soda alone do not bubble and fizz. When they combine, however, a chemical change occurs, causing the bubbling and fizzing.
2. When the classroom tables are dirty, pour some vinegar on the tabletop. Let the children sprinkle baking soda on damp cloths and use these to wipe up the vinegar. The resulting fizz helps loosen dirt. And it's fun!

Watching for Changes

Science

Materials

dry sponges, cut in half ● birdseed ● water

1. Give each child half of a sponge.
2. Ask the children to dip their sponges in water, and then wring them gently.
3. Ask the children to sprinkle birdseed on their damp sponges.
4. Place the sponges in a dark place. Encourage the children to check them every day for changes.
5. Remind the children to add a little water to the sponges every other day.
6. When the seeds begin to sprout, move the sponges to a sunny window. Continue to water the sponges and watch for changes.
7. If desired, the children can plant their sprouting sponges in the ground.

Pineapple Milkshakes

Snack/Cooking

Materials

blender (adult only) • pineapple juice • nonfat, dry milk powder • bananas cut into fourths • vanilla extract • measuring cups and spoons • blunt knives • eyedropper • paper cups

1. Work with one child at a time.
2. Help the child measure ¼ cup pineapple juice, 1 tablespoon dry milk powder, banana slices from ¼ banana, and 1 drop of vanilla extract into the blender container.
3. Put the top on the blender, and then blend the ingredients (adult only).
4. Pour into a cup and enjoy! Makes one drink serving.

Popcorn

Science and Snack/Cooking

Materials

un-popped popcorn kernels • corn popper (adult only)

1. Let the children explore the popcorn kernels before popping it for snack, and again after it pops.
2. Talk about how the heat changed the kernels.

Learning Center Ideas

Materials

dishpans • soapy water • soiled wash rags or cloths • soiled, washable baby dolls • any washable toys from the classroom • sponges • washboard (from hardware store) • small scrubbing brushes • discarded toothbrushes

1. Place a few of the items in the Water Play Area (or Science Area) and encourage the children to observe the changes as they wash and scrub the items day after day.

Related Books

Animals in Winter by Henrietta Bancroft and Richard G. Van Gelder
The Friendship Tree by Kathy Caple
From Caterpillar to Butterfly by Deborah Heiligman
From Seed to Plant by Gail Gibbons
From Tadpole to Frog by Windy Pfeffer
Harry the Dirty Dog by Gene Zion
Joseph Had a Little Overcoat by Simms Taback
A Nest Full of Eggs by Priscilla Belz Jenkins
Sometimes Things Change by Patricia Eastman
Waiting for Wings by Lois Ehlert

Learning With Ladybugs

Introducing the Weekly Curriculum Theme

Weekly Curriculum Vocabulary

aphid

beetle

female

ladybug

male

o'clock

Materials

any children's book about ladybugs

1. Read a book about ladybugs to the children. Discuss ladybugs and how they help us by eating aphids, which are other small insects. Aphids eat plants and destroy them. When ladybugs eat aphids, they protect plants the aphids might have eaten.

2. Ladybugs also carry sticky pollen from one plant to another. This pollen makes the plants produce new seeds so there can be more plants.

3. Ladybugs are a special kind of insect called a beetle. A beetle has hard wing cases that lie over its wings to protect the wings. The red parts of the ladybug are its wing cases.

4. Help the children understand that some ladybugs are male and some are female, but all are called ladybugs.

Ladybug Clock

Art

Materials

white paper plates ● pencil ● scissors ● black poster board ● red, black, and white paint ● paintbrushes ● black construction paper ● glue ● rubber stamps for numerals 0-9 ● stamp pad ● brass paper fasteners (brads)

1. Make a small hole in the center of each paper plate for the clock's hands. On the front of each plate, faintly write the clock numerals in the correct position.
2. Cut out clock hands from black poster board, making a pair of hands for each child and making a small hole at one end of each clock hand. Make the minute hand 3" long and the hour hand 2" long.

Note: Steps 1 and 2 are done by an adult.

3. Give each child a paper plate. Encourage them to use red and black paint to paint the backs of their plates to look like ladybugs. Let these dry thoroughly.
4. Help each child dip his thumb into black paint and then press it onto his bug's red wing cases to make black dots. Then, he dips an index finger into the white paint and presses this, twice, onto the bug's head for eyes.
5. Help the children cut out six strips from black construction paper for their ladybug's legs. Ask them to glue these on their bugs.
6. Help the children stamp their clock's numerals in the correct places, where the adult has written the numerals.
7. Help the children use the paper fastener to attach the clock's hands to the center of the clock's face.

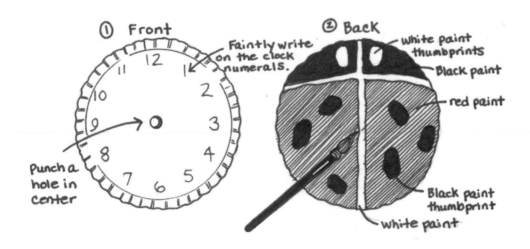

③ 3" Cut clock hands from black poster board. 2"

④ Cut six legs and glue.

⑤ Help children stamp clock's numerals in the correct places. Use paper fastener to attach clock hands to center of clock face.

Retelling the Story

Language

Materials

any story about ladybugs ● variety of art materials including glue ● craft sticks

1. Read a story about ladybugs to the children. Ask each child to make a different stick puppet of a character from the story. Help them glue their characters to a craft stick.
2. Encourage the children to use these puppets to retell the story.

Fingerplay—Five Little Ladybugs

Language and Math

1. Using the fingers of one hand to indicate the correct number, say the rhyme below with the children.

> *Five little ladybugs crawling across the floor,*
> *One flew away, then there were four.*
>
> *Four bright ladybugs looking right at me,*
> *One flew away, then there were three.*
>
> *Three flying ladybugs in the sky so blue.*
> *One flew away, then there were two.*

Two hungry ladybugs eat aphids in the sun.
One flew away, and then there was one.

One brave ladybug might someday be a hero.
She flew away, and then there were zero.

Telling Time to the Hour

Math

Materials

Ladybug Clocks (see page 181) • *The Grouchy Ladybug* by Eric Carle

1. Show the children how an analog clock looks "on the hour," with the hour hand on the hour of the day/night and the minute hand pointing to twelve.
2. Read *The Grouchy Ladybug* to the children. Encourage the children to use their ladybug clocks to show the hour in the story. Have them hold up their clocks each time they change the time so you can check their responses.
3. With or without the book, show the children a time (on the hour) on a clock and ask them to copy that with their clocks. Talk about the time the clock indicates.
4. As the children gain skill, use the clocks to provide more practice. Call out a time (on the hour) and have the children show you that time on their clocks.

Comparing Sizes

Math

Materials

The Grouchy Ladybug by Eric Carle • crayon (or any small item)

1. Use this story to explore size. Read the book, pointing out to children the increase in size of the animals challenged by the grouchy ladybug.
2. Place a crayon where the children can see it. Challenge a child to find something in the room that is slightly larger than the crayon and put it next to the crayon.
3. Next, challenge another child to find something larger than the last item in the line and to add it to the line.
4. Continue until you run out of room, or you run out of ability to move larger items in place.

Ladybug Song

Music

1. Sing the following song with the children.

Tune: ***Twinkle, Twinkle, Little Star***
Ladybug, ladybug,
What do you do?
Do you eat aphids all day through?
You start life as an egg so small,
A larva, then a pupa hanging near the garden wall.
In five days a ladybug you'll be.
Won't you come and visit me?

Ladybugs, Close Up

Science

Materials

ladybugs ● aphids ● zipper-closure plastic bags

1. If your local gardening store sells live ladybugs, bring a few of these to class so the children can hold them and see them up close. Draw the children's attention to the hard wing cases that protect the ladybugs' wings.
2. Help the children see that ladybugs are gentle with people, so people should be gentle with the bugs.
3. If the gardening store has in stock any plants with aphids on them, ask for a few clippings and aphids. Place these in closed plastic bags and bring them to class. (The plastic breathes; the bugs won't smother.)
4. While the children are watching, put some ladybugs into the bags. Observe and discuss what happens next.

Ladybug Rice Cakes

Snack/Cooking

Materials

grape fruit spread or jelly ● seedless raspberry fruit spread or jelly ● rice cakes ● blunt knives ● raisins ● miniature marshmallows

1. Ask each child to make an edible ladybug by spreading a small amount of grape fruit spread on a rice cake for the ladybug's head and raspberry on the rest of the rice cake for the ladybug's body.
2. The children can use raisins for the ladybug's black spots and two marshmallows for its eyes.

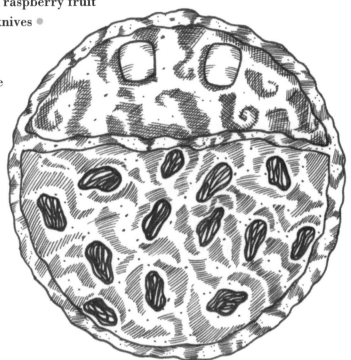

Learning Center Ideas

Dramatic Play Area

Materials

plastic ladybugs and other plastic bugs ● insect field guides ● insect nets ● paper pencils and pens ● clipboards ● magnifying glasses ● small containers for the plastic "specimens" ● bug containers for live "specimens"

1. Provide a few of these items and other items the children request so they can pretend to be *entomologists*, people who study insects.

More Learning Center Ideas

Art Area

Materials

stamp pads • ladybug rubber stamps • numeral rubber stamps

1. Add these to the Art Area and challenge the children to create games using these along with other materials that are already in use.

Related Books

Are You a Ladybug? by Judy Allen

Five Little Ladybugs by Karyn Henley

The Grouchy Ladybug by Eric Carle

Ladybug (Life Cycles) by Sabrina Crewe

The Ladybug and Other Insects by Pascale De Bourgoing (Editor)

Ladybug, Ladybug by Ruth Brown

Ladybug's Birthday by Steve Metzger

A Ladybug's Life by John Himmelman

Ten Little Ladybugs by Melanie Gerth

The Very Lazy Ladybug by Isobel Finn

Mushy Mud

Materials

chart paper ● markers

1. Write the following rhyme on a piece of chart paper:

   Mud, mud, marvelous mud.
   I like to play in mud.

   Squish, squish in my fingers,
   Squish, squish in my toes.
   Mud is all squishy
   Wherever it goes.

   Mud, mud, marvelous mud.
   I like to play in mud.

   Mix dirt and water
   Then stir it around.
   Rain can make mud
   With the dirt on the ground.

   Mud, mud, marvelous mud.
   I like to play in mud.

Weekly Curriculum Vocabulary

mud
pantomime
squish
squishy

2. Read the rhyme with the children. Repeat.

3. Talk about mud and ask if anyone has played in mud. If so, what did the children like best about the experience? Least? Ask them to describe how mud feels.

4. Talk about things children would like to do with mud, such as walk in it, run in it, wiggle in it, sculpt with it, make mud pies, or write their names in it.

Weekly Curriculum Extension Activities

Who's Been Walking on the Wall?

Art and Language

Materials
10' long piece of white bulletin board paper ● 2 chairs ● basins or buckets of water ● terry-cloth towels ● brown tempera paint, several shades ● paintbrush

1. Lay the bulletin paper on the floor. Place a chair at each end of the paper. Place the buckets of water and towels at one end of the paper.

2. Ask the children to remove their shoes and socks. Choose one child to sit in the chair that is not next to the water and towels.

3. Paint the bottoms of the child's feet using several shades of brown tempera paint (mud colors). Hold the child's hands while she stands, then walks along the length of the paper to the other chair, making footprints as she goes.

4. Help the child sit in the chair. Wash and dry her feet.

5. Repeat with each child, having the children start walking at areas where more prints are needed.

6. Encourage the children to talk to each other, describing the experience and how their feet felt.

7. Hang the paper so it appears that people have walked up the wall and onto the ceiling.

Favorite Characters

Art and Math

Materials

any simple storybook about mud ● bulletin board paper ● marker ● drawing
paper ● crayons

1. Choose a story about mud to read to the children.
2. Divide a piece of bulletin board paper into columns for a graph. Label one
   graph column for each character in the book.
3. Read the story to the children, and then ask them to draw a picture of their
   favorite character.
4. Ask the children to put their pictures in the correct column of the graph.
5. Count and compare the results.

Marvelous Mud Day

Art and Outdoors

Materials

shovels ● wading pool or dishpans ● garden hose ● potting soil, if needed ● variety
of everyday items for mud play, such as sieves of different sizes, toy cars and
trucks, pie pans, plastic containers, shells, rocks, colored gravel, leaves, seeds,
sticks, tongue depressors, chopsticks, combs, forks, and scrub brushes ● drawing
paper ● crayons

1. Dedicate a day for exploring mud. Ask the children to bring in bathing suits
   and towels for drying off.
2. Go outside with the children and and let them dig in the dirt and make mud in
   the wading pool or dishpans (filled with water from the garden hose). If needed,
   use potting soil.
3. Encourage the children to play with the mud, experimenting with the sieves and
   making things with the mud.
4. Ask if they can make mud pies. Suggest they decorate the pies before putting
   them in the sun to dry.
5. Show the children how to use sticks, tongue depressors, or chopsticks to draw
   designs in partially dried mud and how to create textures by dragging items,
   such as forks or combs, across the top of it.
6. Before going inside, help the children wash all the "indoor" items. Hose off the
   children and help them put on their dry clothing.
7. Once inside, provide materials for the children to draw several pictures of their
   experiences.
8. Display these where the children and their families can enjoy them.

Visit a Car Wash

Field Trip

1. Arrange a visit to a car wash where the children can observe how the machines remove mud from cars.

Flannel Board Story

Language

Materials

any storybook about mud (see page 192) • Pelon interfacing, medium weight (from fabric store) • colored pencils • scissors • flannel board

1. Place the Pelon interfacing over the picture of any character in the storybook. Trace the character, and then cut it out.
2. Color with colored pencils. Repeat with all of the characters.
3. Read the story to the children, and then show them the Pelon figures and how they stick to the flannel board.
4. Give a figure to each child. Let the children manipulate the characters on the board while you re-read the story.
5. Put the board and the figures where the children can use them, as desired, to retell the story.

Moving in Mud

Movement

1. Ask the children to pantomime how they would walk in mud.
2. Encourage the children to suggest, and then pantomime, other ways they could move in mud (such as swim, jog, run, or any other movement).

Filtering Muddy Water

Science

Materials

2-liter clear soda bottle • sharp scissors (adult only) • coffee filter • spring-type clothespins or clips • muddy water (children can mix this)

1. Cut off the top fourth of the soda bottle (adult only). Invert the cut-off portion, place it in the topless bottle, and use it as a funnel.

2. Ask a child to line the funnel with the coffee filter, using clothespins or clips to hold the filter in place.
3. Pour some muddy water into the filter, saving some muddy water on the side. Encourage the children to observe what happens over time. Discuss their observations.
4. Have the children compare the filtered water and saved muddy water. Discuss their observations.

Eating Mud

Snack/Cooking

Materials

serving spoons ● prepared chocolate and butterscotch pudding ● small, shallow dishes ● chocolate cookie crumbs ● animal crackers

1. Make sure the children wash their hands thoroughly before and after this activity!
2. Ask the children to spoon chocolate pudding into the center of their dishes, and then place butterscotch pudding around the edges. This is pretend mud.
3. Ask them to sprinkle cookie crumbs on top of the pudding for pretend dirt.
4. The children stand animal crackers in the pudding to look like they are playing in the mud.
5. Let the children eat this snack with their fingers, dipping the animal crackers into the pudding, and using them as spoons.

Eat with fingers!

Learning Center Ideas

Outdoor Area

Materials

dishpans of dirt ● water source ● trowels ● plastic aprons ● nature items chosen by children ● soap ● fingernail scrubbing brushes

1. Make these materials available to the children outdoors. Encourage them to mix water with the dirt to make mud.

Note: Supervise carefully.

2. Let them add natural items to the mud, as desired.

3. Supervise cleanup, showing children how to scrub dirt from their hands and fingernails with the soap and brush.

Related Books

Brothers Are for Making Mud Pies by Harriet Ziefert

Ducks in Muck by Lori Haskins

From Mud to House by Bertram T. Knight

Miss Mouse's Day by Jan Ormerod

Mrs. Wishy-Washy by Joy Cowley

Mud by Mary Lyn Ray

Mud Flat April Fool by James Stevenson

Mud Is Cake by Pam Munoz Ryan

Mud Puddle by Robert N. Munsch

The Piggy in the Puddle by Charlotte Pomerantz

Pigs in the Mud in the Middle of the Rud by Lynn Plourde

Pigs Love Mud by Richard Powell

Preschool to the Rescue by Judy Sierra

Real Bears

Materials

teddy bear ● chart paper ● marker

1. Show the teddy bear to the children and let them talk briefly about stuffed bears. Then ask what they know about real bears, not toy bears. On a chart page, write a list of what they know. Include everything they say, even if it is inaccurate. They will re-visit this chart during the week and can correct any misinformation.

2. On another chart page, write the children's responses to the question, "What would you like to learn about real bears?" During the week, explore books and other resources with the children in order to learn the answers to these items.

3. Mount both charts where children can easily refer to them. Re-visit and review these charts daily.

4. Add a third page where you write children's responses to the question, "What have we learned about real bears?" Add to and review this page daily.

Weekly Curriculum Vocabulary

bear
camouflage
grizzly bear
polar bear
zoologist
see "Bear Words" (page 195 in this section)

Magic Polar Bears

Art

Materials

white crayons ● white construction paper ● black tempera paint, thinned with water ● blue tempera paint, thinned with water ● paint brushes

1. After the children learn about camouflage (see page 196), give each child a sheet of white construction paper. Ask them to use a white crayon to draw and heavily color in a polar bear on their white paper. Talk about how the bears are camouflaged against the white "snow" background.
2. Ask the children to paint the top half of their paper black and the bottom half blue. Discuss what happens to the camouflaged polar bears.

Math Bears

Art and Math

Materials

construction paper in white, light brown, reddish-brown, dark brown, and black ● scissors ● crayons ● pictures of bears

1. Cut the white, brown, and black construction paper into 3" x 4" pieces.
2. Remind the children that bears come in many colors.
3. Provide the construction paper squares and crayons and encourage the children to use the pictures of bears to draw one bear on each square.
4. Gather all of the drawings together. Let the children use these for counting, sorting, and creating patterns.

Visit the Bears at the Zoo

Field Trip

1. If there is a nearby zoo with bears in the exhibit, go to see the bears. In advance, request a guide who can tell the children about the bears, and perhaps feed the animals while the children watch.

Bear Words

Language

Materials

chart pages from beginning activity ● sentence strips ● marker

1. Ask the children to look at the chart pages from the opening activity (page 193). Ask them to select words they'd like to learn to read.
2. Use sentence strips to make word cards of these chosen words.
3. Show the cards, one at a time, and encourage the children to match these to the words on the chart pages and say the words as they do so.
4. Make another set of cards, matching the first, so the children can use both together to create matching games.

More Bear Words

Language

Materials

various books about real bears ● charts from opening activity ● marker

1. Read a variety of non-fiction books about bears (see list on page 198).
2. Help the children learn bear facts as well as similarities and differences in the various bears.
3. Encourage the children to suggest facts for you to add to the third chart, "What have we learned about real bears?"

More Math Bears

Math

Materials

teddy bear counters

1. Use teddy bear counters for weighing, measuring, and estimation activities.

The Bear Went Over the Mountain

Music

1. Sing the song "The Bear Went Over the Mountain," using different kinds of bears for each verse.
2. Let the children suggest the substitutions. For example:

   The grizzly went over the mountain (repeat 3 times)
   To see what he could see.

   A field of bright red berries, (repeat 3 times)
   Was all that he could see.

   The polar bear went over the iceberg (repeat 3 times)
   To see what he could see.

   More and more icebergs (repeat 3 times)
   Were all that he could see.

Polar Bear Camouflage

Science

Materials

construction paper in several colors including white ● scissors ● camouflage clothing, if possible

1. Beforehand, cut out polar bear shapes from white construction paper and other colors of paper.
2. After reading about and discussing polar bears, spread sheets of white and other colors of construction paper where children can see them.
3. Place a white bear shape on each sheet of paper. On which color is it most difficult to see the bear?
4. Explain that this is called *camouflage.* When something looks like the place where it is hiding, it is using camouflage. If desired, explore camouflage of other animals and insects.
5. Show camouflage clothing, if possible. Discuss the garments that hunters and soldiers wear. How do these help the hunters or soldiers hide in their surroundings?

Live Bears

Science

Materials

computer ● Internet server

1. Search online for "brown bear," "polar bear," "grizzly bear," and/or "black bear" to find pictures of real bears.
2. These searches will also yield sites with live camera views of bears in zoos and in the wild.

Bear Food

Snack/Cooking

Materials

see below

1. During the week, serve foods that bears like to eat: various berries, honey (on bread), sliced apples the children can dip into honey, and mashed salmon mixed with mayonnaise and chopped celery.

Learning Center Ideas

Dramatic Play Area

Materials

forest ranger-type hats ● clipboards ● binoculars ● name badges or clip-on ID badges ● pictures of real bears ● non-working cameras ● paper grocery bags labeled "bear food"

1. Place these items in the Dramatic Play Area so the children can pretend they are *zoologists* who specialize in studying bears. (A zoologist studies animals.)

Related Books

Bears: Polar Bears, Black Bears and Grizzly Bears by Deborah Hodge
Blueberries for Sal by Robert McCloskey
Grizzlies by Lynn M. Stone (This book is for older readers. For younger children, use the photos and the information.)
Grizzly Bear by Jason Stone and Jody Stone
Growl!: A Book About Bears by Melvin Berger
How Do Bears Sleep? by E.J. Bird
How to Hide a Polar Bear & Other Mammals by Ruth Heller
The Polar Bear by Valerie Tracqui
Polar Bears by Gail Gibbons
Somebody and the Three Blairs by Marilyn Tolhurst
We're Going on a Bear Hunt by Michael Rosen
What Color Is Camouflage? by Carolyn Otto

Shadows on a Sunny Day

Materials

flashlights with strong beams ● high intensity lamps

1. On a sunny day, take the children outdoors to explore their shadows. Point out the children's shadows and encourage them to find the building's shadow, cars' shadows, trees' shadows, and so on.
2. Look at a shadow and see if the children can guess what is casting it. Check their ideas.
3. Help them see that a shadow always falls on the side of the object that is opposite from where the sun is and that the sun or other light source is necessary for shadows to form. Encourage the children to experiment by moving items and their own bodies to see that the item is always between the sun and the shadow.
4. As a follow-up activity, use flashlights to make and explore shadows indoors. Let the children experiment and observe changes when they move the light source up and down. What happens when the light is closer or farther away from the item casting the shadow?

Weekly Curriculum Vocabulary

dark
darker
larger
light
longer
shadow
shorter
smaller
taller
thinner
wider

Shadow Pictures

Art

Materials

plain paper ● crayons and markers ● child-safe scissors ● white chalk ●
black construction paper ● 12" x 18" white construction paper

1. Ask the children to draw a picture of a person or an object using crayons or markers.
2. Help the children cut out their pictures.
3. Show the children how to use white chalk to trace the outline on a piece of black paper.
4. Help the children cut out the black shape and glue both the picture and the black shape on the white construction paper, putting the black shape slightly offset behind the first image. The finished picture will look like the object and its shadow.

① Ask children to draw a picture of a person or object with markers. Cut out picture.

② Use white chalk to trace outline of drawing on black paper. Cut out black shape.

③ Glue both the picture and the black shape on white construction paper, putting the black shape slightly offset behind the first image.

Shadow Games

Games and Outdoors

1. Show the children how to play shadow games. Can they make their shadows jump, run, and climb? Can their shadow "tickle" another child's shadow without either child touching the other?

Shadow Tag

Games and Outdoors

1. Explain how to play Shadow Tag. The child who is "IT" tags another child by stepping on that child's shadow.
2. Help the children discover that this game is more difficult when it is close to noon because the shadows are shorter.

Math Vocabulary

Language and Math

1. While talking about and describing shadows, use words such as *longer, shorter, taller, larger, smaller, wider,* and *thinner.*

Picture This

Language and Science

Materials

digital camera • computer printer • index cards • marker

1. Help the children use a digital camera to take pictures of shadows of familiar objects. Suggestions include a car, a chair, climbing apparatus, swings, and a tree.
2. Enlarge these pictures and print them.
3. Put them on a bulletin board with the caption: "Whose Shadow Am I?" Encourage the children and any classroom visitors to guess and tell what shadow each picture shows.
4. If desired, give hints and increase reading opportunities by posting word cards that tell the names of each shadow.

Number Puzzles

Math

1. Challenge the children to solve number puzzles.
2. For example, can three children together form one shadow? Can four children form two shadows? Can they do this a different way?
3. What is the greatest number of separate shadows that six children can make? The least?

Me and My Shadow

Movement

Materials

recorded music

1. Ask the children to work in pairs. One is the leader, and the other is the leader's shadow.
2. Play slow music, and the leader moves to the music. The shadow's job is to copy every movement done by the leader.
3. Ask the children to switch roles and repeat the activity.
4. The children choose new partners and begin the game again.

Dancing Shadows

Movement

Materials

plain white sheet • projection light from overhead projector or film projector • cellophane • crepe paper • scissors

1. Hang a plain sheet on one wall. Set up a projection light so it shines on the sheet.
2. Encourage the children to dance, pose, and move between the light and the sheet, forming shadows on the sheet.
3. Encourage them to notice what happens to their shadows when they move closer to and farther from the light source.
4. Cut cellophane and crepe paper into streamers. Encourage the children to dance while holding the streamers. What do they notice about shadows of the translucent cellophane and the opaque crepe paper?

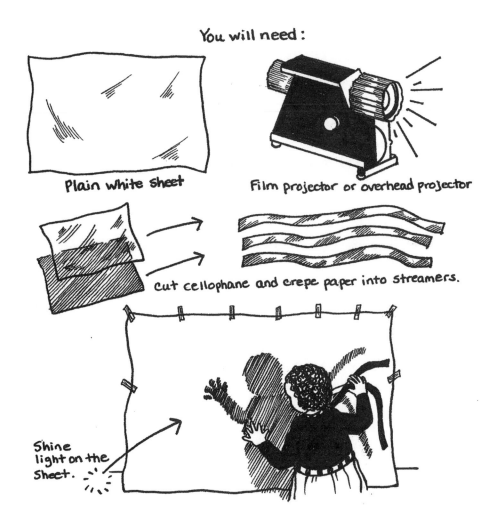

You will need:

Plain white sheet

Film projector or overhead projector

Cut cellophane and crepe paper into streamers.

Shine light on the Sheet.

Does Water Have a Shadow?

Outdoors and Science

Materials

garden hose attached to a spigot

1. On a warm, sunny day, ask the children if they think water has a shadow.
2. Let them predict the answer.
3. Encourage them to turn on a hose outdoors to find out the answer.

Colored Shadows?

Science

Materials

variety of colored items chosen by children • white paper • glass bottle (adult only) • small pane of glass (adult only) • clear plastic bottle • colored plastic bottles

1. Ask the children if they think that colored items make colored shadows. They may draw on their experience and say no, or they may be uncertain. Either way, suggest that they do a science experiment to find out.
2. Ask each child to choose a colored classroom item. Take the items outside and put them on white paper. What color are their shadows?
3. The children will discover that the items do not cast colored shadows. They cast dark shadows because the items are opaque, so they block all light.
4. Place the clear glass bottle on the paper (adult only).

Caution: Supervise carefully when using glass items!

5. Ask the children if its shadow is similar to or different from the other shadows. (The shadow will be lighter than earlier shadows since the bottle doesn't block all of the light. It is translucent so it lets some of the light through.)
6. Hold a pane of glass so the sunlight passes through (adult only). It makes no shadow (or very little) because it is transparent. The light passes through.

Caution: Supervise carefully when using glass items!

7. Let the children experiment with plastic bottles that are clear and those that are colored. Encourage them to use vocabulary such as *lighter, darker, transparent, translucent,* and *opaque.*

Light Table

Science

Materials

light table • various kinds of paper • cellophane • ribbon scraps

1. Use the light table all the time, just like other tables. Use it for art, science exploration, nature exploration, small block constructions, and more.
2. Put various paper, cellophane, and ribbon scraps on the table. Encourage the children to explore these to see which are transparent, which are translucent, and which are opaque.

Learning Center Ideas

Science Area

Materials

overhead projector ● variety of items

1. Place the projector in the Science Area where the children can use it to project shadows on the wall. Encourage them to change the position of the items they use to see how the shadows change.

Caution: Tape the projector's cord flat against the table and the floor so children don't trip on it. Supervise carefully and remind the children that the overhead projector is a tool, not a toy.

Related Books

Bear Shadow by Frank Asch

I Have a Friend by Keiko Narahashi

Little Groundhog's Shadow by Janet Craig

"My Shadow" from *A Child's Garden of Verses* by Robert Louis Stevenson

What Makes a Shadow? by Clyde Robert Bulla

Super Sunflowers

Weekly Curriculum Vocabulary

grow

plant

sun

sunflowers

sway

swaying

Materials

any book about sunflowers (see list on page 212) ● fresh sunflowers (from a supermarket) or artificial sunflowers. (If none are available, show pictures of sunflowers.)

1. Read a book about sunflowers to the children.
2. Show the sunflowers to the children. Ask the children if they can guess why these are called sunflowers. (Because each flower looks like a picture of the sun—the petals look like the sun's rays. Also, sunflowers like to grow in sunshine.)

Great Artists' Sunflowers

Art

Materials

art books containing photographs of van Gogh's "Sunflowers" painted by Vincent van Gogh, Claude Monet, Henri Matisse, Paul Gauguin and others • pictures from the Internet of sunflower paintings by these artists • fresh or artificial sunflowers • vase • paper • paints and paintbrushes • markers • pencils

1. Many artists have created paintings of sunflowers. Show children pictures of these, which you can find in books about the artists. You can also find pictures on the Internet. Search http://www.artcyclopedia.com for the subject "sunflowers." Or search for the above artists by name.
2. Discuss with the children some reasons why sunflowers are good subjects for art. (For example, they have bright, interesting colors, and they are easy to draw because of their circular shape.)
3. Place fresh (from the florist or the grocery store's floral department) or artificial sunflowers in a vase and display them where children can observe them up close.
4. Provide art materials and encourage the children to draw or paint sunflowers.
5. Repeat steps three and four periodically throughout the year, and you'll see the children's observation and representation skills increase.

Dancing Sunflowers

Art and Movement

Materials

plain white paper plates • scissors • yellow tissue paper • white glue

1. Cut out the center from the paper plates (teacher only), leaving a rim that children can wear on their heads (like a halo). When on the children's heads, these will look like sunflowers. Give one to each child.
2. Ask the children to tear the tissue paper into strips for flower petals and glue these to the plate rims.
3. Ask the children to wear their sunflower headpieces. Choose one child to represent the sun. The sun dances around the sunflowers while they act out the rhyme on the following page.

We are happy sunflowers
Growing in the sun.
We start out small, and grow so tall,
Growing in the sun.

We are happy sunflowers
Swaying in the breeze.
We sway to east and sway to west,
Swaying in the breeze.

We are happy sunflowers
Turning to the sun.
We slowly turn the whole day long,
Turning to the sun.

Compound Words

Language

Materials

sentence strips • blue, orange, and black markers • pocket chart

1. Use the sunflower topic to introduce compound words to the children. Using a blue marker, write the word "sun" on a sentence strip. Using an orange marker, write "flower" on a separate sentence strip. Using a black marker, write "sunflower" on a third strip.
2. Show the first two words to the children and help them read the words. Now show the compound word and help the children see that it is made of the two separate words. Help them read the compound word: sunflower.
3. Place the three sentence strips, in order, into one pocket of the chart.
4. Repeat this activity each day, adding other words to pockets in the chart. Choose from the following or other compound words of interest to children:

baseball	cookbook
bathtub	football
bedroom	ladybug
bookmark	sunshine
classroom	

5. Leave the pocket chart where the children can play with it and review their learning.

Sunflower Garden

Language and Science

Materials

sunflower seeds packed for planting ● garden area in a sunny location ● small
garden tools ● garden stakes ● blank books to use as science journals, 1 per child ●
pencils ● crayons

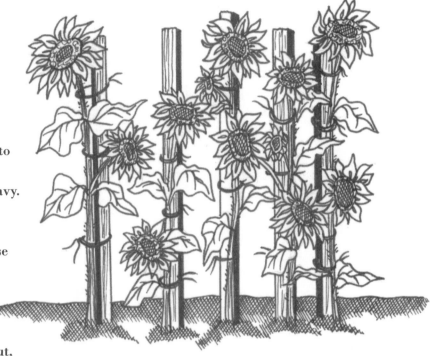

1. With the children, prepare a
   small area outside for a
   sunflower garden. Remove
   grass, weeds, and rocks, and
   loosen the soil.
2. Let each child plant one or
   more seeds. As the seeds
   sprout, thin them according to
   package directions. As the
   plants grow, they become heavy.
   Support them with sturdy
   stakes to keep them upright.
3. Encourage the children to use
   their journals to record the
   seeds' planting and the
   subsequent growth.
   Encourage them to draw a
   picture of a seed's first sprout,
   the same sprout when one leaf appears, when the second leaf appears, when the
   plant is knee-high to a child, when it is waist high, when it is as tall as the
   children, and as it continues to grow.
4. Ask the children to write or dictate their words about the sunflowers and
   their growth.

Sunflower Sequence

Math

1. Provide artificial sunflowers of different heights and challenge the children to
   arrange them in order from shortest to tallest.

Sequence and Ordinal Numbers

Math and Science

Materials

sequence cards with simple drawings showing stages of a sunflower's life: seed; sprout; plant with two leaves; and tall sunflower with blossom

1. After the children have learned about a sunflower's life cycle, show them the sequence cards in mixed-up order.
2. Challenge the children to find the card that shows what happens first, second, third, and last.
3. Ask the children to arrange the cards in order.

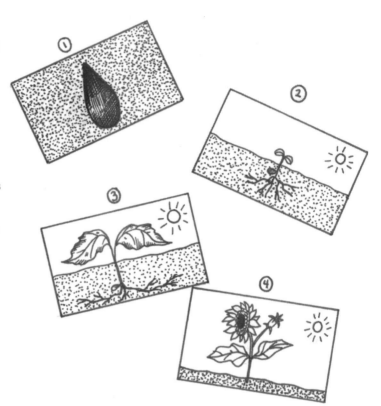

Waltz of the Sunflowers

Movement

Materials

recorded waltz music or "new age" music ● CD or tape player

1. Select one child to be the "gardener," another to be the "sun," and another to be the "rain." The remaining children crouch in a circle and pretend to be sunflower seeds.
2. The sun stands in the middle of the circle and the rain and gardener stand outside the circle.
3. Play the music and narrate a story about a gardener who planted sunflower seeds. The gardener walks around the circle, gently "planting" the seeds.
4. The children act out the parts as you continue the story, saying that the sun

shone down on the seeds and warmed them and the gentle rain gave them water to drink. The seeds wiggled in the ground, then began to sprout.

5. Continue the story until the seeds have become full-grown plants that dry up in autumn and provide seeds for hungry animals and birds.

Sunflower Song

Music

1. As you plant sunflower seeds (see "Sunflower Garden" page 209), sing the first verse of the following "Sunflower Song."
2. When the seeds first sprout, sing both verses.
3. At each step of the plants' development, encourage the children to make up additional verses and sing them.

Tune: *The Farmer in the Dell*
The children plant the seeds.
The children plant the seeds.
Soon we'll have some sunflowers!
The children plant the seeds.

The seeds begin to grow.
The seeds begin to grow.
Soon we'll have some sunflowers!
The seeds begin to grow.

Gardeners' Chores

Outdoors

Materials
watering can

1. Ask the children to take turns watering the sprouts and sunflower plants every day at outdoor time.
2. Show the children which are plants and which are weeds, and have them remove the weeds regularly.

Sunflower Seeds

Snack/Cooking

Materials

sunflower seeds from the grocery store

1. Serve purchased sunflower seeds as a snack.
2. Help the children understand that we don't eat sunflower seeds from sunflowers in the garden because we can't be certain that they are clean.

Learning Center Ideas

Sensory Table Area

Materials

potting soil ● gardening gloves and aprons ● trowels ● plastic cups ● sunflower seeds

1. Place the soil in the sensory table.
2. Place a few of the remaining items beside the table.
3. Encourage the children to plant, dig up, and re-plant the seeds.
4. Let them take planted seeds home, if they wish.
5. At week's end, place the soil and seeds in the play yard and watch to see if the seeds sprout and grow.

Related Books

Camille and the Sunflowers: A Story About Vincent van Gogh by Laurence Anholt—includes reproductions of some of van Gogh's paintings
Cardinal and Sunflower by James Preller
From Seed to Sunflower by Gerald Legg
Sunflower by Miela Ford
Sunflower House by Eve Bunting
Sunflower Sal by Janet S. Anderson
The Sunflower Family by Cherie Winner
This Is the Sunflower by Lola M. Schaefer

Me
and
My World
Themes

Bedtime

Introducing the Weekly Curriculum Theme

Weekly Curriculum Vocabulary

bed
bedtime
least
most
nightgown
pajamas

Materials

your pajamas ● a stuffed animal

1. Wear your sleeping apparel as the children arrive. Carry a stuffed animal, and greet the children sleepily.
2. Tell the children that you are very sleepy, and that the group will spend the week talking about bedtime.
3. Invite the children to talk about their bedtime routines. Discuss why we bathe and brush our teeth at night before going to bed. Discuss other bedtime activities such as reading quiet stories and listening to quiet music.
4. If any of the children talk about nighttime fears, discuss those. Other children may have suggestions about conquering those fears.

Me in My Bed

Art

Materials

drawing paper, 2 sheets per child ● scissors ● markers or crayons ● tape

1. Get two sheets of drawing paper for each child. Cut one of the pieces ⅓ shorter than the other sheet.
2. On the larger paper, suggest that each child draw a picture of himself dressed for bed.
3. The children can decorate and color the smaller piece of paper to look like their own blanket.
4. Ask the children to place the "blanket" page in place on their self-portrait with just the head showing, then tape these together by wrapping a strip of tape on one side edge of the two pieces of paper. Show the children how to "lift the blanket" to see the sleeping child in bed.

Bedtime Stories

Dramatic Play and Language

Materials

furniture or loungewear catalogs ● furniture advertising circulars ● child-safe scissors

1. Encourage the children to cut the following from catalogs and advertising circulars: pictures of bedrooms and/or beds, and pictures of people in sleeping attire.
2. Encourage the children to use the pictures as props for stories they make up about bedtime.

Lazy Mary, Will You Get Up?
Games

1. Ask the children to stand in a circle with one child ("Lazy Mary") in the center. The children sing this traditional song while "Mary" pretends to sleep, substituting the "sleeping" child's name for Mary.

    Lazy (Mary), will you get up?
    Will you get up, will you get up?
    Lazy (Mary), will you get up?
    Will you get up today?

2. At the song's end, if the sleeping child yawns, stretches, and pretends to go back to sleep, the children repeat the song. Or the child may yawn, stretch, and then shout, "Yes!" At this point, she begins chasing the children. The child she catches becomes the next "Lazy Mary" and the game repeats.

The "Ed" Family
Language

Materials
sentence strips • marker • pocket chart

1. Use the bed theme to investigate and learn about the "ed" family of words. Write _ed on a sentence strip. On small pieces of strip, write individual consonants.
2. Place the _ed in a pocket chart. Ask the children, in turn, to select a consonant to place in the blank to form words such as *bed, red, fed, led,* and so on. They can also form nonsense words such as *ged* and *ved.*
3. Ask the group to read each word that is formed.

Five Little Children
Language and Math

Materials
blankets

1. Recite the following fingerplay with the children.

Five little children were jumping on the bed. (Five fingers of right hand
     "jump" on bed made by outstretched left hand.)
One jumped too high and bumped her head. (Hold head with both hands.)
Mother came in and this is what she said,
"Children should not be jumping on the bed." (Shake outstretched index
     finger.)

Four little children were jumping on the bed...
Three little children were jumping on the bed...
Two little children were jumping on the bed...

One little child was jumping on the bed.
She jumped too high and bumped her head.
Daddy came in and this is what he said,
"No more children jumping on the bed." (Hands on hips, looking stern; use
     a deep voice.)

2. After the children learn the rhyme as a fingerplay, encourage them to act it out
   in groups of seven. Designate one child in each group as Mother and another as
   Father. Each "bed" is a blanket placed on the floor.

Every Night

Language and Movement

Materials

chart paper • marker

1. Write the rhyme below on a chart and read it to the children.
2. Have the children act out the rhyme while you re-read it.
3. During the week, read the chart with the children. If desired, they can
   substitute their own stuffed animal's name for the words "teddy bear."

   Every night when I go to bed
   I put my teddy bear next to my head.
   We whisper awhile, then we don't make a peep,
   We just snore and snore when we go to sleep.

4. Pair this activity with A Human Graph on page 219.

My Special Blanket

Language and Music

Materials

chart paper ● marker ● tape recorder ● cassette tape

1. Write the following song on a chart so the children can read while they sing along.

     Tune: *Skip to My Lou*
     I always take my special blanket
     When it's time to go to bed.
     It is soft and warm and cozy
     Tucked in near my head.

     Even if it's very shaggy,
     It's the one I'll always keep.
     'Cause it is the only blanket
     That helps me fall asleep.

2. Record the children singing the song. Place the tape, tape player, and chart in the Listening Area so the children can listen, sing along, and read along.

Pillow Graphs

Math

Materials

four pieces of bulletin board paper, 2' high by 3' wide ● markers

1. Draw a large bed on each piece of bulletin board paper.
2. On one, draw no pillows; on another, draw one pillow; on a third, draw two pillows; on the remaining, draw three or more pillows.
3. Show the children the papers. Ask them to recall how many pillows are on their beds.
4. Ask the children to sign their names on the picture that shows how many pillows are on their beds.
5. Compare the results. Which group has the most? Which group has the least?

A Human Graph

Math

Materials

three large pieces of paper ● markers

1. Label the papers "Stuffed Animal," "Something Else," and "Nothing." Place these side by side on the floor.
2. Read the papers with the children. Explain that when you ask a question, they should all silently walk to the sign that correctly answers the question for them.
3. Ask, "What do you sleep with?"
4. Have each group of children stand shoulder to shoulder, forming a straight line.
5. Compare the lengths of lines. Count the children in each line. Compare, using words such as *more, fewer, less, the same as,* and any other appropriate mathematical terms.

Dancing With Blankets

Movement

Materials

variety of recorded music ● children's blankets

1. Ask the children to bring their blankets to school.
2. Play music so the children can dance with their blankets. Can their blankets dance fast? Slow? High? Low? In circles? As a partner with one other blanket?
3. Repeat, using different kinds of music.

Comparing Blankets

Science

Materials

children's blankets

1. Ask the children to bring their blankets to school to show to the rest of the children.
2. Compare the blankets' textures, and help the children describe them (for example, nubby, smooth, soft, fuzzy, furry, and so on).
3. Let the children feel each blanket as it is being described.
4. Ask the children to find and describe other textures in the room.

Pajama Party
Special Event

1. Ask the children to wear or bring their nightclothes to school for a pretend sleep-over. At story time, read bedtime stories while the children lounge on blankets.
2. Ask the children to suggest other appropriate sleep-over activities.

Learning Center Ideas
Dramatic Play Area

Materials
baby beds ● baby dolls ● stuffed animals ● blankets ● sleeping bags ● small suitcases ● bedtime story books

1. Place a few of these bedtime props and others that the children request in the Dramatic Play Area.

Related Books
Bedtime for Frances by Russell Hoban
D.W.'s Lost Blankie by Marc Brown
Froggy Goes to Bed by Jonathan London
Good Night, Baby Bear by Frank Asch
Goodnight, Moon by Margaret Wise Brown
How Do Dinosaurs Say Goodnight? by Jane Yolen
Hush, Little Alien by Daniel Kirk
Hush, Little Baby: A Folk Song With Pictures by Marla Frazee
Ira Sleeps Over by Bernard Waber
Papa, Please Get the Moon for Me by Eric Carle
Sleep Is for Everyone by Paul Showers
Teddy Bear Tears by Jim Aylesworth
Time for Bed by Mem Fox
Where the Wild Things Are by Maurice Sendak

Charming Chairs

Materials
pictures of chairs

1. Show the children ads and magazine pictures of a variety of chairs. Talk about chairs. What kinds of chairs do they like best? Least? What kinds do their parents like? What kinds do babies like?
2. Talk about places that use unique chairs, for example, a dentist's office, theater, barbershop, or eye doctor.

Weekly Curriculum Vocabulary

chair
chairs
hard
highchair
soft
names of other chairs children talk about in opening activity

How Artists Draw Chairs

Art

Materials

books about chairs • variety of art materials

1. Look at the artwork in the books you read this week. How do different artists depict chairs in the stories?
2. Place the books in the Art Area.
3. Provide a variety of art materials for the children to explore and use while drawing or designing chairs in their own ways or in ways inspired by the books.

Weaving

Art

Materials

several classroom chairs • variety of yarn, ribbons, crepe paper streamers, and other weavable items • scissors

1. Turn over several classroom chairs and place them near each other.
2. Show the children how to weave yarn and other materials in and out and around the chair legs. Encourage them to weave with many different materials.
3. If possible, use the chairs with their decorations intact.
4. When necessary, challenge the children to "un-weave" the items. They can cut stubborn items in several places to facilitate the un-weaving.

Fuzzy Chairs

Art

Materials

pipe cleaners

1. Put pipe cleaners in the Art Area, and challenge the children to use these to make chairs of many kinds.

Dramatic Play With Chairs

Dramatic Play

Materials

classroom chairs • beach towels or fabric

1. Cover several chairs with beach towels or pieces of fabric and place them in the Dramatic Play Area. The children may incorporate these as thrones, fancy chairs, or other items in their play.

Visit a Furniture Store

Field Trip

1. Arrange a short visit to a furniture store to look at and sit in a variety of chairs. Which are most comfortable? Which are largest? Which are smallest?
2. Discuss what materials the chairs are made of. With permission, turn some of the stuffed, fabric chairs on end so the children can see the framework underneath. Point out the wooden framework and metal hardware.
3. Take photos of the children sitting in various chairs. Later, glue these to pages in a blank book and write the children's dictated words on the pages.

The Chair Game

Games

Materials

a child-size chair • small item

1. Place a chair, backwards, in front of the group. Ask a child sit to in the chair with his back to the children, and have him close his eyes.
2. Place the small item on the floor behind the chair.
3. Choose a second child to tiptoe up to the item, pick it up, and go back to her place in the group, hiding the item behind her.
4. While she is doing this, the children chant the following rhyme, substituting the name of the child in the chair for the bracketed name:

   (Patrick), (Patrick), I declare,
   Someone's sneaking 'round your chair.

5. When the chosen child returns to her place, the seated child turns and looks at the children. He has three chances to guess who took the small item.

6. The child who took the small item is next to sit in the chair, and the previously seated child chooses the next child to "sneak 'round the chair."

Who's Been Sitting in My Chair?

Language

Materials

Goldilocks and the Three Bears, any version ● individual baskets of assorted soft and hard everyday items, one basket for each child (Baskets and items do not have to be identical.)

1. Read (or tell) the story of *Goldilocks and the Three Bears*. Before reading, tell the children that they will be hearing about chairs and beds. When they hear the words "too hard," they should say, "Ouch!" When they hear the words "too soft," they should make the sound, "Oo-oo-oo-oo." When they hear the words "just right," they should say, "M-m-m-m-m."

Wooden blocks

Socks

Cotton balls

2. After the story, talk about the chairs. One was too hard, one was too soft, and one was just right. Tell the children they will be exploring items that are hard and soft.

3. Give each child a basket filled with assorted soft and hard items.

4. Ask the children to sort their items into two groups: hard and soft. When they finish, have the children choose partners so they can talk with each other about their work.

Bears in Chairs

Math

Materials

stuffed animals • chairs of different sizes

1. Ask the children to estimate how many stuffed animals can sit in a chair. Encourage them to check their prediction.
2. Repeat the activity with a different-sized chair.
3. Repeat the activity with different-sized animals.

Cooperative Musical Chairs

Movement

Materials

classroom chairs, one fewer than the number of children • recorded music

1. Arrange the chairs in a circle with the children outside the circle. Explain how the game is played (#3 and #4 below). Remind the children to be gentle with each other. Tell them that no one loses in this game, and that everyone has fun when they gently help each other.
2. Start the music. While the music plays, the children walk in a circle outside the chairs. When the music stops, every child sits in a chair. The children will problem solve to help the remaining child find a seat. (This child will have to share a seat with another.)
3. Ask the children to stand. Remove two chairs and begin the game again. This time more children will have to share seats (and they'll share giggles, too.) Continue play, removing one or two chairs each time, until there are three children sharing each chair.
4. As you continue playing this game throughout the year, play until four children are sharing each chair.

The Seats on the Bus

Music

Materials

classroom chairs

1. Encourage the children to set up chairs like seats on a bus. After everyone boards the "bus," sing "The Wheels on the Bus."

Sit Outside

Outdoors

1. Borrow a variety of outdoor chairs from parents. Set these up around the play yard and encourage the children to make up a game using the chairs.

Classifying Chairs

Science

Materials

magazines, furniture ads, and catalogs • scissors

1. Beforehand, cut out pictures of each of the following: father, mother, teen, preschool child, and baby.
2. Provide magazines, ads, and catalogs and ask each child to cut out three pictures of chairs and bring these to group time.
3. Spread out the family pictures in front of the children.
4. In turn, the children place one of their chairs beside the family member they think would like to sit in the chair.
5. There are no wrong answers. Silly answers (for example, dad in the high chair) can add to the fun and result in learning, too.

High Chair Comfort Food

Snack/Cooking

"baby" food (see below)

1. Tell the children that for snack they will be eating a food they ate when they were babies sitting in high chairs. Discuss what kinds of food this might be.
2. Serve applesauce for snack.
3. Repeat this on other days, serving finger foods such as teething cookies, miniature bagels (often given to teething babies), or green beans to dip in ranch dressing.

Learning Center Ideas

Dramatic Play Area

Materials

advertising circulars with pictures of chairs ● home decorating magazines with pictures of chairs ● beach towels or fabric for transforming classroom chairs into thrones or other fancy chairs

1. Add these items to the Dramatic Play Area where children can explore ideas about various kinds of chairs.

Related Books

A Chair for My Mother by Vera B. Williams
The Chair Where Bear Sits by Lee Wardlaw
Goldilocks and the Three Bears by Jan Brett
Mrs. Piccolo's Easy Chair by Jean Jackson
Peter's Chair by Ezra Jack Keats
Poppy's Chair by Karen Hesse
The Wee Little Woman by Byron Barton

First Week—
Cowpokes
and Their
Horses

Introducing the Weekly Curriculum Theme

Weekly Curriculum Vocabulary

bandana
bedroll
boots
breaking (as in taming wild horses)
chaps
hat
mend
mending
round-up
vest

Materials

Cowboy Small by Lois Lenski

1. This short, simple book includes a wealth of information and a glossary about cowboys. Read the book to the children.
2. Read the book again, calling the main character "Cowgirl Small." Introduce the word *cowpokes*, which is used for cowboys and cowgirls.
3. Point out Cowboy Small's clothing items, and discuss the purpose of each:

   - hat with large brim protects from rain, wind, and dust storms
   - boots protect feet from brambles and snakebites
   - chaps protect legs when riding horses
   - bandanas protect neck from sunburn and provide filtered air for breathing during dust storms

4. If you don't have access to *Cowboy Small*, bring in other books (especially those intended for adults) that show authentic clothing and authentic cowpokes.

Sheriff Badges

Art

Materials

silver or gray construction paper ● cardboard five-pointed stars (for tracing)
● markers ● child-safe scissors ● index cards ● masking tape

1. Give each child a piece of silver or gray construction paper. Show the children how to trace around a cardboard star onto the construction paper.
2. Help the children cut out their stars. Show them the easy way to do this—cutting inward from each point.
3. Write the word "Sheriff" on index cards. Help the children copy the word "Sheriff" onto their stars.
4. Attach the stars to clothing with a loop of masking tape with the sticky part of the tape facing out.

Ride 'em, Cowpoke!

Art and Dramatic Play

Materials

tagboard (or file folders) ● horse pattern (see illustration on page 231) ● crayons and markers ● scissors ● tape ● classroom chairs

1. Enlarge the horse pattern on page 231.
2. Encourage the children to draw and color horses' heads on tagboard, to be used in this activity to construct chair horses, and later, to make stick horses. Be certain that several children make more than one of these heads.
3. After the children cut out their horse heads, tape one head onto the back of a child-size chair with the face away from the chair. Make several of these "horses" so the cowpokes can "ride" together.
4. Show the children how to sit astride the chair, facing the chair's back. Children enjoy "riding" these horses. Be certain they understand this is pretend play and the horses are not supposed to really move.
5. Save the remaining horse heads to use in next week's art activity—My Very Own Horse (page 235).

Exploring Bandanas

Art and Science

Materials

old white sheet or fabric • sharp scissors (adult only) • dry sponges • bandana • tempera paints in shallow dishes • fine-tip, permanent markers

1. Pre-cut the sheet into 12" squares (adult only). Pre-cut the sponges into "western" shapes, such as boots, brands, cowpoke hats, and other appropriate shapes (adult only). Dampen the sponges to soften them.
2. Show the real bandana to the children. Give each child a square of fabric. Encourage them to decorate their square so it can be their bandana. They can dip the sponges into paint and make prints on the fabric, or use markers to draw desired decorations.

Note: Supervise carefully while they use permanent markers.

3. When these are dry, show the children how to fold them diagonally and then tie them over their noses and mouths. Remind them of dust storms and the dusty business of branding animals. When they breathe through the fabric, help them realize how the bandana helps the cowpoke avoid breathing dust.

Bedrolls

Language

Materials

items for making a bedroll (see page 244 in the Camping theme for details) • 4" x 6" index cards • marker • chart paper • scissors • glue stick • plain paper, one sheet for each child • markers and paper, if desired

1. Show the children how to make bedrolls. Discuss how cowpokes sleep in these while they are away from the ranch and the bunkhouse.
2. Beforehand, mark the index cards into 1" squares, one for each child. Then write each letter of the word "bedroll" in each square.
3. Write the word "bedroll" on a chart. Give each child an index card.
4. Ask the children to cut the index card into squares. Ask them to glue their letters onto the plain paper, in order, to spell "bedroll." If desired, the children can copy the word onto separate paper.

A Cowpoke's Job and Tools

Language

Materials

real items a cowpoke might use (see below) • books with pictures of cowpokes working and items they use

1. Talk about jobs a cowpoke does, such as mending fences, rounding up cattle, and "breaking" wild horses.
2. Talk about items a cowpoke might take on the trail and how he might use these (utensils for cooking and eating, bedroll, rope, first aid supplies, food, and so on).

Matching Cowpokes and Their Horses

Math

Materials

copy machine that reduces and enlarges • pattern of a cowpoke (see illustration) • pattern of a horse (see illustration) • adult scissors (adult only)

1. Make five different-size copies of the cowpoke and of the horse. Cut out all of the pictures.
2. Challenge the children to place the horse pictures in order of size from smallest to largest. Ask them to put each cowpoke with its matching-size horse.

Rope Seriation

Math

Materials

ropes of different lengths

1. Ask the children to place the ropes in order from longest to shortest or from shortest to longest.

I'm a Little Cowpoke

Music and Movement

1. With the children, act out the following song:

> **I'm a Little Cowpoke**
> Tune: **I'm a Little Teapot**
> I'm a little cowpoke,
> See me smile.
> I ride my horse for miles and miles.
> Dressed up in my chaps and vest and hat,
> I rope cattle just like that!
>
> My horse is just the right size,
> Seven hands tall.
> Some folks think it's much too small.
> But, I'm a little cowpoke; I'm very wise.
> I ride a horse that's just my size.

Cowboy's Beans

Snack/Cooking

Materials

cooking oil • chopped onions • electric skillet (adult only) • cans of pinto beans • chili powder • cooking spoon • small pie plates • spoons • utensils

1. Sauté the onions in medium-hot oil until they are soft and beginning to brown (adult only).
2. Add the un-drained pinto beans and a few shakes of chili powder.
3. Heat thoroughly, simmer 15 minutes, and then serve in small pie plates to hungry cowpokes.

Caution: Supervise closely, and check for possible food allergies.

Learning Center Ideas

Dramatic Play Area

Materials

authentic cowpoke items, if possible, such as boots, chaps, hat, vest, and saddle (borrowed from horseback riding stable) • stuffed horse

1. Add a few of these items and others that the children request to the Dramatic Play Area.

Related Books

Art of the Boot by Tyler Beard

Bootmaker and the Elves by Susan Lowell

Casey's New Hat by Tricia Gardella

The Cowboy and the Black-Eyed Pea by Tony Johnston

The Cowboy Hat Book by William Reynolds

Cowboy Small by Lois Lenski

How I Spent My Summer Vacation by Mark Teague

Just Like My Dad by Tricia Gardella

The Silliest Shapes and Colors Book in the Wild West by Madeline Bennett

Second Week—
Cowpokes
and Their
Horses

Introducing the Weekly Curriculum Theme

Weekly Curriculum Vocabulary

brand
cattle
dance
horse

Materials

chart paper ● marker ● rubber bands

1. Write the words to the following song on a piece of chart paper. Sing "Western Dance" several times with the children so they can become familiar with the words and tune.

2. Slip a rubber band loosely onto each child's right wrist. Talk briefly about right and left and remind them the rubber band is on their right wrist. Explain that everything on that side of their body is also on the right, and everything on the other side is on the left.

3. With children standing in a circle, sing the song again slowly and add the dance movements. Repeat as many times as desired, and then repeat daily.

Western Dance
Tune: ***Turkey in the Straw***
Oh you clap your hands, then you slap your knees.
Then you tap your feet any way you please.

Oh you turn to the right and you stomp the floor.
Turn back to the center, then you stomp some more.

Oh you slide to the right and stamp your feet.
Then you slide to the left and stamp to the beat.
Take two steps forward and bow to a friend;
Take two steps back and then you start again.

Weekly Curriculum Extension Activities

Cowpoke's Vest

Art

Materials

large grocery bags, one for each child, plus a few extra • adult scissors (adult
only) • child-safe scissors • markers • sheriff badges cut from construction paper
(see Sheriff Badges, page 229) • glue

1. Help the children make western vests out of large paper grocery bags. The
   adult turns a bag upside down, cuts the bag up its seam, cuts out the doubled
   area at the seam, and makes a large neck hole in what was the bag's bottom.
2. The adult cuts out armholes and turns the bag inside out to hide the
   store's logo.
3. Encourage the children to cut fringe along the vest's bottom.
4. The children use markers to draw western items on the back of their vests.
5. Help the children glue a sheriff's badge on the part of the bag that will be
   over their left front.

My Very Own Horse

Art

Materials

large paper grocery bags, one for each child • rubber bands • tape • stapler •
8" pieces of yarn • file folders and scissors, if desired • horse heads saved from last
week's art activity (Ride 'em, Cowpoke!, page 229)

1. Have a few children at a time place their bags flat on the table before them.
   Starting with the bag's long side, the children roll their bag into a long log
   shape. Help each child secure the rolls at each end with rubber bands. This

long tube will become the body of their horses.

2. Ask the children to wrap tape tightly around their horses' bodies at each end and in the center. Then remove and discard the rubber bands.

3. Help each child tape or staple her horse's head to one end of her horse's body. (If desired, the child can trace the horse's head onto another piece of file folder and cut it out. These can be attached, sandwich fashion, around the horse's body.) Many children will picture their horse as seen from the front, not from the side as adults do. Encourage all efforts.

4. Show the children how to attach a yarn tail to their horse's tail end.

5. Children "ride" these horses by holding just below the head and pointing the other end towards the ground. If the brown paper rolls are long enough, children can straddle them.

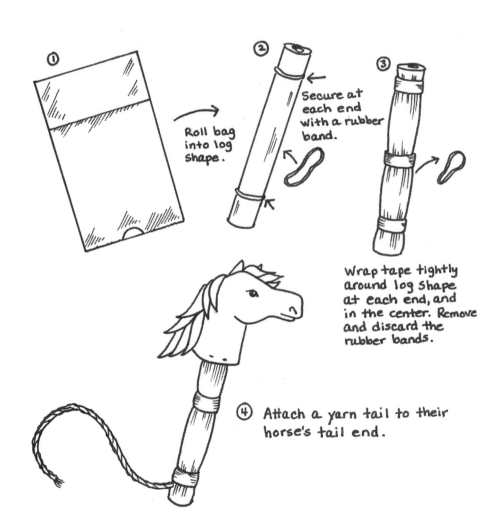

① Roll bag into log shape.

② Secure at each end with a rubber band.

③ Wrap tape tightly around log shape at each end, and in the center. Remove and discard the rubber bands.

④ Attach a yarn tail to their horse's tail end.

Making Western Items and Western Wear

Art and Dramatic Play

Materials

assorted books with pictures of cowpokes and their equipment ● large variety of art materials

1. Encourage the children to use the art materials to make cowpoke clothing and other items for themselves to use in dramatic play. For example, they may use pieces of brown paper grocery bags and masking tape to make a cowpoke's chaps, and they may make cooking equipment by wrapping aluminum foil around margarine tubs. Encourage and value all efforts.

Cattle Brands

Language

Materials

paper ● pencils, markers, or crayons

1. Talk about branding cattle. Each ranch has its own brand, which is usually a simple picture of the ranch's name. Cowpokes apply this symbol to the cattle's fur to identify it as belonging to that particular ranch.
2. Help the children design their own simple brands using the first letters of their names as part of the design. For example, "Rocking R" could be rocking chair rockers below the letter R; "Todd's Tall Trees" could be several tall trees with the initial "T" in a treetop; "Backwards B" could be the letter B printed backwards; "Double D" could be two D's back-to-back, with one of the letters reversed.
3. Label the children's papers with their brands for the rest of the week, and refer to them by their ranch's name.

Measuring With Hands

Math

Materials

paper ● copy machine ● markers

1. Beforehand, draw six classroom items on a piece of paper. (For example, a table, chair, doorknob on a door, tall stuffed animal, short animal, or any other item). Draw a blank line next to each picture. Make a copy for each child.

2. Discuss some of the ways horses help cowpokes, and discuss ways cowpokes take very good care of these valuable animals.

3. Explain that horses are measured using hands. Cowpokes describe their horses as being a certain number of hands tall. To measure height by hands, place one hand at the bottom of the item you wish to measure. Now place your other hand just above this one so the edges of both hands touch. Now move the bottom hand above the top one, again touching edges. Count each time you place a hand on the item. The total number is "how many hands high" the item is.

4. Give each child a sheet of paper with the six classroom items on it.

5. Encourage the children to go around the room and use their hands to measure each item and record the total for each in the corresponding blank.

6. Ask the children to compare their answers. Do small hands and larger hands get the same answer? Why is this a good way for cowpokes to measure? Why is it a poor way to measure?

Variation: Have each child stand against a wall. With chalk, make a mark indicating the top of the child's head. Ask the children to use their hands to measure their own height in hands.

More Cowpokes

Music

1. Continue singing "I'm a Little Cowpoke" on page 232 of Cowpokes and Their Horses—First Week.

Drop the Bandana

Outdoors

Materials

bandana ● stick horse (from My Very Own Horse, page 235)

1. Teach the children to play "Drop the Bandana," which is played like "Drop the Handkerchief." Ask the children to stand in a circle, facing inward.
2. Choose a child to be "IT." IT rides a stick horse around the circle, carrying a bandana.
3. IT drops the bandana behind a child, who picks it up and runs after IT and the horse. If IT gets back to the chosen child's place in the circle without being tagged by the chasing child, he takes that place. If the chasing child catches him, IT must stand in the center of the circle until replaced by another caught cowpoke.
4. The chasing child becomes the new IT and receives the horse from the previous rider.

Tying Ropes

Science

Materials

several kinds and lengths of rope

1. Discuss the ways cowpokes use ropes, such as roping cattle and tying things to secure them.
2. Encourage the children to use the ropes to practice tying knots.
3. Supervise carefully; be sure that no one places rope around their own or another child's neck.

Cowgirl's Tomato and Bean Stew

Snack/Cooking

Materials

canned, diced tomatoes ● cans of pinto beans ● electric skillet (adult only) ● cooking spoon ● chili powder ● small pie plates ● utensils

1. Dump the tomatoes and pinto beans, un-drained, into the skillet. Add in a dash of chili powder. Stir while this warms, and then let it simmer 15 minutes.

Keep the children away from the hot skillet.

2. Serve in small pie plates to hungry cowpokes.

Caution: Supervise closely at all times. Check for possible food allergies.

Learning Center Ideas

Block Area

Materials

plastic horse and rider figures

1. Place these items and other props suggested by children in the Block Area to support ranch play.

Related Books

See Related Books list in Cowpokes and Their Horses—First Week (page 233).

Let's Go Camping—
First Week

Introducing the Weekly Curriculum Theme

Materials

camping equipment, such as a sleeping bag, bedroll, cooler, canteen, cooking kit, flashlight, hiking boots, or any other items used on a camping trip (Borrow these from parents, friends, and scout troops.)

1. Discuss the names of the camping items and their uses.
2. Invite the children to talk about their camping experiences.
3. Discuss what it means to go camping. (This is usually done outdoors, usually with no electricity and no running water.) Discuss how campers cook, how they keep warm, and how they can see at night.
4. Talk about sleeping in a sleeping bag or a bedroll of blankets. Explain that the part of the bedroll under a person keeps her warm by protecting her from the cold ground; the part over her protects her from the cold air.

Weekly Curriculum Vocabulary

bedroll
camping
safe
safety
tent

In Our Bedrolls

Art

Materials

construction paper • scissors • small staplers and staples • markers • craft sticks • glue • art scraps

1. Cut construction paper into 6" squares.
2. Give one square to each child. Ask them to fold their square in half, forming a rectangular bedroll.
3. Show them how to staple near the edge of one open short side (the bottom) and the long open side of the bedroll.
4. Cut construction paper into 2" circles. Give two to each child.
5. Encourage the children to use the circles and craft sticks to make little people to sleep in the bags. They can use markers to make a face on one circle. Show them how to put glue on the back of this circle and on a plain circle, then place the end of the craft stick between the two surfaces with glue on them. Let dry.
6. The children can slide their people in and out of the little bedrolls.

① Fold square in half.

② Staple near the edge of one open short side and the long open side of the bedroll.

③ Make a face on one circle with markers. Put glue on the back of this circle and on a plain circle. Place the craft stick between the two gluey surfaces.

④ Slide people in and out of the little bedrolls.

Let's Go Camping

Bulletin Board

Materials

art scraps • nature materials collected outdoors, if desired • glue • markers • other materials as requested by the children

1. Tell the children they will be making a bulletin board about camping. Discuss what might go on the board, for example, people in sleeping bags, campfires, tents, flashlights, canteens, and so on. Some children may mention stars, clouds, bushes, flowers, trees, small animals, and so on.
2. Encourage the children to use a variety of materials to make items for the board. Encourage all efforts.
3. Help the children glue their creations to a bulletin board with a plain background.
4. Let this be an on-going activity. As children learn more about camping and camp environments, they will be inspired to add other creations. Provide the materials they request, and encourage their creativity.

Visit a Camping Supply Store

Field Trip

1. Arrange a visit to a camping supply store. Ask the clerk to show various kinds of camping equipment and clothing. Allow the children to hold some items and try on some of the outerwear clothing.

Tenting Together

Language

Materials

pop-up tent (or large bedspread) • flashlights

1. Borrow a pop-up tent for the week. Put this in your room and have group meetings in the tent. Use a flashlight to provide light so you can read books with the children. (If no tent is available, substitute a table covered with a large bedspread.)
2. Let the children use the tent for playing and reading. Provide flashlights to light their way.

Camping Safety

Language

1. Discuss camping safety with the children. For example, stay near the campsite, be with an adult at all times, swim only with an adult, beware of the hot fire, and so on.

2. Sing the "Camping Safety Song" below, inviting the children to make up additional verses:

> *Camping Safety Song*
> Tune: *Mary Had a Little Lamb*
> *When I'm camping, I'll be safe,*
> *I'll be safe, I'll be safe.*
> *When I'm camping, I'll be safe,*
> *This is what I'll do.*
>
> *I'll stay near a grownup all the time.*
> *All the time, all the time.*
> *I'll stay near a grownup all the time.*
> *That's what I will do.*
>
> *I'll never run near the hot campfire.*
> *Never run, never run.*
> *I'll never run near the hot campfire.*
> *That's what I will do.*

Making Bedrolls

Math

Materials

blankets ● spring-type clothespins ● belt, rope, or elastic cord

1. Demonstrate to the children how to make a bedroll. Spread two or more blankets on top of each other on the floor.

2. Fold the stack in half, lengthwise, and then use clothespins to close the long, open side and one short side (the bottom). It now looks somewhat like a sleeping bag.

3. Roll this from the bottom to the top and secure the roll with a belt, short rope, or elastic cord. Explain that campers keep their bedroll or sleeping bag rolled up when they are not in it. This keeps bugs out of the bag.

4. Unroll the bag and let the children take turns getting inside.

5. Ask parents to send a blanket to school with their child. Bring extra blankets for children who don't bring any. Help the children fold and clip their blankets into bedrolls.

Our Bedrolls

Math

Materials

children's bedrolls

1. Ask the children to sit in a circle and place their bedrolls in the center of the circle.
2. With the children, count the number of campers present and the number of bedrolls present. Are there enough bedrolls for each camper to use one? Ask the children to pick up their bedrolls. Is there one for each child?
3. Ask the children to return their bedrolls to the center of the circle. Remove two bedrolls from the group. Encourage the children to predict if there are enough bedrolls for each child to have one. Why or why not? The children can check their prediction by each picking up one bedroll.
4. Return all bedrolls to the center; remove one child. Repeat the activity and discuss results.

Variation: Ask the children the following: If we share bedrolls, and two children sleep in each one, how many bedrolls will we need? Children can pair up, and then count the pairs to solve this.

Folding Shapes

Math

Materials

square blanket, any size ● spring-type clothespins

1. Spread a square blanket on the floor. Talk about its shape. Fold it in half. What shape is it now? Talk about how a large square became a smaller rectangle.
2. Spread the blanket again. Fold it in half diagonally. What shape is it now? Talk about how a large square became a triangle.
3. Spread the blanket again, then fold it in half lengthwise and clip it so it becomes a bedroll. Have the children put it in the Dramatic Play Area.
4. Provide squares of paper in the Math Area so children can practice folding them into other shapes.

Nature Sounds

Music

Materials

CDs of nature sounds • CD player

1. Play CDs of nature sounds while the children are working and playing.

Backyard Camping

Outdoors

Materials

tent • camping materials • books

1. Pitch a tent in the school's play yard. Allow the children to play in and around this during outdoor time.
2. Allow the children to bring camping items outdoors for use in this "campground," and return the items when they go indoors.
3. Have story time in the tent.

Where Do People Camp?

Science

Materials

pictures of places where people might camp, optional • pictures of animals people might see when camping, optional

1. Talk about the places people might go camping, such as the woods, lakeside, seashore, mountains, cold and snowy places, hot places, and any other places.
2. Discuss the different kinds of things campers may need in these places (for example, fishing equipment, warm clothes, bathing suits, hiking boots, sunscreen, and so on).
3. Discuss what these places look like. What animals might campers see? If possible, show pictures. If desired, spend a large amount of time discussing places, climates, or animals.

Gorp

Snack/Cooking

Materials

dry cereals ● dried fruits cut into small pieces ● coconut flakes ● chopped nuts
(omit if any child is allergic to these) ● scoop or small cup ● serving bowl ●
3-oz. cups

1. Talk with the children about the kinds of food that would be good snack foods
   on a camping trip—those that are healthy, need no refrigeration, and take up
   little room.
2. Tell the children that some campers combine dry cereal, dried fruits, and nuts
   to make something they call "Gorp."
3. Encourage the children to help pour the food items into the serving bowl. Let
   each child use a scoop or cup to serve himself a cupful of the Gorp for a snack.

Campers' Stew

Snack/Cooking

Materials

canned beef stew ● canned corn ● canned tomatoes ● canned lima beans ● canned potatoes, drained and diced (by the adult) ● canned tomato soup ● can opener ● crock pot (adult only) ● cooking spoon ● bowls ● disposable spoons

1. Ask the children to bring in listed items. The adult opens the cans.
2. Encourage the children to dump their ingredients into a crock pot and gently stir. (Supervise closely.) Encourage the children to pretend the crock pot is heating over a campfire.
3. Heat at high until it is warmed through. Serve to hungry campers.

Learning Center Ideas

Dramatic Play Area

cooking set for camping ● clothing used for camping ● hiking boots ● bedrolls in doll sizes

1. Add camping equipment (such as a cooler, flashlights, water bottles, boots, sleeping bags, and so on) to the Dramatic Play Area.
2. Encourage the children to use these items to act out camping activities.
3. If possible, place a tent in the Dramatic Play Area.

Related Books

Arthur's Camp Out by Lillian Hoban
Bailey Goes Camping by Kevin Henkes
The Berenstain Bears and the Ghost of the Forest by Stan and Jan Berenstain
Henry and Mudge and the Starry Night by Cynthia Rylant
Just Me and My Dad by Mercer Mayer
My Camp Out by Marcia Leonard
What Dads Can't Do by Douglas Wood

Let's Go Camping—
Second Week

Introducing the Weekly Curriculum Theme

Materials

chart paper ● marker

1. Write the words of the song "Let's Go Camping" (below) on a chart, leaving a blank space for each word in parentheses.
2. Sing the song with the children. Invite the children, in turn, to tell what they'll bring on the imaginary camping trip. Insert the child's name and her item in the song.

> *Let's Go Camping*
> Tune: *Are You Sleeping?*
> *Let's go camping. Let's go camping.*
> *Here we go! Here we go!*
> *(name) will bring (item).*
> *(name) will bring (item).*
> *Here we go! Here we go!*
>
> *Let's go camping. Let's go camping.*
> *Here we go! Here we go!*
> *(name) will bring (item).*
> *(name) will bring (item).*
> *Here we go! Here we go!*

Weekly Curriculum Vocabulary

campfire
chocolate
fire
graham cracker
logs
marshmallow
S'mores

Binoculars

Art

Materials

cardboard rolls, 2 per child ● clip-type clothespins ● white glue ● hole punch ● yarn ● scissors

1. Help each child glue two cardboard rolls together, side by side, to form "binoculars." Use the clothespins to hold the rolls together until they dry.
2. Help the children punch one hole on each of the outside edges at one end of the binoculars.
3. Cut yarn into 15" lengths. Tie an end of yarn through each hole to make the binoculars' strap.

Our Campfire

Art

Materials

newspaper ● masking tape ● brown and black paint ● brushes and rags ● tape ● glue ● orange and yellow tissue paper

1. Show the children how to roll the newspaper into log shapes and secure the rolls with masking tape. Ask them to work in pairs to make logs.
2. The children paint the logs brown. After the "logs" are dry, the children use rags to dab black paint on top of the brown.
3. When the logs are dry again, help the children arrange them into a campfire shape and join them to each other with tape.
4. Help the children glue on orange and yellow tissue paper flames.
5. Encourage the children to nap in sleeping bags around this "fire."

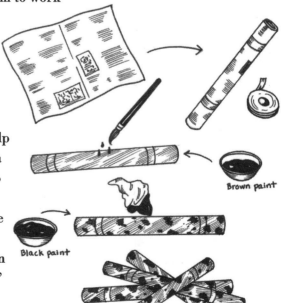

Brown paint

Black paint

Campfire Meetings

Language

Materials

campfire (see previous activity, Our Campfire)

1. Hold group meetings around the "campfire." Sing favorite songs.
2. Encourage the children to tell simple true or made-up stories about any topic. Let the group guess whether the story is true or make believe.

Camping Words

Language

Materials

camping props • markers • chart paper • plain paper • blank books • crayons

1. Look at the camping props with the children. As the children name each prop, write the word on the chart and draw a simple picture of the prop beside the word.
2. Place the chart in the Writing Area and provide paper and markers for children who wish to copy the chart.
3. Some children may wish to fill blank books with camping words and illustrations.

Venn Diagram

Math

Materials

markers • bulletin board paper • index cards • tape

1. Use a marker to draw a large tent shape on the bulletin board paper.
2. Use a marker of a different color to draw a large house shape, partially overlapping the tent shape.
3. With the children, discuss camping and staying at home.
4. Ask the children to tell you some things about camping. Write these on individual index cards and tape them inside the tent shape.
5. Ask the children to tell you some things about staying at home. Write these on individual index cards and tape them inside the house shape.
6. Finally, ask the children to help you identify identical cards that are in both

shapes. Remove one of these, and put the other in the overlapping part of the picture. Help the children "see" that these are in both pictures at the same time.

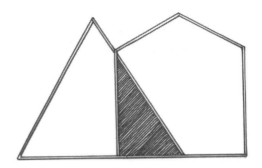

7. If the children tell you something that isn't correct about either staying at home or going camping, discuss the answers and ask the children where to place those cards (outside both pictures).

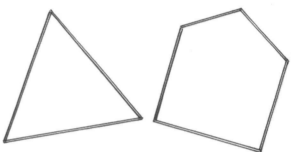

S'mores

Science and Snack/Cooking

Materials

milk chocolate candy bars divided into squares ● graham crackers ● marshmallows ● microwave oven (adult only)

1. Tell the children how this snack got its name. When people finish eating it, they say quickly, "I want some more." When they say the words quickly, it sounds like, "I want s'more."

2. Let the children watch you put four squares of chocolate atop a graham cracker and place a marshmallow on top of that. Encourage them to look carefully at this.

3. Put this into a microwave oven and heat it until the marshmallow begins to melt. Remove it, and let the children observe any changes. Let them watch as the marshmallow's heat melts the chocolate. If necessary, return the S'more to the microwave and heat it a few seconds longer.

4. Tell children that a S'more is very hot. It must cool completely before it is eaten.

5. Follow up by helping each child, in turn, make a S'more for snack. Do not allow children to operate the microwave oven or to touch the hot S'mores.

Related Books

See Related Books list on page 248 of Let's Go Camping—First Week.

Library

Materials

Stella Louella's Runaway Book by Lisa Campbell Ernst ● variety of books from the library

1. Read the story to the group. See if the children can guess from the clues the name of the book that Stella lost. If you don't have *Stella Louella's Runaway Book*, begin with step number two.
2. With the children, discuss the library. Encourage the children to tell you what they know about it.
3. Help the children understand that they can borrow and read books from the library, but they must promise to return the books by a specific time. If a person returns a book late, he has to pay money. We must take good care of library books so they don't become damaged.
4. Review ways to care for books.
5. Help the children understand that libraries have books that help us learn about many real things. They also have lots of books about make-believe things.
6. Show the children the covers and a few inside pages of several books that you have borrowed from the library for their use. Tell them a few sentences about each book. Emphasize that these books belong to the library and that the children must help you take good care of them.
7. Give the children 5-10 minutes to look at books you've brought from the library. If desired, they can pair up with a friend to look at the books together. Have them return the book they've just completed before getting another book.

Weekly Curriculum Vocabulary

books
librarian
library
recorded book

Our Favorite Books

Art

Materials

drawing paper ● crayons

1. Encourage the children to talk about their favorite books.
2. Provide paper and crayons and ask each child to draw a picture of her favorite book. Write the child's dictated title on the page.
3. Use these pictures for a bulletin board titled "Our Favorite Books." Later, put the pictures in the children's assessment portfolios.

A Visit to the Library

Field Trip

1. Arrange a trip to the library, requesting a short tour of the library and a story time for the children. Allow each child to choose a book to take back to the classroom. Do not send these books home with the children. Read them to the children during story time and return them to the library when they are due.

Paper Bag Theaters

Language

Materials

lunch-size paper bags ● variety of art supplies

1. Encourage each child to make a paper bag theater of his favorite story. Ask them to decorate a bag as though it is the book's cover, front and back.
2. The children can use a variety of materials to represent individual characters and some of the props from their story. Tell them that they can store the characters and props in the bag.
3. Have them use the characters and props to tell the story to others.

Recorded Books

Language

Materials

recorded books • tape player or CD player

1. Borrow recorded books from the library, or use some you have on hand.
2. Play a recording while you hold up the matching book. Page through as the narrator reads the book.
3. Help the children understand that they can listen to these books and read along by turning pages when directed to do so by the signal in the recording.
4. Have the materials available for the children's use.

Estimation

Math

1. Encourage the children to estimate how many books you have in your class library. Count the books to check the estimates.
2. To practice counting by fives, place the books in stacks of five, and then count the total.

Comparing Sizes

Math

Materials

picture books in several sizes

1. Ask the children to compare the sizes of several picture books—small, medium, and large. Ask the children to decide which group each book belongs in.

Singing About My Favorite Book

Music

1. Ask the children to name their favorite books. Then, sing the song below, letting each child in turn tell what book title to sing in place of the blank lines.

> Tune: *The Wheels on the Bus*
> *I like to go to the library*
> *The library, the library.*
> *I like to go to the library*
> *Where I can read some books.*
>
> *My favorite book is _____.*
> *_____, _____.*
> *My favorite book is _____.*
> *It's at the library.*

Sing a Story

Music

Materials

any storybook that is also a song

1. Choose any book that is also a song. These are located in Dewey Decimal section 782 in the children's section of the library. The musical notation is often at the back of the book.
2. Read the book as a story, then repeat it as a song. Repeat it regularly so the children can learn the song.
3. Place the book where the children can use it.
4. The following are examples of books that are songs:

   - *Baby Beluga* by Raffi
   - *She'll Be Coming Around the Mountain* by Emily Coplon, Doris Orgel, and Ellen Schecter

Book Snacks

Snack/Cooking

1. Serve snacks that are related to the children's favorite books, such as:

   - fresh wheat bread (*The Little Red Hen* by J.P. Miller)
   - blueberries (*Blueberries for Sal* by Robert McCloskey)
   - pancakes (*Pancakes, Pancakes!* by Eric Carle)
   - spaghetti and meatballs (*Cloudy With a Chance of Meatballs* by Judi Barrett)
   - any soup (*Today Is Monday* by Eric Carle)

Learning Center Ideas

Dramatic Play Area

Materials
items to support dramatic play about libraries

1. Provide materials that children request so they can turn the Dramatic Play Area into a library. Some children may want these:

   - a pen-size flashlight for the scanner used when checking out books
   - bins for sorting books into categories
   - pencils and pads of paper
   - bags for carrying books

2. Encourage the children to be librarians, and read to other children and to dolls and stuffed animals.

Related Books
Any book is appropriate for the Library theme since books can be found in a library. Remember to include non-fiction selections, too.
I Took My Frog to the Library by Eric A. Kimmel
The Library by Sarah Stewart
The Library Dragon by Carmen Agra Deedy
Library Lil by Suzanne Williams
My Aunt Came Back by Pat Cummings
Stella Louella's Runaway Book by Lisa Campbell Ernst
The True Story of the 3 Little Pigs by A. Wolf by Jon Scieszka

Quaint Quilts

Introducing the Weekly Curriculum Theme

Weekly Curriculum Vocabulary

cloth

clothing

design

quilt

quilter

Materials

any children's storybook about a quilt (see book list on page 263) ● adult books with many photos of quilts ● a real quilt, if possible

1. Read a story about quilts to the children.
2. After reading, point out the illustrations of quilts in the children's storybook and talk about quilts. Explain that today many are made from new fabrics, and they are created as works of art. In earlier times, they were made from worn-out clothing (the parts of garments that were still strong). This was a form of recycling—using the clothing's fabric in a new way.
3. Show the real quilt. Call attention to the way fabrics are joined together to form patterns or pictures.
4. Use the adult book(s) to show pictures of various quilts and their patterns. Talk about the patterns' names and discuss whether children think the name describes the pattern.

Colorful Classroom Quilt

Art and Bulletin Board

Materials

black construction paper ● scissors ● commercially available pattern block shapes cut from bright colors ● glue sticks ● bulletin board paper

1. Cut black construction paper into 8" squares. Give each child a black square.
2. Encourage the children to choose a variety of colorful shapes and arrange them on their square to create a quilt pattern of their own. Help them glue the shapes in place.
3. Glue the squares to the bulletin board paper to make a large, classroom quilt.
4. Display this by hanging it flat against the ceiling or on a wall or bulletin board.

A Quilter Comes to Visit

Classroom Visitor

1. Contact one or more quilters in your area. (Ask for names at a quilting shop or fabric store.) Invite quilters to visit your class and bring finished quilts and quilt blocks with them. Ask them to tell the stories behind their quilts.
2. Ask if they can demonstrate the way they make a simple quilt block.

Quilt Pattern Names

Language

Materials

pictures of simple quilt squares (in adult quilting books)

1. Show the children pictures of a few simple quilt patterns (for example, a log cabin, broken dishes, bear paw, nine-patch, or four-patch) and tell them the name of each.
2. Ask the children to name the quilt patterns they created in the previous activity, "Colorful Classroom Quilt."

Some Quilts

Language

Materials

sentence strips ● marker ● pocket chart

1. On individual sentence strips, write the following words: *some, quilts, have.* On additional individual strips, write color names and shape names. Leave two strips blank.
2. In a pocket chart arrange the cards to read: "Some quilts have (blank) (blank)."
3. Place the strips with the names of colors together in one pile and the strips with names of shapes in another. In turn, ask a child to choose one color word and one shape word. Ask them to add these to the pocket sentence so the sentence reads: "Some quilts have (color word) (shape word)." For example, "Some quilts have orange squares."
4. Have the group read each sentence.

Shapes in Quilts

Math

Materials

real quilts, if possible ● books with quilt illustrations

1. Use the quilt theme to explore and learn about geometric shapes.
2. Look at real quilts and pictures of real quilts. Talk about the shapes the children see in the quilts and how these are combined to make other shapes.
3. As you do other activities in this section, discuss the shapes children discover in their work and in quilts.

Quilt Block Shapes

Math

Materials

construction paper in many colors ● scissors ● 9" square of paper ● glue sticks

1. Cut construction paper into 3" squares and 6" squares. Have each child choose two 3" squares of paper and one 6" square. Distribute child-safe scissors and glue to the children.

2. Using a 9" square of paper, show the children how to fold a square in half horizontally and cut on the fold to form two rectangles. Encourage the children to do this with one of their 3" squares.

3. Demonstrate how to fold a square in half diagonally, then cut on the fold to form two triangles. Ask the children to do this with their other 3" square.

4. Ask the children to place their cut shapes onto their 6" square, forming a pattern of their own creation. Help them glue the smaller shapes in place, forming a quilt square.

5. If desired, join these squares together to form a quilt.

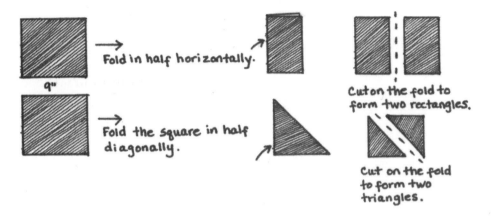

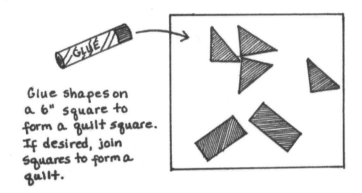

Matching Quilt Designs

Math

Materials

quilt pattern magazine ● drawing paper ● markers ● laminating machine or clear contact paper, optional

1. Using patterns from a quilt magazine, copy simple patterns onto drawing paper, making two copies of each. Color the matching pairs identically. Laminate, if desired.

2. Place the group of pairs in the Manipulatives Area for the children to use as a matching game.

3. Encourage the children to play in pairs, taking turns holding up a design for their friend to find the match.

Dancing Quilt

Movement

Materials

scarves in many colors and patterns • music

1. Let each child choose one or two scarves to wave and dance with while you play music. They will look like a dancing quilt.

Toasted Quilt Squares

Snack/Cooking

Materials

bread, one slice per child • aluminum foil • yellow and white cheese, ½ slice each per child • serrated-blade plastic knives • toaster oven (adult only) • paper plates • camera, if desired

1. Give each child a slice of bread. Ask them to place their bread on a piece of foil.

2. Give each child ½ slice of yellow cheese and ½ slice of white cheese. Help them cut their cheese slices into squares and triangles and arrange these in a design on the bread.

3. Toast the creations to melt the cheese (adult only).

4. Serve on individual paper plates.

5. If desired, take photos of each creation so the children can compare their designs.

Caution: Supervise closely.

Learning Center Ideas

Dramatic Play Area

Materials

quilts • quilting magazines • fabric scraps

1. Place the quilting items in the Dramatic Play Area where children can explore them.

Related Books

The Boy and the Quilt by Shirley Kurtz

Eight Hands Round: A Patchwork Alphabet by Ann Whitford Paul

Joseph Had a Little Overcoat by Simms Taback

Luka's Quilt by Georgia Guback

The Quilt by Ann Jonas

The Quilt Story by Tony Johnston

Quilting Now & Then by Karen B. Willing and Julie B. Dock

The Quiltmaker's Gift by Jeff Brumbeau

Sam Johnson and the Blue Ribbon Quilt by Lisa Campbell Ernst

The text in the following picture books is too advanced for preschoolers and kindergarteners, but the books have high-quality pictures of quilts, quilt squares, and times past.

Generous Quiltmakers by Joanne Larsen Line and Nancy Loving Tubesing (This adult book shows finished quilts from *The Quiltmaker's Gift* by Jeff Brumbeau.)

The Quilt-Block History of Pioneer Days: With Projects Kids Can Make by Mary Cobb

Quilts from the Quiltmaker's Gift: 20 Traditional Patterns for a New Generation of Generous Quiltmakers by Joanne Larsen Line

Selina and the Bear Paw Quilt by Barbara Smucker

The Seasons Sewn: A Year in Patchwork by Ann Whitford Paul

Royalty—
First Week

Introducing the Weekly Curriculum Theme

Weekly Curriculum Vocabulary

dragon
king
prince
princess
queen
royal
royalty
scepter

Materials

costume crown and jewelry

1. Wear the crown (a paper one is fine) and lots of jewelry. Introduce yourself as a queen/king or princess/prince.
2. Encourage the children to talk about their ideas about royalty.

Drawing Dragons

Art

Materials

paper • crayons and markers

1. Talk with the children about dragons, which play a prominent role in some "Once upon a time" stories about royalty. The prince or king becomes a hero by killing (slaying) the dragon.
2. Be certain the children understand that dragons and dinosaurs are not the same thing.
3. Show the children an easy way to draw a dragon. Begin by drawing an uppercase letter D. Turn the page so the D is lying on its back with the hump in the air. This is the dragon's body.
4. Add an S-shaped neck and a triangle head and an S-shaped tail.
5. Add triangle plates sticking up on the dragon's back.
6. Draw facial features and fire coming from the dragon's mouth.

Scepters

Art

Materials

paint-stirring sticks (from paint store) • aluminum foil • variety of ribbons

1. Give each child a paint-stirring stick to make a royal scepter.
2. Show them how to wrap the stick with aluminum foil, then tie ribbons around the stick's indented area.
3. Encourage them to use these in dramatic play.

Princess and the Pea

Art and Language

Materials

The Princess and the Pea (any version) • variety of wallpaper samples • glue sticks • drawing paper • markers • hole punch • green construction paper scraps

1. Read or tell the story of *The Princess and the Pea*.
2. Make the art materials available to the children. Encourage them to cut out mattress shapes from the wallpaper and glue these to their drawing paper in a tall stack.
3. Encourage them to draw a princess on top of the mattresses.
4. Help the children use the hole punch to make a green circle and glue that below the mattresses for the pea.

Royal Crowns

Art and Math

Materials

tagboard ● scissors ● child-safe scissors ● construction paper ● holographic wrapping paper ● glue stick ● stapler (adult only)

1. Cut out strips of tagboard 5" high and long enough to encircle a child's head and overlap by 2".
2. Give each child a strip of tagboard to make a crown. Encourage each child to cut the top of her tagboard to resemble a crown's top.
3. Beforehand, cut construction paper and holographic wrapping paper into diamonds and circles. Invite the children to select paper shapes and make a repeating pattern with them. Ask them to glue the pattern to their crown.
4. Help fit the crowns to the children's heads by overlapping and stapling the ends (adult only).

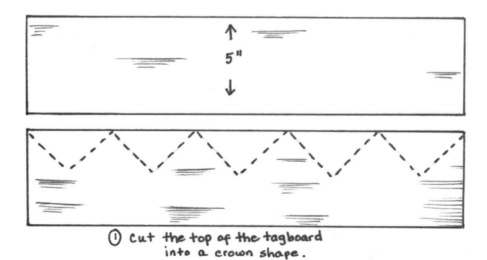

① Cut the top of the tagboard into a crown shape.

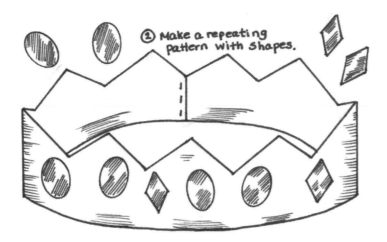

The Princess and the Pea

Language

Materials

The Princess and the Pea (any version) ● pillows ● small wad of green construction paper ● doll or stuffed animal

1. Read or tell the story of *The Princess and the Pea*. Show the pictures to the children.
2. Let the children re-tell the story using the dolls and animals as props. At the proper place in the story, encourage them to stack up the pillows and put the "pea" (wad of green construction paper) under these. Have them put the doll on top, and move it around and around while it tries to get comfortable. Let them continue to the story's conclusion.
3. Place the props and books where the children can use them to retell the story.

Old King Cole

Language

Materials

any Mother Goose book containing the rhyme "Old King Cole" ● chart paper ● marker ● scissors

1. Read the Mother Goose rhyme, "Old King Cole."
2. Write the rhyme on chart paper. Read the chart with the children, then cut the paper into strips with one line of the rhyme on each strip.
3. Give one strip to each of several children and ask them to place the strips in the correct order. Have the group re-read the rhyme from the strips. If the strips are out of order, help the children discover that as they read.
4. Repeat daily until every child has a turn.

The Royal Ball
Movement and Music

Materials
old fancy dresses and men's shirts ● old jewelry for males and females ● music ● mirrors

1. Find old fancy dresses, men's shirts, and jewelry from yard sales and thrift stores. Cut off the bottoms of the dresses (ball gowns) to fit the children.
2. To make royal capes, cut off the sleeves of the shirts and the front below the second button from the top, leaving the collar. The children can button the top two buttons to hold the cape in place.
3. Play music and encourage the children to dress up for a royal ball. Children will enjoy dancing together or alone and acting out scenes from familiar royal stories.
4. Leave the dress-up props where the children can use them during free play.

Exploring Gems
Science

Materials
old jewelry—donated from parents or purchased at yard sales ● "jewels" from craft/fabric store (sold to decorate clothing) ● plastic dishpans or storage containers ● tweezers ● magnifying glasses ● sorting trays or egg cartons

1. Put the old jewelry and "jewels" into plastic dishpans or storage containers. Show the children how to pick up a "gem" using tweezers or their fingers and use the magnifiers to enlarge their view.
2. Encourage the children to arrange the gems in the sorting trays. They may classify them by color or size, or they may choose another criteria. Ask them to explain their choices.

Caution: Supervise closely if children still put objects in their mouths.

Pretzel Scepter
Snack/Cooking

Materials
large rod pretzels ● canned vanilla frosting ● edible candy sparkles

1. Encourage each child to make an edible scepter by dipping a rod pretzel into vanilla frosting, then into edible candy sparkles.

Fruity Scepter

Snack/Cooking

Materials

sanitized, new Popsicle sticks, 1 for each child ● bananas, ½ for each child ● honey poured onto several plates ● crushed corn flakes or graham cracker crumbs ● freezer, if possible

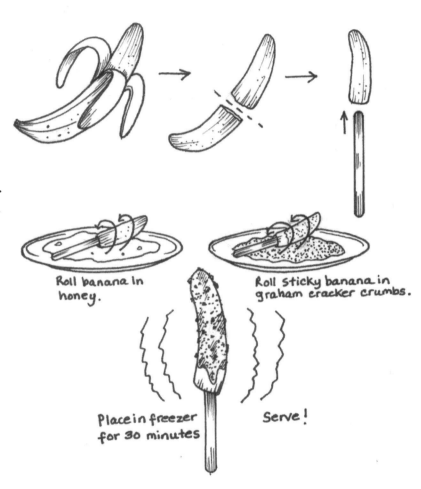

Roll banana in honey.

Roll sticky banana in graham cracker crumbs.

Place in freezer for 30 minutes

Serve!

1. Give each child ½ of a banana. Ask them to peel their banana halves and push the Popsicle stick into the flat end.
2. Ask them to roll the banana in honey until it is coated and then roll the sticky banana in the crushed crumbs.
3. If possible, place these in a freezer for 30 minutes, and then serve.
4. Yum!

Learning Center Ideas

Dramatic Play Area

Materials

bath towels for royal capes ● paper crowns ● scepters (have a few children make additional ones during art)

1. Place these materials in the Dramatic Play Area to enhance royal play.

Related Books (Also see list on page 276 in Royalty—Second Week.)

Cinderella by Charles Perrault. Choose several versions and have the children compare the illustrations.

Cinder-Elly by Frances Minters

The Frog Prince by Jacob Grimm (There are many illustrated versions; choose several and compare illustrations.)

King Bidgood's in the Bathtub by Audrey Wood

Mud Is Cake by Pam Munoz Ryan

The Paper Bag Princess by Robert N. Munsch

The Paper Princess by Elisa Kleven

The Princess and the Pea by Hans Christian Andersen (Choose several versions and have the children compare the illustrations.)

Royalty—
Second Week

Introducing the Weekly Curriculum Theme

Materials

any version of *The Frog Prince*

1. Read the story to the children. (This is a long story; you might prefer to tell a shortened story while showing the illustrations.)
2. Discuss the story and how the princess wasn't honest with the frog. Discuss the importance of keeping promises and only making promises you intend to keep.
3. Read or tell the story again on another day. Encourage the children to add motions and sound effects when you say the following:
   - princess—Children stroke their hair, bat their eyelashes, and say, "Ooooooh, I'm soooo pretty."
   - ball—Children pantomime bouncing a ball and say, "B-bounce, b-bounce, b-bounce."
   - frog—Children say, "Ribit, ribit."
   - king—Children look stern and say, "I am the king!"
   - prince—Children smile and say, "I told you so."

Weekly Curriculum Vocabulary

frog
castle
sand castle
tarts

Royal Castle

Art

Materials

large appliance boxes with ends removed ● pencil ● craft knife (adult only) ● duct tape ● tempera paint in tall plastic cups ● paintbrushes ● wallpaper sample books ● scissors ● glue

1. Cut several appliance boxes from top to bottom along one corner so the boxes can be opened and laid out flat, side by side (adult only).
2. Draw a simple castle shape along the tops of the boxes, then cut along this line with the craft knife (adult only). The finished castle should be no more than 4' tall (so you can see inside.)
3. Cut out a few windows and two doors (adults only).
4. Tape the flat boxes together, and then stand them upright.
5. Let the children paint the castle. Encourage them to cut items from wallpaper samples to glue to the insides and outsides of the castle.
6. They can use the finished castle in their dramatic play indoors and out.

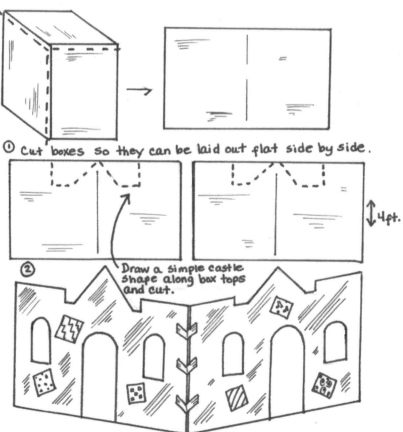

① Cut boxes so they can be laid out flat side by side.

② Draw a simple castle shape along box tops and cut.

↕ 4ft.

③ Cut out doors and windows. Let children paint and decorate with wallpaper samples. Stand upright and tape together.

Royalty Rhymes

Language

Materials

any book of Mother Goose rhymes

1. Many Mother Goose rhymes are about royalty. Read these to the children and use them to explore rhyming words.

Royal Questions

Language

Materials

chart paper • marker

1. Write the following Mother Goose rhyme on the chart:

   Pussycat, pussycat where have you been?
   I've been to London to visit the queen.
   Pussycat, pussycat what did you there?
   I frightened a little mouse under the chair.

2. Use the written rhyme to explore question marks.
3. Ask the children to read and act out the rhyme.

Castles

Language

Materials

pictures of castles • picture books about castles (see page 276)

1. Discuss the idea of castles as people's homes. What sorts of rooms do the children think they would find in castles? Bedrooms? Dining rooms? Look in the books to find out what's inside real castles.

Kings and Queens

Math

Materials

chalkboard and chalk (or chart and marker)

1. Practice counting and comparing with this activity. Pose this question, "If everyone in our class today was either a king or a queen, how many kings would we have and how many queens?"
2. Count, and then record the results on the chalkboard. Count each day and compare results with previous days. Do the numbers stay the same or do they change? Why?

The Frog Prince

Outdoors

1. Add a ball to outdoor play so the children can act out the story of *The Frog Prince*.

Sandcastles

Science

Materials

sand table or deep containers ● damp sand (you can buy "play sand" at building supply stores) ● colored plastic beads ● shells and pebbles ● plaster of Paris ● water ● disposable containers and stirring implements

1. Ask the children to look at pictures of real castles.
2. Add enough sand to the sand table (or deep container) so the sand is more than 8" deep. The sand should be damp (not wet) enough to hold its shape when the children dig in it.
3. In turn, ask each child to dig a hole in the sand and line the walls with colored beads and shells or pebbles. Some of these should stick partially into the sand.
4. In a disposable container, mix a small amount of plaster of Paris (just enough to fill the hole) according to package directions. When it thickens, pour this into the hole. Repeat with each child. Write each child's name in his castle's damp plaster.

Caution: Do not pour plaster mixture down a drain. It will solidify and block the drain. Dispose of all plaster in plastic bags in a trashcan.

5. Let the plaster harden over night. The next day, let the children dig out the creations—their very own sandcastles.

6. Provide a soft brush for brushing off excess, loose sand. Encourage the children to use their castles in the Block Area to enhance their royal constructions.

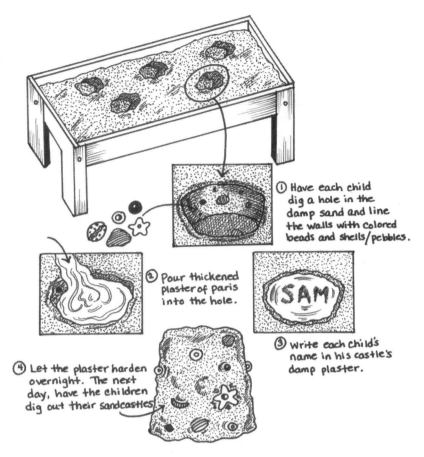

① Have each child dig a hole in the damp sand and line the walls with colored beads and shells/pebbles.

② Pour thickened plaster of paris into the hole.

③ Write each child's name in his castle's damp plaster.

④ Let the plaster harden overnight. The next day, have the children dig out their sandcastles.

Royal Fruit Compote

Snack/Cooking

Materials

can opener (adult only) • canned peach and pear slices • paper plates • plastic knives with serrated blades • individual plastic bowls, one for each child • raisins • tablespoon for serving raisins • plastic spoons, one for each child

1. The adult opens the cans and partially drains the fruits.
2. Give each child a peach slice and a pear half on a paper plate.
3. Using the plastic knife, the child cuts the fruit into small bits.
4. Each child puts her fruit bits into a into a plastic bowl, and then adds a tablespoonful of raisins to the bowl.
5. Encourage the children to stir their fruit with a spoon, then eat the royal concoction.

The Queen's Tarts

Snack/Cooking

Materials

Mother Goose book with *The Queen of Hearts* ● aluminum foil ● refrigerated biscuits ● red jelly or jam ● teaspoon ● toaster oven/regular oven (adult only) ● lemonade made from a mix

1. Read "The Queen of Hearts" to the children. Talk about tarts, which are small pastries with red jam inside.
2. Working in small groups, give each child a piece of foil and a refrigerated biscuit. Ask them to place their biscuit on their foil.
3. Show each child how make a heart indentation in his biscuit by placing his thumb tip just to the left of the biscuit's center and pressing down. Tell him to raise just the very tip of his thumb, move that slightly to the right, and press down again. This will form a heart.
4. Have the children put a small amount of jelly in the heart indentations. Show them how to use the thumb and forefinger to crimp the edges of their tarts, slightly pulling the edges upwards.
5. Write each child's name on his piece of foil.
6. Bake the tarts (on the foil) according to the directions on the biscuit can (adult only).
7. Cool thoroughly, and then serve with "royal" lemonade.

Learning Center Ideas

Block Area

1. Inspire young architects by putting books with pictures of castles in the Block Area.

Related Books (See also list on page 270 of Royalty—First Week.)

1-2-3 Draw Knights Castles & Dragons: A Step by Step Guide by Freddie Levin
Castle by David MacAulay
Castles and Fortresses by Robin S. Oggins (adult "coffee table book")
Country Series: Castles of England, Scotland & Wales by Paul Johnson (adult "coffee table book")
Great Irish Houses and Castles by Jacqueline O'Brien (adult "coffee table book")
Living in Castle Times by Robyn Gee
What Were Castles For? by Phil Roxbee Cox

Table Talk

Materials

pictures of tables

1. Show the children pictures of a variety of tables (from furniture store advertisements, home and antiques magazines, interior decorating and art books, storybooks, and so on).
2. Talk about the tables and about places where people might see tables.
3. Discuss ways that people use tables and how tables in different locations are used in different ways. (For example, tables in the kitchen are used for preparing food, eating meals, and so on; tables in department stores hold stacks of clothes or other items.)

Weekly Curriculum Vocabulary

estimate
table
under
underneath

Mosaics

Art

Materials

pictures of mosaics ● colorful scrap paper ● scissors ● construction paper ● glue sticks ● clear plastic tablecloth

1. Show the children pictures of mosaics and if possible, mosaic tabletops. Tell them that some tabletops are made of mosaic tiles or mosaic wood shapes.
2. Beforehand, cut colorful scrap paper into small, random shapes. Show the children how to glue the small paper scraps on the larger paper, leaving space in between the shapes to look like mosaics.
3. Challenge them to create a mosaic design for a tabletop.
4. Display these on a classroom tabletop and cover them with a clear plastic tablecloth, creating your own classroom mosaic tabletop.

Drawing Upside Down

Art

Materials

pictures of the mural on the ceiling of the Sistine Chapel, optional ● classroom tables ● large paper ● masking tape ● crayons and markers

1. If possible, show pictures of the Sistine Chapel. Tell the children that the artist, Michelangelo, had to lie on his back on a high scaffold in order to draw and paint this famous work of art on a very high ceiling.
2. Tape paper to the underside of the tables.
3. In this group activity, ask the children to go underneath the tables to draw and color on the paper.
4. Display their finished creations, or leave them on the tables' undersides and invite people to observe them there.

If Tables Could Talk

Bulletin Board and Language

Materials

large classroom table ● digital or instant camera ● sentence strips ● marker

1. Take a photograph of the classroom table, enlarge it (if possible), and hang the enlarged photo in the center of a bulletin board.
2. Hold a group meeting under the real table and discuss things the children remember doing at that table during the school day and year.
3. Ask the children, "What would this table say if it could talk?"
4. Write their answers on sentence strips and put these on the bulletin board around the photo of the table.

Under the Tables

Dramatic Play

Materials

classroom tables ● bedspreads, sheets, or tablecloths ● classroom toys ● flashlights

1. Cover each classroom table with a bedspread, sheet, or cloth that hangs almost to the floor.
2. Allow the children to take toys and flashlights under the covered tables and play under them.
3. For safety, be sure that you can see and supervise what is going on under each table.

A Visit to a Furniture Store

Field Trip

Materials

drawing paper ● markers and crayons

1. Arrange a short visit to a furniture store to look at the variety of tables. Discuss the sizes and uses of each.
2. When you return to school, encourage the children to draw pictures of what they saw. Write their dictated words.
3. Display the pictures so the children can see and compare all of them.

Story Time

Language

1. Have story time with the group sitting or lying under the classroom tables.

The "Able" Family

Language

Materials

sentence strips ● marker

1. On sentence strips, make word cards of words in the __"able" family. They can be real words or nonsense words.
2. Show the children the word "table." Cover the initial consonant, T. Read the word's remaining sound: able. Repeat.
3. Show the children additional words, one at a time. Encourage the children to "guess-read" them—*cable, dable, fable, gable,* and so on.
4. Add additional words the children suggest.
5. Place these in a learning area where children can play with them and practice their reading skills.

How Many?

Math

Materials

classroom tables

1. Ask the children to estimate how many children can fit under a designated table. Check their prediction.
2. Repeat the activity using a different table.

Estimating Table Sizes

Math

Materials

classroom tables • yarn • scissors

1. Ask the children to look at a classroom table from all sides. Ask them whether they think the table is taller than it is wide.
2. Use the yarn to measure both distances; compare yarn lengths. Were the children's estimations correct?
3. Repeat with another table.
4. Repeat comparing the table's height and its length.

Follow the Leader

Movement

1. Choose a child to be leader. Encourage the leader to lead their friends *under, around, beside,* and *over* the classroom tables.
2. Choose new leaders. Challenge each new leader to think of a different way to move—sideways, on tiptoes, crawling, and other ways.

"We Have a Table"

Music

1. With the children, sing the following song:

> Tune: ***Bingo***
> *We have a table at our school,*
> *And table is its name, oh!*
> *T-A-B-L-E, T-A-B-L-E, T-A-B-L-E,*
> *A table at our school.*

Outdoor Art

Outdoors

Materials

art supplies, including paper • picnic table or card table • masking tape

1. Bring the art supplies outdoors and set them up on a picnic table or card table.

2. If it is windy, tape the paper to the table's surface.

3. Tape finished art work to the play yard fence.

Eating at a Table
Snack/Cooking

Materials
instant oatmeal ● hot water ● bowls and spoons

1. Remind the children that the Three Bears ate their porridge while sitting at a table in their kitchen.

2. Tell the children that porridge is a cooked cereal like oatmeal. Serve the children porridge (oatmeal) for today's snack and eat at the table, just like the bears.

Tabletops
Center Activities

1. This week, emphasize tabletop activities, such as working on puzzles, building with table blocks, reading at the table, listening to tapes, serving pretend meals, and so on.

Learning Center Ideas
Dramatic Play Area

Materials
advertising circulars and home decorating magazines with pictures of tables ● tablecloths ● place mats ● napkins ● plastic vase and plastic flowers

1. Add a few of these items to the Dramatic Play Area so the children can explore ideas about tables and can beautify the tables in the classroom.

Related Books
Bread and Jam for Frances by Russell Hoban
The Table Where Rich People Sit by Byrd Baylor
The Wee Little Woman by Byron Barton

Art Themes

Exploring Color

Introducing the Weekly Curriculum Theme

Weekly Curriculum Vocabulary

blue
color
dark
green
light
orange
purple
red
yellow

Materials

un-colored modeling dough or playdough from your favorite recipe •
red, blue, and yellow food coloring

1. Before presenting this weekly theme to the children, make Magic Color Dough Balls. Flatten out approximately two tablespoons of freshly made modeling dough or playdough. Add a few drops of one color of food coloring to the center of this. Fold over the dough, hiding the color within. Without kneading, gently squeeze the dough into a ball shape. Repeat, making a ball of color-added dough for each child. Make an equal number of each color.

2. Show the balls to the children and ask them to describe what they see, including the balls' neutral color.

3. Give a ball of dough to each child and encourage her to play with the dough. As the children knead, squeeze, and flatten the dough, the colors will appear, causing much excitement.

4. When the children finish playing with their dough, ask them to place the separate pieces in the Art Area.

5. When the children later begin combining colors, encourage them to observe and talk about any changes.

Color Wheels—A Three-Day Activity

Art

Day One

Materials

white paper plates, 1 per child • pencil • red, blue, and yellow tempera paint • paintbrushes

1. On each plate, lightly draw a small circle at "12:00", "4:00", and "8:00".
2. Give one plate to each child and call their attention to the penciled circles.
3. Ask the children to put red paint at "12:00", yellow paint at "4:00", and blue paint at "8:00".
4. Explain that these are *primary colors* and when combined, they make other colors.

Day Two

Materials

color wheels from Day One • yellow, blue, and red tempera paint • teaspoons • cotton swabs

1. Review the primary colors—red, blue, and yellow.
2. Ask the children to spoon a small amount of red paint and a small amount of blue paint halfway between the red and blue circles on their color wheel. Show them how to mix the two colors with a cotton swab, yielding a new color. Discuss the changes.
3. Repeat step #2, blending blue and yellow halfway between the blue and yellow circles.
4. Repeat step #2 again, blending yellow and red halfway between the yellow and red circles.
5. Introduce these three new colors as *secondary colors*, those formed by combining any two primary colors.
6. Let the children compare their resulting colors. Each will be slightly different, depending on the proportions of original colors they used.

Day Three—Exploring Warm and Cool Colors

Materials

color wheel ● white drawing paper folded in half, then opened ● orange and blue crayons ● *Rabbit's Good News* by Ruth Lercher Bornstein, optional

1. Hold the color wheel with red at the top. Ask the children to look at the colors on the right side of the wheel. These are called "warm colors." Discuss why this is so. What color is fire? What color do we think of for the sun?
2. Ask the children to look at the colors on the left side of the wheel. These are called "cool colors." Discuss why this is so. What color do we think of for cold swimming pool water?
3. Give each child a piece of white drawing paper that has been folded in half, then opened. Provide crayons, and ask the children to draw an orange sun in a blue sky on one half of their paper.
4. Ask the children to draw a blue sun in a yellow sky on the other half.
5. Display all of the pictures and discuss how they look. Which ones "feel" right? Which colors "feel" warm? Which colors "feel" cool?
6. If possible, read *Rabbit's Good News* by Ruth Lercher Bornstein. Call the children's attention to the change of colors from winter's cool blues and grays to early summer's warm yellows.

Mixing Our Own Colors

Art

Materials

tempera paint in red, yellow, and blue ● three plastic bowls ● plastic spoons ● small paper cups, 3 per child ● cotton swabs ● bulletin board paper ● marker ● drawing paper

1. Pour the red, yellow, and blue paint in individual bowls.
2. Give each child three small paper cups. Ask children, in turn, to spoon a bit of one color into each of their three cups.
3. Tell the children to add one or two additional colors to their cups, allowing each child to add the proportions he desires.
4. Ask the children to stir their paints with cotton swabs.
5. Encourage the children to use the swab and their paints to paint three small areas of the bulletin board paper, using a different color for each.
6. Display the resulting creation with the caption "Our Colors."
7. Let the children use their remaining paint on drawing paper.

Color Values

Art and Science

Materials

white and blue paint ● eyedroppers ● long piece of white bulletin board paper ●
cotton swabs

1. *Value* refers to the darkness or lightness of a color. Encourage the children to experiment with changing the value of a primary color.
2. Working with one child at a time, ask her to drop one drop of white and one drop of blue paint close together on white paper. Then ask her to use a clean swab to stir the colors together.
3. Repeat, but this time, ask the child to drop one drop of white and two drops of blue paint, and then stir with a swab. Repeat using other proportions.
4. Ask the child which one makes a lighter value: mixing a small amount of white and a larger amount of blue, or mixing a small amount of blue and a larger amount of white?
5. Repeat this with all of the children, and then display the paper where all can see it. Encourage them to look at the variety of values they produced. Can they find any matching colors?
6. Invite families and others to see the display.

Color Addition

Math

Materials

tempera paints in primary colors ● 3 paintbrushes, one for each color ● long sheets
of white paper ● marker

1. Use color mixing to help children practice using the mathematical symbols "plus" and "equals."
2. Working with one child at a time, paint the child's left hand with a primary color of his choosing. Help the child make a handprint on the left edge of the paper.
3. Write a "plus" sign to the right of the handprint.
4. Paint the child's right hand with a different primary color of his choosing. Help the child make a handprint to the right of the plus sign.
5. Write an "equals" sign to the right of this print.
6. Re-paint both of the child's hands with the two original colors. Ask the child to vigorously rub his hands together, forming a new color on both. Help the child make both handprints to the right of the equals sign. Then ask the child to wash his hands.

7. Repeat with every child.

8. When the paint dries, write the appropriate words under each equation. Display the pictures where families can admire them.

9. Later, gather the pages into a book for children to read to each other.

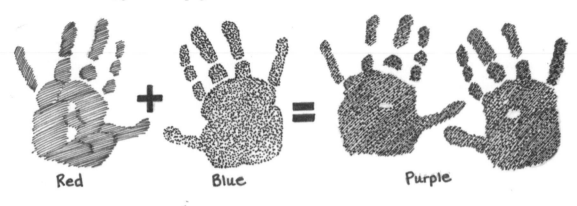

Red, Yellow, and Blue

Music

1. Sing the following song with the children.

> Tune: ***Three Blind Mice***
> *Red, yellow, blue. (repeat)*
> *What can you do? (repeat)*
> *We make other colors, oh, yes we do.*
> *Orange and green and purple too.*
> *Mix us together. It's fun to do.*
> *Red, yellow, blue.*

Colorful Surprise Cookies

Snack/Cooking

Materials

canned vanilla frosting • blue, red, and yellow food coloring • 3 bowls • 3 teaspoons • vanilla wafers, 2 for each child

1. Divide the frosting into three batches. Use food color to tint each batch a different primary color.

2. Put a spoon into each bowl of frosting.

3. Give two vanilla wafers to each child.

4. Encourage the children to choose two colors of frosting and put a small amount of one color on the bottom of one wafer and a small amount of the other color on the bottom of the other wafer.

5. Ask them to touch their wafers together gently so the two colors of frosting touch, and then rub them together.

6. Talk about what happened.

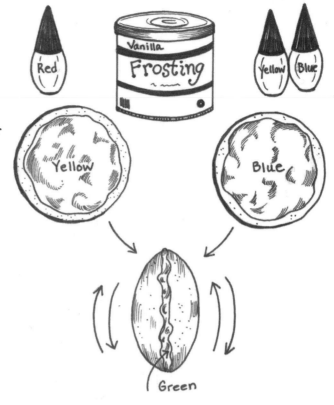

Learning Center Ideas

Art Area

Materials

home decorating magazines ● paint sample chips ● decorative paper scraps

1. Place these materials in the Art Area where the children can explore them and use the colors in their artwork.

Related Books

The Art Lesson by Tomie dePaola
Brown Bear, Brown Bear, What Do You See? by Bill Martin, Jr.
Color Dance by Ann Jonas
A Color of His Own by Leo Lionni
Growing Colors by Bruce McMillan
Is It Red? Is It Yellow? Is It Blue? by Tana Hoban
Little Mouse's Painting by Diane Wolkstein
Mouse Paint by Ellen Stoll Walsh
My Colors/Mis Colores by Rebecca Emberley (a book in two languages)
Rabbit's Good News by Ruth Lercher Bornstein
Red, Blue, Yellow Shoe by Tana Hoban

Art Museum

Weekly Curriculum Vocabulary

art
frame
Jackson Pollock
Jasper Johns
museum
portrait
Thomas Gainsborough
Thomas Lawrence

Materials

paper • crayons

1. Visit an art museum with the children. Arrange in advance for a guide who has experience working with young children to take you through the museum.
2. When you return, ask the children to draw a picture of something they saw at the museum.
3. Write the children's dictated words on their papers.

Fancy Portraits

Art

Materials

drawing paper ● markers and crayons

1. Explain to the children that before cameras were invented, some people asked artists to paint their portraits so they would have lasting pictures of themselves. Sometimes the artist would paint them in fancy clothes, wearing a lot of jewelry, so they would appear to be very rich.
2. Challenge the children to draw portraits of themselves in fancy clothes and jewelry.
3. Display the pictures where all can enjoy them.

Painting Our Pets

Art

Materials

easel paper ● easel paint ● brushes

1. Tell the children that some people like to have portraits painted of their pets.
2. Encourage them to paint their own pets (or their pretend pets) at the easel.
3. Display the portraits and invite parents and others to view the exhibition.

In the Style of Jackson Pollock

Art and Bulletin Board

Materials

Olivia by Ian Falconer ● examples of Jackson Pollock's work from art books or the Internet ● shower curtains or shower curtain liners ● large pieces of bulletin board paper ● tempera paint ● turkey basters ● squeeze bottles, such as detergent, ketchup, and so on ● paint-stirring sticks ● paint smocks

1. Read *Olivia*, the story of a pig that spends rainy days at the art museum. Impressed with Jackson Pollock's work, Olivia makes a reproduction on her family's living room wall.

2. Show the children pictures of Jackson Pollock's work with its many drips, splashes, and dribbles.

3. Set up an area where the children can drip and dribble paint over large pieces of bulletin board paper. Cover the area with shower curtains and put the paper on top.

4. Provide paint, turkey basters, squeeze bottles, paint-stirring sticks, and a lot of encouragement. Let several children work on each creation.

5. Display the completed works as bulletin boards with the title "In the Style of Jackson Pollock."

6. Ask the artists to sign their names to their creations.

Choosing Colors for Mounting Our Art

Art and Language

Materials

several picture books • construction paper in a variety of colors • several pieces of child-produced art • drawing paper • scissors • crayons or markers • glue

1. Tell the children that they are going to pretend to be people who frame pictures. They must choose a color frame that will look best with each picture.

2. Open a picture book to any color illustration and show it to the group.

3. One at a time, hold different colors of construction paper behind the page so a few inches of the paper show around the page's edges.

4. Discuss each choice. With the children, narrow the choices to the ones that best complement the illustration. If possible, choose one color.

5. Repeat with other illustrations, other books, and other styles of art.

6. On another day, cut drawing paper into 6 ½" x 9" pieces. Give one to each child to draw a picture.

7. With the group, experiment using different colors of construction paper to see which color provides the best backing for each child's picture.

8. Show the children how to center their pictures on the chosen construction paper.

9. Help the children glue their art to the construction paper.

What Did You Say?

Language

Materials

picture of "Blue Boy" by Thomas Gainsborough ● picture of "Pinkie" by Thomas Lawrence ● (Note: Both of these paintings hang at The Huntington Gallery and can be seen on that website. Search for "Huntington Gallery." You can also look in art books in the library.) ● easel ● paper ● blue, pink, and other colors of tempera paint ● paintbrushes

1. Show the children a picture of "Blue Boy." Ask them why they think he might be called that. Explain to the children that he was painted by a man named Thomas Gainsborough and that he is dressed in clothes from a long, long time ago.
2. Encourage the children to imagine and discuss what he might be thinking or where he might be going.
3. Show the children a picture of "Pinkie." Why do they think she is called that? Tell the children that a man named Thomas Lawrence painted her and that she is dressed in clothes from a long, long time ago.
4. Encourage the children to imagine and discuss what she might be thinking or where she might be going.
5. Ask the children if they think these two might be friends. Tell them that these pictures hang side-by-side in an art museum, and they have been together a long time.
6. Encourage the children to imagine and discuss what "Blue Boy" and "Pinkie" talk about when no one is at the museum.
7. Put blue and pink paint with other colors at the easel so the children can experiment with portraits, if desired.

Jasper Johns' Numbers

Math

Materials

books of Jasper Johns' work ● Jasper Johns' art on the Internet ● drawing paper ● crayons, markers, colored pencils, and paint ● paintbrushes

1. Jasper Johns did many paintings filled with numerals. Find some of these in art books (from the library) and on the Internet.
2. Show these pictures to the children and talk about them.
3. Provide them with the drawing materials and encourage them to make pictures in the style of Jasper Johns.

Posing

Movement

Materials

pictures of any paintings that have people in them

1. Show the pictures, one at a time, to the children. Challenge them to pose like the people in pictures.

A Salty Painting

Science

Materials

paper ● tempera paint, any colors ● paintbrushes ● table salt or kosher salt

1. Give each child a piece of paper. Encourage them to paint bands of color on their papers.
2. While the paint is wet, ask them to sprinkle salt generously over part of the painting.
3. Talk about what they see happening.
4. Discuss how the paintings look when they are dry. Compare the "salted" and "unsalted" areas.

Learning Center Ideas

Language Area

Materials
books with pictures of paintings by well-known artists • catalogs from art museums • pictures of art from the Internet

1. Place the books, catalogs, and pictures in the Library Area and encourage the children to read the books in pairs or small groups and to talk about what they see, such as what they like and what they don't care for.

Related Books
A Is for Artist: A Getty Museum Alphabet by John Harris
Child's Book of Art by Lucy Micklethwait
A Child's Book of Art: Discover Great Paintings by Lucy Micklethwait
Getting to Know the World's Greatest Artists by Mike Venezia (Any in the series, which are individual books for children about great artists and their work)
Jackson Pollock by Ellen G. Landau
Olivia by Ian Falconer
Squeaking of Art: The Mice Go to the Museum by Monica Wellington

We Are Artists, Too

Introducing the Weekly Curriculum Theme

Weekly Curriculum Vocabulary

art
art critic
Eric Carle
Mondrian
still life

Materials

books by Eric Carle ● fingerpaint ● drawing paper ● tempera paint ● crayons ● scissors ● glue

1. Give the children a variety of books by Eric Carle to explore together. Focus on examining the illustrations. What do the children notice?
2. Explain that Eric Carle's illustrations are collage creations made with painted and colored paper. Some are fingerpainted, some are crayon on top of dry paint, and some are paint over crayon strokes. Other papers look like the artist dragged a comb or other implement through the wet paint. What other techniques can you and the children find?
3. Accept all possibilities that the children suggest. Tell the children to remember these techniques, because they will be using them, too. Explain that they will decorate paper that will later be cut up and shared with the whole class. Everyone will make a collage with decorated paper.
4. Provide the children with the art materials and support their efforts to create interesting patterns on the paper.
5. When all of the artwork is dry, cut each picture into 4" x 5" rectangles, 1" x 2" rectangles, and triangles and circles of several sizes. Save all scraps.
6. Offer these to the children with glue and more drawing paper. Challenge them to make a collage from the shapes and the scraps.
7. Display the children's creations with a few of Eric Carle's books and invite families and others to view the exhibit of "Art in the Style of Eric Carle."

Inspired Art

Art

Materials

books with pictures of paintings by well-known artists ● catalogs from art museums ● pictures of art from the Internet ● drawing paper ● markers

1. Show children a simple picture of a painting with a few colors.
2. Encourage the children to make a picture using some of the colors they see in the picture you are showing.

More Inspired Art

Art

Materials

books with pictures of paintings by well-known artists ● catalogs from art museums ● pictures of art from the Internet ● drawing paper ● markers

1. Show the children a picture with a realistic theme.
2. Encourage the children to draw a picture of something they are reminded of when they look at the picture you are showing. Accept all responses.
3. On another day, show the children an abstract picture and encourage them to draw a picture of something that is similar (not identical) to the picture you are showing. Accept all responses.

My Mona Lisa

Art and Language

Materials

picture of "Mona Lisa" by Leonardo Da Vinci ● any children's picture books illustrated by Don Wood (or other artist who includes backgrounds in his or her work) ● oil pastels or crayons ● pastel shades of construction paper

1. Show the children a picture of "Mona Lisa" and tell them that it was painted by Leonardo Da Vinci.
2. Tell the children this is called a *portrait*. Paintings of people are called portraits.

3. Explore the picture together, noticing details such as the color in her face, color of her eyes and hair, and the way she is posing with her hands crossed.

4. With the children, re-examine a picture of "Mona Lisa." Examine the picture's background and explain that many artists include a background in their pictures.

5. Show picture books illustrated by Don Wood, or other books illustrated with art that has backgrounds.

6. Put the children into pairs. Ask one child in each pair to sit in a chair and pose like Mona Lisa. Ask the other child to study the first, noticing eye and hair coloring, hairstyle, and clothing colors and style.

7. Encourage this child to use the art materials to draw a portrait of the posing child. Remind the artist to add an interesting background.

8. On another day, have the children switch roles.

My Mondrian

Art and Language

Materials

picture of "Composition in Blue and Yellow" by Piet Mondrian ● picture of "Composition in Red, Yellow and Blue" by Piet Mondrian ● white construction paper ● blue, yellow, red, and black crayons ● black construction paper ● blue, yellow, and red construction paper ● scissors ● glue sticks

1. Show the children the "Composition in Blue and Yellow" picture. Tell them it was painted by Piet Mondrian. Discuss whether the picture looks complicated or easy to make. Ask if they think they could make a picture like that.

2. Ask the children if they think Piet Mondrian drew the black areas first or last. Why do they think that?

3. Talk about the shapes in the painting. Remind the children that they can find shapes in many paintings.

4. Repeat steps one through three with "Composition in Red, Yellow and Blue."

5. Put the pictures where children can see them.

6. Give white paper and crayons to the children and challenge them to make a picture "in the style of Piet Mondrian."

7. On another day, give them whole sheets of black construction paper and smaller pre-cut squares and rectangles of blue, yellow, and red construction paper. Provide glue sticks and challenge the children to glue the smaller shapes to the black paper to create more art "in the style of Piet Mondrian."

8. Display the art where children, visitors, and families can enjoy it.

Exploring and Drawing Flowers

Art, Language, and Science

Materials

pictures of floral still-life paintings (in adult art books and from the Internet) ●
flowers (from the yard or the grocery store, or artificial) ● non-breakable vases ●
drawing paper ● oil pastels or crayons ● children's picture books about gardens

1. Show the children pictures of paintings of floral arrangements.
2. Compare a few of these. Do they have the same kinds of flowers or different flowers? Do they have the same numbers of flowers, or different? Which do the children think are most interesting? Why?
3. Encourage the children to explore the fresh or artificial flowers. Ask them to look for and compare shapes, colors, and number of blossoms on the stems.
4. Encourage the children to make floral arrangements using the flowers and vases. Challenge them to use the art materials to draw pictures of their arrangements.
5. Place children's books with garden illustrations in the Art Area to inspire floral artists.

Art Critiques

Language

Materials

variety of children's picture books with different kinds of illustrations

1. Show the children the illustrations in a variety of picture books. Some are very simple, such as *Harold and the Purple Crayon* by Crockett Johnson and any by Byron Barton or Frank Asch. Some are ornate, such as Don Wood's *Heckedy Peg* and *King Bidgood's in the Bathtub*. Some are colorful collage pictures like those by Eric Carle or Ezra Jack Keats.
2. Discuss the illustrations and how each artist's style is unique, just like the children's illustration styles are unique. Help the children understand that all of the illustrations are "right." There is no "wrong" in art.
3. Encourage the children to talk about what they like about the different styles.
4. Help them understand that "liking" and "not liking" are individual feelings. Neither is wrong.

Art Themes

299

Talking About Leonardo Da Vinci's "Mona Lisa"

Language

Materials

pictures of Da Vinci's paintings and sculptures • picture of "Mona Lisa" painting • cassette recorder and tape • sentence strips

1. Do an Internet search for "Da Vinci" to find pictures of his paintings and sculptures.
2. Show the pictures to the children and tell them the artist's name. Encourage their discussion about the artwork.
3. Show the children a picture of "Mona Lisa." Ask the children what they believe she is thinking about.
4. Ask the children why they think she is smiling. Tell them that people have wondered this ever since Da Vinci first painted the portrait. Encourage them to discuss their thoughts with each other.
5. Record the children's discussion. Later, write their thoughts on sentence strips and display these with a picture of "Mona Lisa."

Learning Center Ideas

Art Area

Materials

books with pictures of paintings by well-known artists • catalogs from art museums • pictures of art from the Internet

1. Place the books and pictures in the Art Area where they can inspire your artists.

Related Books

Art Dog by Thatcher Hurd
The Art Lesson by Tomie dePaola
A Child's Book of Art: Discover Great Paintings by Lucy Micklethwait
Da Vinci by Mike Venezia
Leonardo Da Vinci by Diane Stanley (Although the text is difficult for preschoolers, pre-read the book, explore the artwork together, and tell the children what you read.)
Michelangelo by Diane Stanley
Piet Mondrian by Hans Ludwig C. Jaffe
Any illustrated children's books

Sculptures and Statues

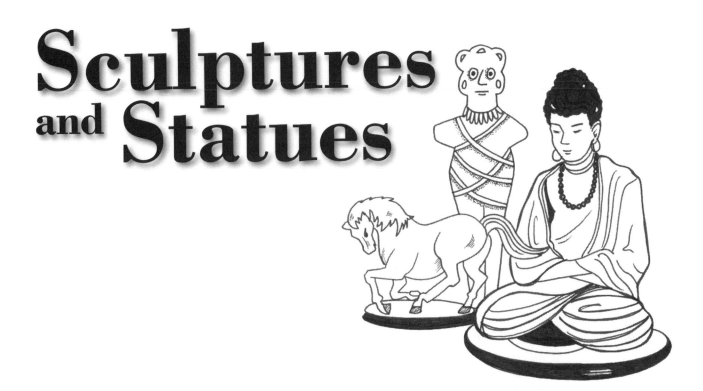

Materials
books with pictures of realistic and abstract sculptures ● a small sculpture (or model of one) ● a simple line drawing of the sculpture

Weekly Curriculum Vocabulary

abstract
realistic
sculpture
statue

1. Show the children several pictures of realistic sculptures. The children may be familiar with the word "statue." Help them understand that statues are a name for sculptures of people or animals.

2. Discuss the meaning of *two-dimensional* and *three-dimensional* as applied to art. Show the children a small sculpture and a drawing of it. Help them see that the flat drawing has two "directions" or dimensions:

   ● "up-and-down" or height
   ● "side-to-side" or width

3. Help them see that the sculpture has three "directions" or dimensions:

   ● "up-and-down" or height
   ● "side-to-side" or width
   ● "back-to-front" or depth

4. Children will probably better understand this if you refer to two-dimensional as "flat" and three-dimensional as "fat."

Small Sculptures

Art

Materials

modeling dough or plastic clay ● plastic knives, forks, and spoons ● plastic tools for shaping clay, optional ● small everyday items, such as toys, wood scraps, bottle caps, paper clips, small blooms cut from artificial flowers, yarn, and so on ● heavy paper plates ● marker ● poster board

1. Provide the materials and challenge the children to create realistic or abstract sculptures. Begin by putting modeling dough on their plates so the creations can be easily moved later.
2. Show the children how they can use the dough to hold the small items in place.
3. Ask the children to label the finished creations with the artist's name.
4. Place these on display in a classroom area labeled "Art Museum" and invite others in to see them.

Berry Basket Sculptures

Art

Materials

plastic berry baskets ● pipe cleaners ● scissors ● construction paper ● hole punch ● ribbons ● plastic beads ● 1" lengths of drinking straws ● aluminum foil strips ● assorted art supplies and recycled materials

1. Cut pipe cleaners into various lengths, leaving some of them uncut. Show the children how to attach berry baskets to each other using the pipe cleaner pieces.
2. Cut construction paper into 1" squares and/or circles. Demonstrate how to use a hole punch to make holes in the construction paper shapes.
3. Encourage the children to brainstorm ways to attach the construction paper shapes and other items to the baskets, creating sculptures. Have them test their ideas.

Abstract Sculptures

Art

Materials

art books written for adults with pictures of modern, abstract sculptures • art books with pictures of realistic sculptures • variety of art materials that can be used for making sculptures, such as clay, foil, paper, tape, ribbon with wire in it, and so on

1. With the children, look at pictures of modern, abstract sculptures.
2. Introduce the word *abstract*. Explain to the children that abstract sculptures might remind us of something we've seen, but they don't look exactly like those things. Sculptures that look like real things are called *realistic* sculptures.
3. Look at more pictures of sculptures and decide if they are realistic or abstract.
4. Challenge the children to use the materials to copy some of these sculptures or to create some of their own.

Giant Sculpture

Art, Math, and Movement

Materials

newspaper (ask parents to donate) • dowel sticks in different diameters • masking tape • crepe paper streamers

1. Ask parent volunteers to help with this activity. Ask the parents to roll tubes of newspaper diagonally on the dowels, tape them with masking tape, and then slide them off the dowels. Make A LOT of these. The more you have, the larger the sculpture can be.
2. Ask the children to help bend some of these newspaper rolls into triangles, with the parents taping the ends together.
3. Ask the parents and children, together, to tape together the tubes in any form— the larger, the better.
4. Show the children how to weave the streamers through the construction to add color and movement.
5. If the sculpture is sturdy, let the children play "Follow the Leader" carefully through the sculpture.

Statues

Field Trip

Materials

camera, optional

1. Take a field trip to see one or more nearby sculptures, statues, or monuments.
2. If you see statues of people, encourage the children to pose their bodies in the same pose as each statue.
3. If possible, take pictures of the children posing and post them where parents and children can see them.

Sculpted Letters and Numerals

Language and Math

Materials

index cards ● marker ● modeling dough

1. Write a numeral or a letter of the alphabet on each of the index cards. Use first letters of children's names and other letters and numerals that the children are learning.
2. Show the children how to roll modeling dough into a "snake" shape.
3. Let them practice doing this with you.
4. Challenge the children to turn their snakes into letter and numeral sculptures, using the index cards as guides.

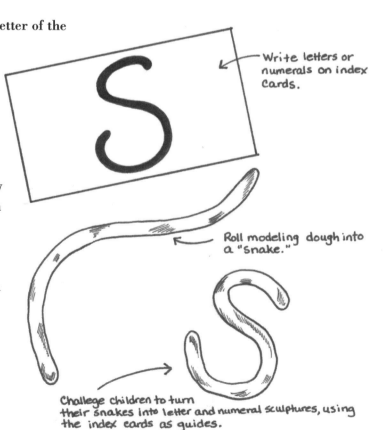

Write letters or numerals on index cards.

Roll modeling dough into a "snake."

Challenge children to turn their snakes into letter and numeral sculptures, using the index cards as guides.

Human Sculptures

Movement

Materials

camera, optional

1. Select one child to strike any kind of pose while standing solidly on two feet.
2. In turn, ask several more children to volunteer to attach themselves to the first child in some way, creating a human sculpture. Children may lean on the first, simply touch one part of their body to a part of the first child, or entwine arms or legs with the first. These children may stand, sit, or lie down.
3. Repeat with the remaining children. Use only a few children each time so the other children can view the sculpture.
4. Over several days, have more children be a part of each sculpture until all the children are a part of one sculpture.
5. If possible, take photos of the human sculptures so the children can see what they created. Enlarged photos can be gathered into a big book titled "Human Sculptures." Let the children take turns taking the book home to share with their families.

Freeze

Music

Materials

any recorded music

1. Encourage the children to dance to the beat as you play any music. Stop the music every 10 to 30 seconds.
2. When the music stops, everyone must "freeze" in position. When the music resumes, they may resume dancing.
3. Looking at everyone's frozen position provides lots of giggles.

Sand Area

Outdoors

Materials

water • containers in a variety of shapes and sizes • shovels and scoops • spatulas

1. In good weather, dampen the sand in a sandbox.
2. Provide containers, shovels, and spatulas, and challenge the children to use them to mold sand for sand sculpting.

Standing Sculptures

Science

Materials

aluminum foil

1. Encourage the children to practice making fist-size balls of foil.
2. Have them twist or fold other pieces of foil into long shapes.
3. Challenge the children to make a foil sculpture that will stand up. Ask them to discuss their efforts, successes, and failures with each other.
4. Children will learn through trial and error that sculptures with a broad base and narrow top will stand; sculptures with a narrow base and wider top will not.

Edible Sculptures

Snack/Cooking

Materials

peanut butter • whipped cream cheese • crackers • cereal pieces in various shapes • thin pretzel sticks • raisins • blunt knives

1. Provide all of the ingredients and challenge each child to use them to construct a sculpture.

Caution: Check for any food allergies, especially peanut allergies, before doing this activity.

2. Put the sculptures on display for all to see before each child eats her own "edible sculpture."
3. Encourage the children to tell each other about their sculptures.

Icy Sculpture

Water Table

Materials

many plastic containers of different shapes and sizes • water • food coloring • kosher salt and table salt in unbreakable saltshakers • turkey basters • gloves and mittens

1. Several days before this activity, freeze water in many different plastic containers. For extra interest, add food coloring to some of the water. Ask the parents to help with the freezing—this activity requires a lot of freezer space.
2. Unmold the ice in the sensory table and provide saltshakers filled with table and kosher salt.
3. Challenge the children to work together to build sculptures with the ice.
4. Let them experiment with the salt to see how it affects the ice. (It helps the pieces stick together.)
5. Have gloves and mittens available to protect the children's hands from the cold ice.

Learning Center Ideas

Art and Language Areas

Materials

masking tape and mailing tape • recyclable plastic containers • small boxes, such as gelatin, rice, and cereal • medium boxes, such as small appliance or mailing cartons • newspaper tubes rolled diagonally on a dowel • cardboard tubes • egg cartons • crepe paper streamers • yarn • scarves • shredded paper • camera and photo album

1. Add a few of these and a variety of other items to the Art Area and encourage the children to use them to create sculptures and constructions.
2. Take photos of the sculptures and display them in a photo album.

Related Books

The Big Brown Box by Marisabina Russo
Look What You Can Make With Tubes by Margie Hayes Richmond
Watch Me Build a Sandcastle (Making Things) by Jack Otten
Any variety of art books written for adults with pictures of realistic and abstract sculptures (available at the library). Place these where children can use them.

Miscellaneous Themes

Fasteners

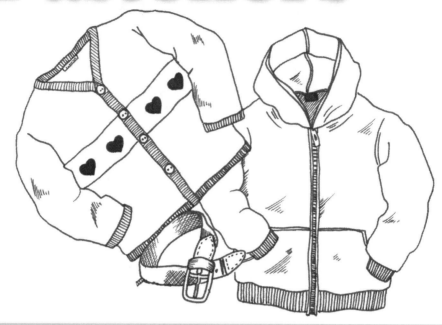

Weekly Curriculum Vocabulary

buckle
button
fasten
fastener
lace
less
more
nail
paper clip
screw
staple
zipper
other types of fasteners suggested by the children

Materials

several pieces of clothing that "fasten" in different ways, such as ones with zippers, buttons, laces, hooks and eyes, buckles, and others

1. Show the clothing items to the children, pointing out some fasteners and demonstrating how they work.
2. Ask the children to think of other ways to fasten clothing.
3. Ask each child, in turn, to stand in front of the group. Ask the group to point out fasteners that the child is wearing and sing the following about one of the fasteners. Substitute the child's name, the name of the fastener, and the name of the garment in the appropriate places in the song:

Tune: *Mary Had a Red Dress*
[Jimmy] has a [button],
[Button], [button].
[Jimmy] has a [button]
On his [shirt].

[LaToya] has [laces],
[Laces], [laces].
[LaToya] has [laces]
On her [shoes].

Fastening Beads to Canvas

Art

Materials

plastic needlepoint/rug canvas with large holes ● pipe cleaners ● plastic pony beads

1. Show the children how to fasten the beads to the canvas. Start by fastening one end of a pipe cleaner to the top of the needlepoint canvas. String a bead onto the pipe cleaner, and then thread the end of the pipe cleaner through a hole in the canvas and bring it up through another hole.
2. Repeat as desired. Use several colors of pipe cleaners to add interest to the project.

Clothespin Holders

Art

Materials

spring-type clothespins ● crayons ● paper

1. Ask each child to choose a crayon and clip a clothespin around it, midway up the crayon's length.
2. Encourage them to hold the clothespin, not the crayon, to color on a piece of paper.

Looking for Fasteners

Field Trip

1. Take the children for a walk around the school building to look for fasteners. Possible fasteners include door hinges, cabinet hinges, mortar between bricks, paper tacked onto bulletin board, and a bulletin board nailed to a wall.

Clothespin Toss

Games

Materials

clothespins ● large coffee can ● smaller coffee can

1. Start the game with each child taking turns standing over the coffee can. Ask the child to drop three clothespins to see how many he can get into the can.
2. Ask the child to step backwards one step, and then try to toss the three clothespins into the can. Each time the child succeeds, he takes a step backwards and repeats until he can no longer get the clothespins in the can.
3. Repeat the game as many times as children are interested, then bring the materials outdoors so the children can practice and play as desired.
4. As skill increases, use the smaller coffee can to add more challenge.

Button, Button

Games

Materials

a button ● other fasteners, optional

1. Choose one child to be "IT." Everyone else sits in a circle, facing inward, with their hands cupped together behind their backs.
2. IT holds a button, hidden in her hands. IT walks around the outside of the circle, pretending to put the button into each child's hands. The rest of the children do not indicate whether they have or have not received the button.
3. At some point, IT does put the button into someone's hands, and continues pretending to place the button in a few more children's hands.
4. IT now goes to the circle's center and asks the children, in turn, "Button, button, who has the button?" The first player to guess correctly becomes IT for the next game.
5. For variety, use other fasteners instead of a button, such as paper clips, bolts, shoelaces, rubber bands, or thread.

Put the Zipper on the Jacket

Games

Materials

bulletin board paper ● jacket shape pattern (see illustration) ● scissors ● construction paper ● markers ● masking tape ● child-size sweater ● glue stick ● string, optional

1. Ask the children to help you make a simple game similar to "Pin the Tail on the Donkey." Cut out a large jacket shape from bulletin board paper, and cut out zipper-size strips of construction paper. Ask each child to draw zigzags on a zipper shape and write his name on the back.

2. Hang the jacket shape on the wall at the children's level. Place a line of masking tape on the floor about 10 feet from the jacket "target."

3. Using the sweater as a blindfold, tie the sleeves around a child's head with the sweater's body hanging over her eyes.

4. Rub the glue stick on the back of the child's paper zipper strip.

5. Stand the blindfolded child behind the masking tape line. Gently turn her one rotation and point her toward the jacket shape. Have her walk, blindfolded, to the jacket to place her zipper where she thinks it belongs.

6. After everyone has had a turn, compare to see which zippers are closest, farthest away, and the same distance. If desired, use pieces of string to measure the distances.

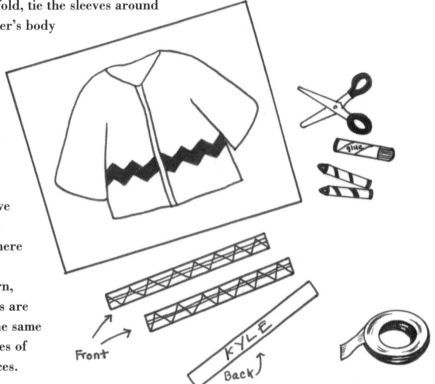

Front

KYLE
Back

Other Fasteners

Language

Materials

variety of fasteners, see below

1. Show the children a variety of fasteners that are used for items other than clothing, such as paper clips, staples, tape, glue, clothespins, nails, screws, and nuts and bolts.

2. Discuss these items and talk about the things they are used to fasten, such as paper, wood, or metal.

3. Make the items available for children to explore and incorporate into their work and play.

Using a Balance Scale

Math

Materials

variety of fasteners ● containers ● balance scale ● measuring cups and scoop

1. Sort a variety of fasteners into separate containers.
2. Show the children how to weigh and compare weights using a balance scale.
3. Ask the children to predict, then check, which will weigh more:

   - 1 cup of buttons or 1 cup of paper clips?
   - 8 clothespins or 4 roofing nails?
   - 1 scoop of screws or 2 scoops of paper clips?
   - 1 cup of blue buttons or 1 cup of white buttons?
   - 15 rubber bands or ½ cup of paper clips?
   - 10 shoelaces or 1 roll of tape?

Fastener Patterns

Math

Materials

variety of fasteners

1. Challenge the children to use a variety of fasteners to make patterns. For example, button/paper clip/button/paper clip, and so on.
2. For variety, ask the children to work opposite each other, in pairs. One child begins a fastener pattern, then the two children trade places and each extends the other's pattern.

Fasten Us

Movement

1. Put the children in pairs, and challenge them to move together as if they are fasteners or as if they are items being fastened together. For example, two children can be a zipper; two can be a shirt being buttoned; two can be a hook and eye or a belt and a belt buckle. Three can be a bottle of glue and two pieces of paper being glued together; three can move as if one is a pushpin attaching paper (the second child) to a bulletin board (the third child).
2. Encourage the children to think of other fastenings to act out.

Exploring and Classifying Fasteners

Science

Materials

sensory table ● assorted buttons (sold in tubs at craft or sewing stores) ● sorting trays, ice cube trays, or egg cartons ● tweezers ● other fasteners

1. Place buttons, sorting trays, and tweezers in the sensory table and encourage the children to explore them freely.

Caution: Supervise closely if children still put small items, such as buttons, in their mouths.

2. Each day, add more sorting trays and one or more of the following items: vinyl-coated paper clips, paper fasteners, metal screws, rolls of tape, and rubber bands.

Cheesy Fastener

Snack/Cooking

Materials

cheese spread or cream cheese ● crackers ● O-shaped dry cereal ● raisins ● small pieces of diced pineapple

1. Provide the foods and challenge the children to use the cheese spread or cream cheese to "fasten together" these snack foods.

Edible Buttons

Snack/Cooking

Materials

refrigerated cookie dough ● tablespoon ● paper plates ● raisins and/or chocolate chips

1. Give each child three tablespoons of cookie dough on a paper plate to shape into a cookie person. Encourage them to use raisins or chocolate chips for buttons.
2. Bake as directed on the dough package.

Learning Center Ideas

Dramatic Play Area

Materials

recycled computer paper ● office supplies, including fasteners ● paper clips, tape, double-faced tape, and glue stick ● real clothing with a variety of fasteners, including buttons, zippers, Velcro, hook and eye, buckles, and snaps

1. Put office supplies, including the fasteners in the Dramatic Play Area and encourage the children to install a "home office."
2. Provide dress-up clothes for the children to wear in their office.

Related Books

All by Myself! by Aliki
Corduroy by Don Freeman
Join it! by Henry Pluckrose
Joseph Had a Little Overcoat by Simms Taback
The Magical, Mystical, Marvelous Coat by Catherine Ann Cullen
Mrs. Toggle's Zipper by Robin Pulver

Happy Un-Birthday

Materials

cupcake ● birthday candle

1. Choose a week when no one in the class, including the teachers, has a birthday. Have a week-long "Happy Un-Birthday" celebration.
2. Show the children a cupcake with a birthday candle in it. Discuss birthdays with the children and how they change as they grow older.

Weekly Curriculum Vocabulary

April
August
birthday
December
February
January
July
June
March
May
November
October
September

Wrapping Two-Dimensional Presents
Art and Language

Materials
paper strips ● white construction paper ● crayons ● markers ● tape

1. Write each child's name on a separate paper strip and fold each one.
2. Ask each child to select a paper strip, open it, and read it. Encourage them to keep this name secret.
3. Give art materials to the children. Ask them to use crayons to draw a picture of something they would like to give as a birthday present to the friend whose name they selected.
4. Write their dictated words beside the picture.
5. Ask the children to turn their papers over and use markers to make wrapping paper designs on this side of their paper.
6. Invite the children to fold their papers as they desire, with the wrapping paper designs on the outside. Have them tape these closed.
7. When everyone's "gift" is finished, the children deliver the presents to the recipients. Let everyone open the presents.

A Visit to the Grocery Store or Bakery
Field Trip

1. Take a short trip to a grocery store bakery (or a freestanding bakery) to watch the baker decorate birthday cakes. Arrange this with the bakery ahead of time.
2. Arrange for someone to be available to answer the children's questions about the bakery and about decorating cakes.
3. If possible, arrange for the children to watch the baker decorate sugar cookies—one for each child.

Birthday Words

Language

Materials

Bruno the Baker by Lars Klinting (or any other simple birthday book—see list on page 324) ● marker ● sentence strips

1. Beforehand, read the book to yourself. Use a marker and sentence strips to make word cards of important single words in the story: birthday, cake, sugar, eggs, bowl, and others. Make matching cards for each of these words. On one set, draw a simple picture to illustrate the word.
2. Read the book about Bruno and his friend Felix and how they baked a cake. (Or read any simple birthday book.)
3. Challenge the children to "guess read" the cards without pictures. If they need help, show them the matching illustrated card.
4. Place these cards where the children can use them.

Happy Birthday Song Chart

Language

Materials

chart paper ● marker ● long candle

1. Write the words of the following song on a piece of chart paper.
2. With the children, sing the song several times, using the candle to point to the words.
3. Let the children volunteer to use the candle to point to the words.

> *No One's Birthday*
> Tune: *London Bridge*
> *It is no one's birthday today,*
> *Birthday today, birthday today.*
> *It is no one's birthday today,*
> *Happy Birthday!*
>
> *March around and shout, "Hooray!"*
> *Shout, "Hooray," shout, "Hooray!"*
> *March around and shout, "Hooray!"*
> *Happy Birthday!*

Practicing Beginning Sounds

Language

1. Sing the song "No One's Birthday" (see previous activity), substituting a chosen letter sound for the first sound of every syllable. For example:

   - F sounds like this—"Fit fis fo funs firthfay foofay...."
   - B sounds like this—"Bit bis bo buns birthbay boobay...."

Birthday Book

Language

Materials

white paper ● stapler or hole punch and string ● marker ● pencils/pens

1. Make a 12-page book entitled "Months of the Year." Staple together 12 pieces of paper, or punch holes in the side and fasten with string. Write the name of a different month on each page, in order, from January through December.
2. Show the children the book, and then work with the children individually. Ask each child to sign his name on the page that indicates his birthday month.
3. After their names, ask the children to write the numeral that indicates which day of the month their birthday is. For example, Sydney - 21.
4. Put the book in the class library where children can read it at will.
5. For writing practice, encourage children to copy pages from the book.

Reading and Matching the Months of the Year

Language

Materials

markers ● manila envelope ● index cards

1. Write the months of the year, in order, on the envelope. Write the name of each month on index cards, one month per card. Mix these up and store them in the envelope.
2. Encourage the children to arrange the index cards in order, using the list on the envelope for help.

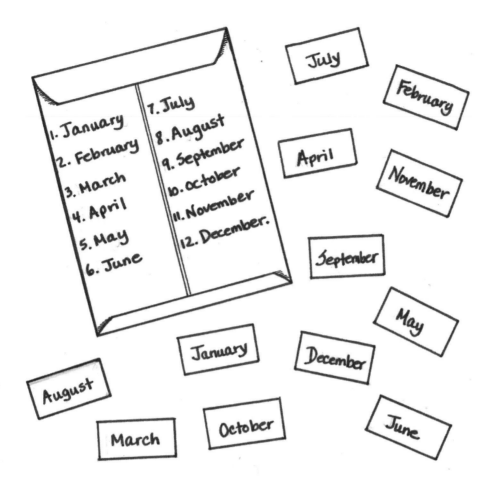

Wrapping (and Sorting) Three-Dimensional Birthday Presents

Math

Materials

3 pieces of plain paper ● marker ● small- to medium-sized empty boxes ● wrapping paper or newspaper ● tape ● recycled bows

1. Label the three pieces of plain paper "small," "medium," and "large" and spread them out on a table.
2. Make the remaining materials available for the children to wrap presents for "no one." Ask the children to place their wrapped gifts beside the paper they think best describes their present's size.
3. Together, examine the wrapped presents in each group. Compare the presents and the groupings using words such as *larger, smaller, largest, smallest, more than, less than*, and other comparative terms.

4. If there are any disagreements about where a gift belongs, encourage the children to discuss their ideas.

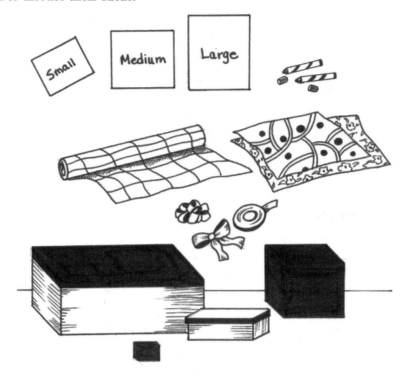

Human Graph

Math

1. Have the children sort themselves into three groups: those who are four years old, those who are five years old, and those who are six years old (or appropriate ages for your group).
2. Ask the children in each group to stand in a line to see which group has the most, the least, and so on.

Matching Real Items to Numerals

Math

Materials

paper ● scissors ● birthday candles

1. Cut out six birthday cake shapes from paper. Write the numerals 0-5 (or appropriate numerals for your group) on the cake shapes, one numeral per cake shape.
2. Challenge the children to put the correct number of candles on each numbered birthday cake.

Pantomiming

Movement

1. Encourage the children to pantomime making a birthday cake.
2. Sing the Happy Birthday song, and then let them pantomime eating the cake.

Birthday Cupcakes

Snack/Cooking

Materials

purchased, unfrosted cupcakes • blunt plastic knives, one for each child • canned frosting • tubes of cake-decorating icing • birthday candles

1. Working with a small group of children, let them decorate their own cupcakes. Encourage them to spread canned frosting on their cupcakes, and then decorate them with the tubes of decorating icing. Give each child a birthday candle to put in the cupcake.
2. Have the children pretend to light their candles. Sing the Birthday Song "to everyone," blow out the candles, and eat the cupcakes.

Learning Center Ideas

Writing Area

Materials

calendars • date books/appointment books of various sizes

1. Place the calendars and date books in the Writing Area so the children can sign their names to dates that indicate their birthdays and the birthdays of others in their families.
2. Encourage the children to also mark the pretend birthdays of their dolls and stuffed animals.

Related Books

Ask Mr. Bear by Marjorie Flack

Bruno the Baker by Lars Klinting

Bunny Cakes by Rosemary Wells

The Flying Garbanzos by Barney Saltzberg

Happy Birthday to You! by Dr. Seuss

Happy Birthday, Moon by Frank Asch

It's My Birthday by Helen Oxenbury

Little Bear by Else Holmelund Minarik

Max's Birthday by Rosemary Wells

Shawn and Keeper and the Birthday Party by Jonathan London

Something Special for Me by Vera B. Williams

Hiding Places

Materials

filled donuts—enough for ¼ donut for each child, plus an additional donut ●
a knife (adult only) ● spoon ● bowl ● flat toothpicks ● napkins

1. Show a filled donut to the children. Talk about it. Have they ever seen this kind of product before? What do they think it is? Do they think it's the same outside and inside?
2. Cut open the donut. Show the filling. What is this? Scoop out the filling into a bowl. Let each child dip the end of a flat toothpick into the filling to get just a small amount to taste.
3. Ask the children if they are surprised to find this hiding inside. What do they think it is?
4. Ask the children what other things might have something hidden *inside*, *behind*, or *under* them.
5. Discuss their answers. If they can't think of items, use the following ideas to start the discussion: mittens hide hands, mailboxes hide envelopes, envelopes hide letters, and covered cooking pots hide what's cooking inside of them.
6. Ask the children these questions: "What might be hiding in a cupboard?" "What might be hiding in a drawer?" "What might be hiding in a pocket?"

Weekly Curriculum Vocabulary

behind
beside
hide
hiding
in
over
under

7. Ask the children to name some places they can hide. Let them try out as many of their suggestions as possible to see if they work. Here are a few suggestions:

- Behind another child
- Behind a door
- Under a table
- Under a table that has a sheet over it
- Behind a bush or a big tree
- Under a beach towel

8. Give each child ¼ of a donut and a napkin. Ask how they like eating a "hiding place."

Weekly Curriculum Extension Activities

Hidden Art

Art

Materials
small paper bags, 1 for each child ● plain paper ● scissors ● crayons or markers

1. Cut plain paper to fit easily inside each paper bag. Give each child a piece of paper. Ask the children to draw a picture of something they'd like to hide.
2. Give the paper bags to the children and ask them to place their pictures into their bags. Their items are now "hiding."

Who Hid What?

Games and Language

Materials
classroom items chosen by children ● chart paper ● marker

1. Let each child choose a classroom object to later hide in the room. Each object should be different.
2. One child at a time (the hider) shows and names her object to the rest of the children. Then she chooses a child (the finder) to find it. (Be certain each child has a chance to hide and to search.)
3. The hider hides her item while the finder turns his back and covers his eyes.

4. When the item is hidden, the finder searches for it. When he finds it, he tells what he found and where he found it.

5. Write each finder's report on a chart using the same sentence framework (below) for each sentence:

   [Child's name] found a [item's name] [where the child found it].

   For example, "Tara found a puppet under the table." "Carlos found a unit block beside the crayons."

6. Call the children's attention to the positional words that describe where the objects were, such as *under, in, behind, inside,* and so on.

7. Continue the game with the finder becoming the next hider and choosing the next finder. Continue until each child has had a turn to do both jobs.

8. Read all of the sentences as a group and challenge the children to continue to use the chart. They may want to read parts of it to each other, or they may enjoy copying the sentence that tells what they found.

Guess What's Hiding?

Games and Music

Materials
bags from previous activity (see Hidden Art)

1. Ask the children to hold their bags of hidden pictures while they sing the song below.

2. Repeat the song until each child, in turn, has an opportunity to reveal her hidden picture as they all sing the final line of the song.

   Tune: *Mary Had a Little Lamb*
   Guess what's hiding in my bag,
   In my bag, in my bag.
   Guess what's hiding in my bag.
   It's a [child sings name of item].

Guess Who's Hiding?

Games and Music

Materials

large beach towel or dark-colored sheet

1. Ask the children to cover their eyes. Choose one child to sit or lie down in front of the group. Cover the child with a large beach towel or a dark-colored sheet. Ask the children to uncover their eyes and sing this song together:

   Tune: *London Bridge*
   Someone's hiding under there,
   Under there, under there.
   Someone's hiding under there,
   Who can it be?

2. Choose another child to guess the hidden child's identity. If he guesses incorrectly, uncover a small part of the hidden child—an arm, a shoe, a section of clothing, or a bit of hair.
3. Have the guessing child choose the next child to guess, and continue playing until someone guesses the correct identity. Repeat the game as before, choosing a different child to hide.

Hidden Estimates

Math

Materials

many identical classroom objects, such as crayons and table blocks • variety of containers

1. Ask the children to estimate how many crayons (or other identical objects) can "hide" in different containers such as a shoebox, cottage cheese container, small cooking pot, plastic storage tub, or any other container.
2. Ask the children to check their estimations.
3. The children's estimating skills will increase when you repeat the activity on other days.

Outdoor Hiding Places

Outdoors and Science

1. Tell the children they will be explorers looking for hidden things. Take them outdoors and encourage them to find what's hiding under rocks or other objects. In winter, what's hiding under the snow? Under the sand? Dig up a weed to see what's hiding under the ground.
2. Let the children describe what they've found and where they found it. What other "hidden" items can they find outdoors?

What's Inside?

Science

Materials

items that hold other items which, in turn, hide another item (see below)

1. Show the children the items that are hiding inside other items, and then in a third item. For example:

   - a canister with a lid; inside is a wrapped candy such as a chocolate kiss
   - a purse with a clasp or zipper; inside is an envelope with a card inside
   - a beach bag; inside is a plastic bottle with lotion inside

2. Challenge them to think of other items that hide things that are, in turn, hiding other things. Here are few to get you started:

   - A diaper bag hides a container that hides baby wipes.
   - The refrigerator hides a bottle that hides milk inside.
   - The cupboard hides a box that hides cereal inside.
   - The cupboard hides a can that hides ravioli that hides cheese filling inside.

Hidden Snacks

Snack/Cooking

Materials

canned ravioli • plates • forks

1. Serve canned ravioli for snack. What do the children find hidden inside?

Learning Center Ideas

Block Area

Materials

blocks ● small people figures

1. Encourage the children to build block structures and to hide small figures in and around them.

More Learning Center Ideas

Science Area

1. Ask the children to bring in items that hide other items. Put these in a special area titled "Hiding Places" where the children can explore the contents and return them for others to explore.

Related Books

Hiding in a Fort: Backyard Retreats for Kids by G. Lawson Drinkard III and George Drinkard
A House Is a House for Me by Mary Ann Hoberman
Where's Spot? by Eric Hill

Keeping Myself Clean

Materials

a bottle of liquid hand soap

1. Show the children the bottle of soap. Talk about the importance of washing hands thoroughly.
2. While you lead, encourage the group to pantomime the complete procedure for washing hands (below).

Turn on water.

Wet hands.

Turn off water.

Put a squirt of soap on one hand.

Spread soap over the front and back of hands.

Rub hands together to form lather.

Scrub back and front of both hands; scrub fingers, thumbs, and between fingers.

Scrub the nails of each hand against the other hand.

Scrub for at least 30 seconds. (Sing a favorite song to pass the time.)

Rinse hands in clean water.

Dry with paper towel.

Dispose of paper towel.

Weekly Curriculum Vocabulary

clean

dirty

soap

wash

words children generate in "These Help Us Wash" (page 333)

names of body parts children generate in "Body Parts" (page 334)

Clean and Dirty Hands

Art and Language

Materials

paper • marker • easel • tempera paints • paintbrushes

1. Draw two large hand shapes on pieces of paper. (Trace your own hands.) Put the papers on the easel.
2. Discuss the kinds of dirt children might have on their hands, such as paint, mud, sticky food, and so on.
3. Challenge the children to visit the easel and paint one dirty hand and leave one hand clean.

A Visit to a Building Supply Store

Art, Field Trip, and Language

Materials

drawing paper • clipboards • markers

1. Take the children to a building supply store to see the large variety of sinks, bathtubs, and shower stalls.
2. Bring along paper, clipboards, and markers, and let the children sit and draw pictures of some of the items they see.
3. Write their dictated words on their papers, then gather these together as pages for a "Washing" book.

Keeping Our Clothes Clean

Dramatic Play

Materials

large appliance box (dishwasher, washing machine, or dryer) • duct tape • craft knife (adult only) • hot glue gun (adult only) • large button • marker • empty laundry detergent container • various dress-up clothes

1. Make a washing machine for the Dramatic Play Area. Close the bottom and top flaps of the appliance box and use duct tape to hold the flaps closed.
2. With the craft knife (adult only), cut an upside down U-shape into one side of the box to serve as the door to the washing machine. Open this outward.
3. Use a hot glue gun (adult only) to attach a large button on the door's outside to serve as a handle.
4. Draw "On/Off" controls on the washing machine.
5. Discuss with the children the importance of wearing clean clothes on a clean body, and the importance of washing dirty clothes.
6. Place the washing machine and dress-up clothes in the Dramatic Play Area so the children can practice washing their clothes.
7. If desired, make a matching dryer from an additional box.

These Help Us Wash

Language

Materials

marker • chart paper • sentence strips • pencils • index cards

1. Encourage the children to generate a list of all the items used to help us as we clean ourselves: soap, washcloth, brush, tub, tub mat, sink, tub stopper, and so on. Write their words on the chart.
2. On sentence strips, write matching words and encourage the children to match each strip with its identical chart word.
3. Provide pencils and index cards for the children who want to copy some of these words for their own cards.

Body Parts

Language

Materials

marker • chart paper • index cards • bulletin board paper

1. On the chart paper, draw a simple stick figure or outline of a child.
2. Ask the children to name body parts they keep clean by washing. Label these parts on the stick figure as the children name them.
3. Make matching word cards on the index cards.
4. Place a piece of bulletin board paper on the floor and choose a child to lie on top of it.
5. Trace the outline of the child's body.
6. Encourage the children to label the body parts on the outline by placing the index cards where they belong on the body. For example, put the card with "hand" written on it next to the hand on the outline.

Why Use Soap?

Language and Science

Materials

dirty rags/cloths • dishpans of clear, clean water • timer • liquid detergent

1. With a small group of children, give each child a dirty rag or cloth. Have them share dishpans of water.
2. Ask the children to wash their rags for one minute in the clear water, wring them out, and examine them for cleanliness. Discuss their findings.
3. Put a large squirt of liquid detergent on each rag and have the children continue washing the rags for one minute.
4. Again, examine the rags for cleanliness. Discuss the children's observations.
5. Ask the children what they conclude about washing with or without soap.

Scrubbing Song

Music

1. While the children sing the following song, encourage them to pantomime bathing the body part mentioned in the verse.
2. Let each child, in turn, name a body part to substitute for the words in parentheses.

Tune: *Turkey in the Straw*
Every night when I get in my tub,
I use my bath brush and I scrub, scrub, scrub.
First I scrub my [back],
Yes, my [back] I scrub,
Every night when I get in my tub.

Cleaning Classroom Items

Outdoors

Materials

dishpans ● water ● liquid dishwashing soap ● small brushes ● washcloths ● towels ●
washable classroom toys

1. In warm weather, put dishpans of soapy water outside at the children's level.
2. Provide cleaning items, such as brushes and washcloths, and let the children
   select washable classroom toys to bring outdoors. Encourage them to wash and
   dry the items.

Caution: Supervise carefully when children are using water.

Oh, Those Nasty Germs!

Science

Materials

potato ● potato peeler (adult only) ● sharp knife (adult only) ● zipper-closure
plastic bags ● marker ● masking tape ● picture of a potato

1. For a dramatic example of germ growth, peel a large potato and cut it in half
   (adult only).
2. While the children have dirty hands, pass one potato half from child to child,
   and ask them to rub their hands all over the potato.
3. Put the soiled potato half into a plastic zipper-closure bag. Seal the bag and use
   a marker and masking tape to label it "Dirty Hands."
4. **Make sure the children thoroughly wash their hands.**
5. Pass the remaining potato half from child to child, having them rub their hands
   over it before they pass it on.
6. Place this potato half in a plastic zipper-closure bag, seal the bag, and label it
   "Clean Hands."
7. **Ask the children to wash their hands again.**

8. Watch the bags over several days and talk about the differences in the potatoes. What do the children conclude about dirty hands?

Caution: Do not open the bags for any reason. Dispose of both bags carefully. They may contain dangerous germs!

9. Put a picture of a potato near the bathroom sink to remind the children to wash their hands carefully.

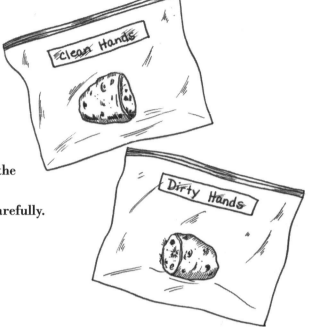

Always Wash Hands First!

Snack/Cooking

1. Stress the importance of washing hands before and after eating snacks and meals and before any food preparation activity. (We wash after a meal or snack because our hands have been at our mouths and our hands could spread our germs to others.)

Learning Center Ideas

Dramatic Play Area

Materials

brush for scrubbing hands, fingers, and fingernails ● empty plastic bottles, such as shampoo, body wash, liquid dishwashing detergent, and liquid laundry detergent

1. Place these items in the Dramatic Play Area to encourage play about keeping ourselves and our surroundings clean.

Related Books

Harry Takes a Bath by Harriet Ziefert
Harry the Dirty Dog by Gene Zion
Mortimer Mooner Stopped Taking a Bath! by Frank B. Edwards

Marvelous Monsters

Materials

Where the Wild Things Are by Maurice Sendak

1. Read the book to the children.
2. Discuss the story. Ask the children if they think the story is real or make believe and why. Ask the children if monsters are real or make believe.
3. Tell the children that they will be reading about monsters and pretending to be monsters this week. Assure them that all will be make-believe, and that no one needs to be afraid.

Weekly Curriculum Vocabulary

feet

hairy

legs

monster

monsters

Monster Feet and Hairy Legs

Art

Materials

adult-size white tube socks, 1 pair for each child • permanent markers, any colors • newspaper • red felt • scissors • tacky glue (available at craft stores and office supply stores)

1. Give each child a pair of white tube socks. Supervise carefully while the children use permanent markers to draw squiggly lines (hair) on the leg portions of their socks. Hang the socks to dry.

2. Ask the children to put a large wad of newspaper in the toe of each of their dry socks.

3. Pre-cut red felt into toenail-size geometric or irregular shapes. Encourage the children to select some red felt shapes for their monster's toenails. Remember— monsters can have any number of toes! Working with one child at a time, help the children use the tacky glue to attach toenails to each sock foot. Lay the stuffed socks aside to dry.

4. When dry, ask the children to remove the newspaper and put these socks on over their shoes. Now they have monster feet! Children wear these while acting out stories and for the Wild Rumpus activity (page 339).

Monster Faces

Art

Materials

scissors • paper plates • art supplies, such as paints, paintbrushes, and scrap paper • glue • tongue depressors • stapler

1. The adult cuts large eyeholes in each plate. Give one plate (with eyeholes) to each child.

2. Encourage the children to create monster masks using the provided materials. Help each child staple a tongue depressor to the bottom of his mask as a handle.

3. Children hold these faces during the Wild Rumpus activity (see page 339) and other monster activities.

Wild Rumpus

Language

Materials

monster feet (see page 338) ● *Where the Wild Things Are* by Maurice Sendak

1. Ask the children to wear their monster feet and masks while you re-read the story. Encourage them to act out the parts of the wild things. They can do this while remaining seated, standing in one place, or moving anywhere within a designated area.
2. End the acting by having the wild things crawl into their pretend beds after Max discovers his dinner waiting.
3. Encourage them to think about their wild rumpus, remembering that they are now very tired, and then pretend to go to sleep to dream about quiet things.

Monsters at Home (Conserving Numbers With Monsters)

Math

Materials

plain paper ● marker ● dried beans (monsters)

1. Divide a piece of paper in half by drawing a line through the middle of it, forming two "monster homes." Make one for each child.
2. Give each child a dozen beans and a piece of divided paper. Encourage the children to put three monsters (beans) into one monster home (half of the paper) and three monsters into the other home.

Caution: Supervise closely, especially if children still put small objects in their mouths.

3. Help the children count the monsters in each home.
4. Ask individual children if one home has more monsters than the other. Answers will vary from child to child.
5. Ask the children to empty their homes and repeat the game, using a new number (use small numbers).

Variation: Ask the children to put four monsters close together in one home and four monsters far apart in the other. Many children will think there are more monsters in the "far apart" home because it looks like more. Encourage the children to count and re-count. Don't try to correct or convince them. Through many repetitions of similar games over time, they will learn that the number is the same even though the beans are arranged differently.

Monster Freeze

Music

Materials

CD player ● CD with recorded spooky music or any lively music

1. Play the recorded music. Encourage the children to dance together or independently, the way monsters might dance, remembering to treat each other gently.
2. From time to time, stop the music. When the music stops, children "freeze" in place, not moving at all until the music begins again.
3. Enjoy the fun of children who keep moving after the music stops. Don't put them out of the game; they are the ones who most need to develop the listening skills encouraged by games of this sort.

Monster Tag

Outdoors

1. Let the children make up their own rules for a game of Monster Tag.

Paper Cup Monsters

Science

Materials

small plastic cups ● permanent markers ● cotton balls ● small container of water ● potting soil ● grass seed or radish seeds ● eyedroppers ● plastic bags

1. Give each child a plastic cup. Working in small groups, supervise carefully while each child uses permanent markers to draw a monster face on her cup.
2. Ask each child to dip a cotton ball in the water and place it in the bottom of her cup. Ask the children to put potting soil on top of the balls, stopping ¼" below the cup's rim.
3. Help the children sprinkle seeds on top and lightly pat them into the soil. Show the children how to use eyedroppers to gently add water to the cup. Soil should be damp, not wet, or seeds will rot.
4. Ask the children to put their cups near a window and put a plastic bag loosely over each cup. Observe carefully for growth—monsters' hair.

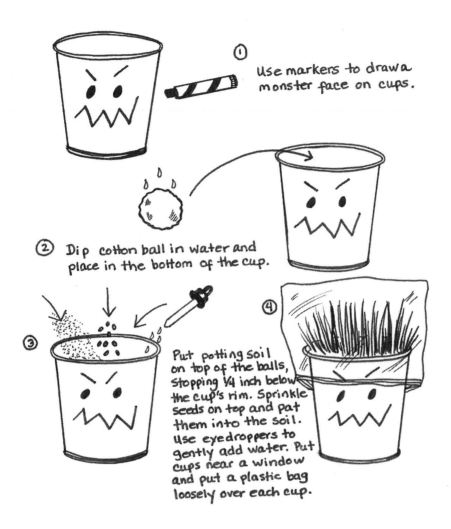

① Use markers to draw a monster face on cups.

② Dip cotton ball in water and place in the bottom of the cup.

③ Put potting soil on top of the balls, stopping ¼ inch below the cup's rim. Sprinkle seeds on top and pat them into the soil. Use eyedroppers to gently add water. Put cups near a window and put a plastic bag loosely over each cup.

④

Edible Monsters

Snack/Cooking

Materials

green gelatin, 3 boxes ● 9" x 13" pan ● water ● plastic knife ● spatula ● paper plates ● raisins ● slivered almonds

1. Make gelatin using half the water called for on the box. Pour this into the pan and refrigerate until congealed.
2. Cut the gelatin into squares or irregular shapes, one per child, and serve on paper plates.
3. Encourage the children to use raisins and slivered almonds to turn their shape into a monster's face. Display the results so everyone can enjoy seeing them, and then eat the scary creations.

Painted Monster Toast

Snack/Cooking

Materials

small, shallow dishes ● milk ● food coloring ● white bread slices ● sterile cotton swabs ● toaster oven (for adult use only)

1. Pour milk into shallow dishes. Put a different color of food coloring into each dish of milk, making strong colors. Place several cotton swabs next to each bowl.
2. Encourage the children to dip the cotton swabs in the colored milk and use this to "paint" a monster face on a slice of bread. They should use a clean swab for each color. Supervise to be sure they don't saturate the bread.
3. Toast (adults only) the "painted" bread in the toaster oven. When it is cool, the children can enjoy their Painted Monster Toast.

Learning Center Ideas

Dramatic Play Area

Materials

Monster Faces (see page 338) ● Monster Feet and Hairy Legs (see page 338) ● unbreakable mirrors

1. When making Monster Faces and Monster Feet and Hairy Legs, have several children make extras.
2. Place these, and the mirrors, in the Dramatic Play Area where the children can enjoy dressing up for impromptu "wild rumpuses."

Related Books

The Boy Under the Bed by Preston McClear
Dogzilla by Dav Pilkey
Go Away, Big Green Monster! by Ed Emberley
Junie B. Jones Has a Monster Under Her Bed by Barbara Park
Kat Kong by Dav Pilkey
Laura Numeroff's 10-Step Guide to Living with Your Monster by Laura Joffe Numeroff
Monster Manners by Bethany Roberts
My Mama Says There Aren't Any Zombies, Ghosts, Vampires, Creatures, Demons, Monsters, Fiends, Goblins or Things by Judith Viorst
There's a Monster Under My Bed by James Howe
There's Something in My Attic (A Pied Piper Book) by Mercer Mayer
Where the Wild Things Are by Maurice Sendak

Mischievous Mice

Materials

any storybook about a mouse/mice (see suggestions on page 349) ● copy paper ● markers

1. Read the book to the children and discuss the story.
2. Tell the children that you will show them one easy way to draw a mouse.
3. Draw a large letter "D" on the paper and show it to the children. Slowly turn the paper so the D is lying on its back with the curved portion in the air. This is now a side view of the mouse's body.
4. Add a triangle to one end for the head and pointed nose; add a long, curved line for a tail at the other end. Add small triangle ears, an eye, and whiskers.
5. Give paper and markers to the children so they can practice drawing mice.

Weekly Curriculum Vocabulary

bottom

mice

mouse

nibbling

over

top

under

other words children generate in "Where Is the Mouse?" (page 345) and "How Mice Move" (page 346)

Nice Mice Bulletin Board

Art and Bulletin Board

Materials

construction paper ● markers ● scissors ● yarn ● glue ● clear tape

1. Encourage the children to make several mice from construction paper and yarn. Remind them that they can draw and then cut out a letter D for the body. Then they can cut out a triangle for the head and cut a piece of yarn for a tail.
2. Ask them to glue on the head and use tape to attach the tail. They can add ears and facial features made from construction paper scraps.
3. Ask them to place their mice on the bulletin board with the title: "These Mice Are Nice."

Pet Store

Field Trip

Materials

disposable plastic gloves

1. Go to a pet store to buy (or borrow) mice to keep for a while as classroom pets. Ask the pet store employee to tell the children how to care for the mice.
2. Let the children help you care for the mice. Be certain they wear gloves while holding the mice or cleaning their cage. Make sure they dispose of the gloves immediately after use.

Can You Guess, Little Mousie?

Games

Materials

a small yellow or orange block

1. Ask the children to sit in a circle, facing the center. Select a child (the mouse) to sit in the center with his eyes closed.
2. Place the yellow or orange block (the cheese) behind the "mouse."
3. Point to a child in the circle. This child quietly creeps to the center, takes the "cheese," and returns to her place in the circle.
4. All the children put their hands behind their backs as if they are hiding the cheese. Together they say, "Can you guess, Little Mousie, who took cheese from your housie?"
5. The mouse opens his eyes and tries to guess who is hiding the cheese. The child with the cheese becomes the next mouse.

Where Is the Mouse?—Creating Big Books

Language

Materials

12" x 18" sturdy paper • construction paper • markers • stapler

1. Ask the children to help create pages for big books depicting positional words. Discuss the idea of drawing pictures that show a mouse *under* something, *over* something, *in front of* something, *behind* something, *near* something, *far away from* something, and so on.
2. Ask each child to volunteer to illustrate a page. For example, a child might illustrate: "A mouse is under a rainbow." Another might illustrate: "A mouse is on top of a chair."
3. Encourage the children to "write" the description, and then add your written words to the page.
4. Gather several pages, add a construction paper cover, and staple the book together. Make several books so each child can contribute one or more pages.

How Mice Move, Part I

Language

Materials

construction paper • scissors • glue • tongue depressor • chart paper • marker

1. Beforehand, make a "mouse pointer" by cutting out a mouse shape from construction paper and gluing it to the end of a tongue depressor.
2. With the children, talk about the many ways mice move. List these ways on the chart.
3. Let children take turns using the pointer to point to letters or words on the chart that their friends designate.

One Mouse and Many Mice

Language

Materials

chart paper • marker

1. In this brief introduction to plurals, show the children how words such as *cat*, *dog*, *sweater*, and *car* become plural (show more than one) by adding the letter "s" to the end of them.
2. Talk about the word *mouse* and how more than one mouse is *mice*, not mouses. Explain that there are other words that show more than one in this way and that they will learn about those at other times.

Five Little Mice

Language and Math

1. Ask the children to hold up one hand, with their fingers and thumb extended.
2. Help the children count their five fingers (including thumb), then recite the rhyme below.
3. At the end of each stanza, the children fold down one finger (or thumb) and count again. At the final line, children shout, "Hooray!"

> *Five little mice were nibbling rice*
> *In the kitchen cupboard one day.*
> *The cat crept by and winked his eye,*
> *And one mouse scampered away.*

Four little mice....

(Repeat until no mice remain.)

> *No little mice were nibbling rice*
> *In the kitchen cupboard one day.*
> *The cat crept by and winked his eye,*
> *And Mother shouted, "Hooray!"*

A Story in a Circle— A Sequence Activity

Math

Materials

a circular story (see examples below) ● 4" squares of paper ● colored pencils ● glue ● long strip of paper from adding machine roll ● fine-tip marker

1. Read a circular story, such as *Lunch* by Denise Fleming or *If You Give a Mouse a Cookie* by Laura Joffe Numeroff, to the children.
2. Give each child a paper square and colored pencils. Challenge the children to draw a picture about the story.
3. Gather the pictures and, with the group, place them in the correct order. If any parts of the story are missing, ask for volunteers to illustrate those parts. Place them in the story where they belong.
4. Ask several children to glue the paper squares, in order, to the adding machine paper. Use the fine-tip marker to write the children's dictated words on each square.
5. Arrange the long strip in a circle with pictures on the outside, and glue the two ends together. When the glue dries, the children can start at any part of the circle and read/tell the story, going around and around.

How Mice Move, Part II

Movement

Materials

chart from How Mice Move, Part I (see page 346)

1. With the children, review the chart "How Mice Move."
2. Challenge the children to read the chart and move in each of the listed ways.

Hickory Dickory Dock

Music

1. Sing "Hickory Dickory Dock" with the children. Encourage the children to make up words for additional verses about other numbers on the clock.

   Hickory Dickory Dock
   Hickory dickory dock
   The mouse ran up the clock.
   The clock struck one,
   The mouse ran down.
   Hickory dickory dock.

Mouse Crackers

Snack/Cooking

Materials

wax paper ● large and small round crackers ● cheese spread ● blunt knives ● black olive slices ● raisins ● thin pretzel sticks

1. Give each child some wax paper to use as a work surface. Put out all the ingredients where the children can serve themselves.
2. Ask the children to select one large cracker and two small crackers. Ask them to spread cheese spread on the large cracker (for a mouse face) and place the small crackers in place for mouse ears.
3. Encourage the children to use the remaining ingredients to add eyes, a nose, and whiskers.
4. Ask the children to count the circles before eating the snack. Some children will have black olive circles to count in addition to the three crackers.

Learning Center Ideas

Library Area

Materials

books about mice (see list on next page)

1. Place the books in the class library for the children to enjoy alone or in small groups.

Related Books

Aunt Isabel Tells a Good One by Kate Duke

Boats for Bedtime by Olga Litowinsky

Dogzilla by Dav Pilkey

Frederick by Leo Leonni

If You Give a Mouse a Cookie by Laura Joffe Numeroff

Is This the House of Mistress Mouse? by Richard Scarry

Kat Kong by Dav Pilkey

Look Out Kindergarten, Here I Come! by Nancy L. Carlson

Lunch by Denise Fleming

Maisy Goes to Bed by Lucy Cousins (lift the flaps)

Mouse Paint by Ellen Stoll Walsh

The Mouse That Snored by Bernard Waber

A Mouse Told His Mother by Bethany Roberts

Naughty Nancy Goes to School by John S. Goodall (a wordless picture book)

Seven Blind Mice by Ed Young

The Very Noisy Night by Diana Hendry

Picnic Time

Weekly Curriculum Vocabulary

ants

basket

estimate

napkin

picnic

plate

tablecloth

Materials

sentence strip ● pen ● picnic basket (or a cooler)

1. Beforehand, write the word "picnic" on a sentence strip and place it inside the basket.
2. Open the basket, remove the sentence strip, and show it to the children. Can they guess the word? If not, tell them what it is.
3. Discuss picnics. Encourage the children to describe their memories of picnics. Prepare the children to have picnic fun all week!

The Order of Things

Art and Language

Materials

We're Going on a Picnic by Pat Hutchins (or other picnic book) ● paper ● drawing materials

1. Before doing this activity with the children, draw simple sketches of five parts of the story—the beginning, three events in the middle, and the end.
2. Read the book to the children. (The activity can be done with other books.) Ask them to name the main characters and recall the story.
3. Display the sketches out of order and have the children tell you the proper sequence for the pictures.
4. Read the story again. At the end, ask the children what might happen next, after the book ends.
5. Encourage the children to draw a picture of what they think might happen next in the story.
6. Encourage the children to show their pictures to the group and tell what their pictures depict.

Picnic Area

Bulletin Board

Materials

bulletin board covered with solid color paper ● wrapping paper or wallpaper in a colorful design ● variety of art supplies ● glue or thumbtacks

1. Place a large square of wrapping paper or wallpaper on the solid background on the bulletin board. Tell the children this is a tablecloth at a picnic site.
2. Discuss what could be added to the scene to make it look more like a picnic and a picnic area. (Repeat this step every day as the scene grows and changes.) If necessary, ask leading questions: Who will eat all this food? What do you think the weather is like? What kinds of animals might be nearby?
3. During the week, provide a variety of materials for children to make items to add to the scene. Help them glue or tack their items to the board.

Picnic in the Park

Field Trip

Materials

blanket • handwashing towelettes • simple snack

1. Take a short trip to a nearby park with a playground.
2. After the children play on the playground for a while, spread the blanket on the ground.
3. Make sure the children clean their hands, and then sit on the blanket to enjoy a picnic snack.

What's Missing?

Games

Materials

picnic cooler • tablecloth • picnic items, such as a cup, napkin, and paper plate

1. Put six picnic items inside a cooler. Include a tablecloth and five other items.
2. Open the cooler. Spread the tablecloth in front of the children. Take out the remaining items and put them on the cloth, naming each as you do.
3. Re-pack the cooler with all the items, including the cloth.
4. Choose a child and ask him to remove all but one item from the cooler. Help the child spread these on the cloth in front of the group, keeping the remaining item in the closed cooler.
5. The children try to guess which item is missing.
6. Repeat the activity until each child has had a turn. Change some of the items to keep the game challenging and interesting.
7. Whisper to the final child, suggesting that she leave the tablecloth in the cooler.

Estimation

Math

Materials

picnic tablecloth

1. Spread the tablecloth on the floor. Ask the children to estimate how many children could fit on the tablecloth if all are standing. Test this to see if their answers are close.

2. Ask the children to estimate how many children can fit on the tablecloth if all are sitting with their legs crossed. Ask them to guess if this will be more or less than the previous grouping. Again, test their answers.

3. Repeat with the children sitting in an L-shape. Repeat with the children reclining.

Numbers in Order

Math

Materials

11 paper plates ● marker

1. Write the numerals 0-10 on individual paper plates. Mix these up and ask the children to place them in order from 0-10.

Picnic Ants

Math

Materials

plates from Ordinal Numbers (previous activity) ● 55 plastic ants

1. Encourage the children to put the correct number of ants on each plate.

2. Have them ask another child to "check" their work, providing counting practice for the second child.

Patterned Tablecloths

Math

Materials

ruler ● marker or pen ● paper ● copy machine ● two colors of construction paper ● scissors ● glue sticks

1. Make a 5" x 5" square grid of 1" squares on a piece of paper. Make a copy for each child. Cut out 1" squares of two colors of construction paper.

2. Demonstrate several ways to create a pattern or design in the grids, using 1" squares of colored paper.

3. Give each child a grid and encourage them to use the 1" squares and glue sticks to design a picnic tablecloth.

4. Display the finished products.

Picnic Pantomime

Movement

1. Tell the children that *pantomime* means telling a story with our bodies instead of words. One person may narrate (tell the story with words), but the others act it out without a sound. Tell them that you will tell a story, and they can act it out.

2. Tell the children the following story:

We are going to have a picnic at the park. Let's pack the picnic basket. Oh! That's heavy! We are so excited! You can see how excited we are while we walk to the park. Here we are. We spread out the blanket and sit down. We unpack the picnic basket. Let's eat! Here comes a bee! What will we do? Swat it! Swat it! Now let's eat. Here comes a squirrel begging for food. What will we do? Shoo it away! Shoo it away! Here come the ants! What will we do? Ooooo, so many ants! Let's pack up the food and move to another spot. NOW let's eat. (Pause.) M-m-m-m-m, that was good. Let's pack up the trash. Who wants to play baseball? Strike one! Strike two! A hit! A home run! (Pause.) What a good game. Time to walk home. We are so tired. (Pause.) Home at last. Let's wash up and go to sleep. Good night!

3. Let the children make up stories for the group to pantomime.

Ants Love Picnics

Music

1. Sing the following song. Ask the children to suggest names of picnic foods to substitute for the words in parentheses.

2. Repeat until each child has a turn.

> *Ants Love Picinics*
> Tune: *Are You Sleeping?*
> *Ants love picnics.*
> *Ants love picnics.*
> *Yes they do.*
> *Yes they do.*
> *Some are coming now*
> *To eat my (picnic dinner)*
> *Go away! Go away!*

More Ants!

Sand and Water

Materials

sand ● sand and water table ● plastic ants

1. Hide plastic ants in the sand in the sand table.

Active Ants

Science

Materials

paper plates ● markers ● paper clips ● pre-cut, black oval shapes (ants) ● magnets

1. Give each child a paper plate. Invite them to draw pictures of picnic foods on their plates.
2. Give each child a paper clip and black oval shape. Show them how to slide the clips onto their "ants."
3. Ask them to put the ants on their paper plates and hold a magnet under the plate. As they move the magnets, their ants will move around their plates.
4. Sing "Ants Love Picnics" (see page 354).

① Draw pictures of picnic foods on paper plates.

② Slide paper clip onto oval "ant."

③ Hold magnet under plate. As magnet is moved, "ants" will move around the plate.

Picnic!

Snack/Cooking

Materials

tablecloth ● simple snacks

1. Let the children eat snack while sitting on a tablecloth spread on the floor.
2. Serve simple snacks such as pretzels or animal crackers on napkins. Provide water to drink. Spilled water will cause no damage to the tablecloth or the floor.

Learning Center Ideas

Dramatic Play Area

Materials

picnic baskets ● paper plates and napkins ● plastic cutlery

1. Place a few of the items in the Dramatic Play Area so the children can pretend to prepare for and go on pretend picnics in the classroom or (supervised) outdoors.

Related Books

It's the Bear! by Jez Alborough
Picnic by Emily Arnold McCully
Rattlebang Picnic by Margaret Mahy
We're Going on a Picnic! by Pat Hutchins

Pizza

Materials

spice shaker of oregano (from the spice section of the supermarket)

1. At group time, show the spice shaker to the children. Shake a small amount of oregano into each child's open hands.
2. Ask the children to rub their hands together, releasing the spice's aroma. Invite them to smell their hands and talk about what they smell. Where have they smelled that before?
3. Guide the children to talk about flavorful foods and guide their talk to pizza.

Weekly Curriculum Vocabulary

pizza
pizza parlor
pizzeria
spice

Making Pizzas

Art

Materials

small plastic dish • red tempera paint • white glue • large and small inexpensive white paper plates • plastic spoons • scissors • shredded white and yellow paper scraps of construction paper, including brown and red

1. Mix a small amount of red paint with an equal amount of white glue in a small plastic dish.
2. Give each child a large paper plate. Ask the children to spoon the paint (pizza sauce) onto their paper plate "crusts" and spread the "sauce" with the spoon.
3. They can cut out brown mushroom shapes and red circles for pepperoni and add these to their pizza.
4. Ask them to add shredded paper for cheese.
5. Provide other scrap paper for children who want different toppings. Ask the children to press all of their toppings into the sticky "sauce."
6. Repeat the procedure, using the small plates.
7. When the pizzas dry, use them for the math activity "Exploring Fractions" (see page 360) and in the Dramatic Play Area's "Pizza Parlor" (below).

Pizza Parlor

Dramatic Play

Materials

pen • paper • copy machine

1. Support children's efforts to turn the Dramatic Play Area into a pizza restaurant.
2. Ask the children to generate a list of items they need for their restaurant.
3. Incorporate this list into a letter to families, asking if they can send in any items. Make a copy of the letter and send it home to parents.

A Visit to a Pizza Restaurant

Field Trip

1. If possible, tour a pizza restaurant including the kitchen and the big refrigerator. Arrange with the manager in advance so you can come at a time when they aren't busy. Some restaurants allow the children to knead pizza dough and make their own pizzas. Ask if this restaurant will do so.

Move to the Pizza

Language and Movement

Materials

dark marker ● 26 red paper plates ● 26 index cards

1. With the marker, write a different letter of the alphabet on each red plate (pizza).
2. Write a different letter of the alphabet on each index card.
3. Place the "pizzas" at random on the floor. Ask each child to stand next to a letter of his choice.
4. Mix up the index cards and hold them face down. Ask the children, in turn, to select a card from your hand.
5. At a given signal, ask the children to move in a designated way (for example, crawling, hopping, walking sideways, and so on) to the pizza whose letter matches the letter on their index card. Remind the children to move carefully and to choose a path that will help them avoid bumping into others.
6. Have several children hold up and identify the pizza letters they have moved to.
7. Ask the children to put their pizza letters back on the floor and return their index cards to you.
8. Repeat so the children have an opportunity to move to several different letters and until every child has an opportunity to identify one or more letters.

Song About Pizza

Language and Music

Materials

one large paper plate pizza (see Making Pizzas on page 358)

1. Talk about different kinds of pizza that the children like to eat: pepperoni, cheese, sausage, vegetable, barbecue chicken, pineapple, and so on.

2. Ask a child to hold the paper plate pizza as the children sing the song below (singing the appropriate girl or boy version). On the last word of the song, the child holding the pizza tells what kind of pizza she is bringing.

3. At the end of the song, the child passes the pizza to another child, and the group sings the song again. Continue the game until each child has had a turn to tell what kind of pizza she is bringing.

Tune: ***Do You Know the Muffin Man?***
Oh do you know the pizza girl,
The pizza girl, the pizza girl?
Oh do you know the pizza girl?
She's bringing [_____].

Or sing this:
Oh do you know the pizza boy,
The pizza boy, the pizza boy?
Oh do you know the pizza boy?
He's bringing [_____].

Exploring Fractions

Math

Materials

small paper plate pizzas • large paper plate pizzas • paper plates in two different colors • felt and felt board, if desired

1. To explore fractions, use two paper plate pizzas that are the same size. Leave one whole and cut the other in half. Write "½" on the backs of the cut pieces.

2. Give each child two same-size paper plates in two different colors. Cut one of them in half and write "½" on the backs of the cut pieces.

3. Place your pizza plates in front of a small group of children with both pizzas intact.

4. Divide the cut pizza, and then put it back together on top of the whole pizza. Talk about how the two pieces are each one half of a pizza.

5. Ask the children to do the same thing with their plates.

6. Repeat several times.

7. At another time, repeat the activity using pizzas (and paper plates) that are whole and matching ones cut into fourths.

8. Place all of these pizzas (and paper plates) where the children can explore them at will. Help the children discover, through playing, that two quarter pieces make up one half piece.

9. If desired, make similar felt pizzas for the children to manipulate on the felt board.

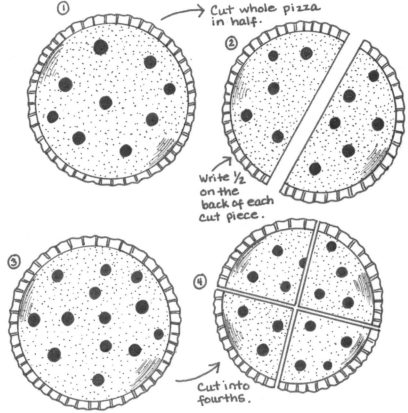

Who's a Pizza?

Movement

Materials

Pete's a Pizza by William Steig ● stuffed animals

1. Read the book to the children. In this story, Pete's parents pretend he is a pizza and they play with him accordingly.
2. After reading the story, ask each child to hold a stuffed animal. While you re-read the book, have the children act out the story with their animal as the pizza.

Pizza Parlor Tag

Outdoors

1. Suggest that the children play tag in the usual way, except that when IT tags someone, he must also call out the name of a kind of pizza.
2. Designate a spot in the play area as the pizza parlor. Children are "safe" if they are inside this area.

How Heat Changes Pizza
Science and Snack/Cooking

Materials

paper plates • small bagels cut in half (or English muffin halves), one for each child • spoon • small dish of pizza sauce • canned mushroom slices • sliced black olives • pepperoni slices cut in fourths • shredded mozzarella and cheddar cheese • toaster oven (adult only)

1. Give each child ½ of a bagel or English muffin on a paper plate. Encourage them to spoon just enough sauce on their bagel to thinly cover it.
2. Let them select desired toppings to place on the bagel pizza, ending with the shredded cheese.
3. Toast the pizzas in a toaster oven, just until the cheese begins to melt and bubble (adult only). Remove and let the children observe the bubbling cheese from a safe distance.
4. When the pizza is thoroughly cool, serve it for snack.
5. While the children eat, encourage them to discuss the changes they observed.

Learning Center Ideas
Dramatic Play Area

Materials

empty pizza boxes • order pads • pencils • poster board (for pizzeria signs) • markers

1. Place a few of the items in the Dramatic Play Area so the children can pretend to prepare and eat pizzas.

Related Books
Eating Fractions by Bruce McMillan
"Hi, Pizza Man!" by Virginia Walter
Little Nino's Pizzeria by Karen Barbour
Pete's a Pizza by William Steig

Teddy Bears

Materials

any version of *The Three Bears* or *Goldilocks and the Three Bears* • children's teddy bears

1. Before introducing this topic, invite the children to bring their teddy bears to school for the week's activities. Provide extras for children without bears.
2. Hold a bear in your lap while you read the book to the children. Let them hold their bears, also.
3. Ask the children to tell you, in order, what happened in the story. Use words like *first*, *second*, *next*, and *last*.
4. Let each child introduce her bear to the group, telling something special about the bear.

Weekly Curriculum Vocabulary

bear
bears
bed
Goldilocks
jumping
Teddy
three

Our Bears

Art

Materials

large and small white paper plates ● stapler ● construction paper ● scissors ● markers ● construction paper scraps

1. Give each child one small paper plate and one large paper plate. Help each child staple together the rims of the two plates. This will be a bear's body and head.
2. Let the children use the remaining materials to add arms, legs, ears, and facial features.
3. Use these bears with the bulletin board activity Teddy Bears Jumping on the Bed (see page 365).

Spend-the-Night Bears

Art and Language

Materials

children's teddy bears ● camera, optional ● plain paper ● crayons

1. Encourage the children to leave their bears at school overnight for a bear's spend-the-night party—only bears allowed!
2. Before the children arrive the next day, place bears in odd places around the room. For example, upside down on top of cabinets, amidst puzzle pieces, surrounded by potted plants, in the Book Area with open books in front of them, in the Snack Area with cookie crumbs strewn around, under tables, at the easel with a painted picture of a honey jar, sleeping under blanket, and so on.
3. If possible, take photos of the bears so the children can revisit the experience from time to time.
4. As the children arrive, encourage them to observe the "chaos." Briefly discuss what might have happened overnight.
5. Give paper and crayons to the children and ask them to draw pictures of what they think their own bear did overnight. Write their dictated words on their papers, and then gather the papers into a book titled "Spend-the-Night Bears."
6. Read the book to the group, and then put it in the class library so the children can read it alone or with their friends.

Teddy Bears Jumping on the Bed

Bulletin Board

Materials

drawing paper squares (size determined by your bulletin board) • crayons

1. Let the children choose two different colors of crayons.
2. Ask each child to color a pattern of stripes on his square.
3. Mount these squares to make a quilt on a bulletin board. This is the teddy bears' bed.
4. Let the children help you mount their paper plate teddy bears on the board with most of the bears "jumping on the bed" and a few falling off or flying through the air.

Doctor's Office for Teddy Bears

Dramatic Play

Materials

bandages • strips of old sheets, clean pantyhose, and ace bandages for wrapping wounds • gauze • toy syringes • tongue depressors • disposable gloves • stethoscope • an egg carton cup attached to a pipe cleaner (for examining ears) • message pads • calendar • pencils

1. Give the materials to the children to set up a doctor's office for sick bears to visit.
2. Show the children how to wrap "broken arms" with strips of sheets or pantyhose, or with ace bandages.
3. Encourage the children to make up activities based on their own experiences with illness, injury, and doctors.
4. Remind them to treat their patients gently.

Interactive Bear Stories

Language

Materials

any storybooks about bears • children's teddy bears

1. Ask the children to hold their bears when you read stories about bears. Encourage them to listen carefully for parts of the story where the bear characters speak. At those times, have the children "help" their bears speak by growling with them.
2. If the story has more than one bear character (for example, "The Three Bears"), divide the group into smaller groups, each growling with only one character. For example, one group would growl when the daddy bear speaks, another for the mama, and a third for the baby.

"Five Little Teddy Bears Jumping on the Bed"

Math

1. This variation of the traditional fingerplay provides experience in subtracting by one.
2. Ask the children to hold one hand out, palm up, for the bed. The other hand, fingers outstretched, becomes five bears.
3. As the children recite the following rhyme, they do the motions described.

> *Five little teddy bears jumping on the bed.* (Bear fingers "jump" on the outstretched palm.)
> *One fell off and bumped his head.* (Show one bear finger and point to head.)
> *He went to the doctor and the doctor said,* (Swish palms together to indicate walking motion.)
> *"That's what you get for jumping on the bed."* (With a stern look, shake the index finger as if scolding a naughty bear.)

> *Four little teddy bears jumping on the bed.* (Repeat as above, with one bear falling off the bed at each verse.)

> (Final verse follows; same motions as above:)
> *One little teddy bear jumping on the bed.*
> *He fell off and bumped his head.*
> *He went to the doctor and the doctor said,*
> *"No more teddy bears jumping on the bed."*

Teddy Bears Jumping on Beds

Movement

1. Divide the children into groups of six. Five children in each group are bears and one is the doctor.
2. Designate areas for each group. While everyone recites the rhyme about bears jumping on the bed (see previous activity), all groups act out the rhyme.

Teddy Bear Flight

Outdoors

Materials
parachute (or full-size bed sheet) ● children's teddy bears

1. Ask the children to stand around a parachute (or sheet), holding the edge with both hands. Place a teddy bear in the center of the parachute. On the signal, the children raise and lower the chute, bouncing the bear. Do this slowly, and then do it rapidly. Compare the results. The goal is to keep the bear from flying off the parachute.
2. Add more bears and repeat the activity, letting the bears fly within the perimeter of the parachute.
3. Repeat the activity, making the bears fly as high as possible, even if they fly away from the parachute.

Real Bears

Science

1. See the theme "Real Bears" on pages 193-198. After the children have learned about real bears and teddy bears, encourage them to compare the two groups.

Bear Faces

Snack/Cooking

Materials

large and small round crackers • dull, plastic knives • peanut butter (check for allergies) • O-shaped cereal • raisins

1. Encourage the children to make bear faces by spreading peanut butter on a round cracker and sticking the remaining items into the peanut butter to form the facial features.

Caution: Check for any food allergies (especially peanut) before doing this activity.

2. If the children in your group have peanut allergies, substitute whipped cream cheese mixed with brown food coloring (available in cake decorating departments).

More Jumping Teddy Bears

Snack/Cooking

Materials

teddy bear-shaped graham cookies • napkins

1. Give each child five cookies and one napkin. Ask them to place the napkins (bears' beds) on the table and the cookies on the napkin.
2. Together, recite the rhyme "Five Little Teddy Bears Jumping On the Bed" (see page 366). Have children remove one bear when they say, "One fell off and bumped his head." At the end of each verse, the children eat the bear that "fell off" the bed.

Learning Center Ideas

Art Area

Materials

teddy bear rubber stamps • stamp pads • paper • pencils

1. Place these items in the Art Area so the children can explore them.
2. Encourage the children to tell about their pictures by writing their own words on their pictures.

Related Books

Beady Bear by Don Freeman

Bear at Home by Stella Blackstone

Blueberries for Sal by Robert McCloskey

Corduroy by Don Freeman

Drawing Lessons from a Bear by David McPhail

Goldilocks and the Three Bears by Jan Brett

Good Night, Baby Bear by Frank Asch (also, any other bear books by Asch)

Little Bear by Else Holmelund Minarik (also, any in this series)

A Pocket for Corduroy by Don Freeman

Somebody and the Three Blairs by Marilyn Tolhurst

Teddy Bear Tears by Jim Aylesworth

Teddy Bear, Teddy Bear: A Classic Action Rhyme by Michael Hague

The Three Bears by Paul Galdone

We're Going on a Bear Hunt by Michael Rosen

Index

Book Index